Ecological Literacy

SUNY Series in Constructive Postmodern Thought
David Ray Griffin, editor

Ecological Literacy

Education and the Transition
to a Postmodern World

David W. Orr

State University of New York Press

The author gratefully acknowledges the following for permission to reprint articles that appeared in HOLISTIC EDUCATION REVIEW (Chapter 5); HARVARD EDUCATIONAL REVIEW (Chapter 6); CONSERVATION BIOLOGY (Chapters 11 and 12); and BIOSCIENCE (Chapter 14).

Published by
State University of New York Press, Albany

© 1992   State University of New York

Printed in the United States of America

For information, address State University of New York
Press, State University Plaza, Albany, N.Y. 12246

Production by Dana Foote
Marketing by Dana E. Yanulavich

Library of Congress Cataloging-in-Publication Data

Orr, David W., 1944–
    Ecological Literacy : education and the transition to a postmodern
world / David W. Orr.
        p.   cm.   — (SUNY series in constructive postmodern thought)
    Includes bibliographical references and index.
    ISBN 0–7914–0873–6 (alk. paper). — ISBN 0–7914–0874–4 (pbk. :
alk. paper)
        1. Education—Aims and objectives.   2. Environmental education.
3. Human ecology.   I. Title.   II. Series.
LB41.0745   1992
375' .0083—dc20
                                                                90–28767
                                                                    CIP

10 9 8

For Elaine, Michael,
and Daniel

INTRODUCTION TO SUNY SERIES IN CONSTRUCTIVE POSTMODERN THOUGHT

The rapid spread of the term *postmodern* in recent years witnesses to a growing dissatisfaction with modernity and to an increasing sense that the modern age not only had a beginning but can have an end as well. Whereas the word *modern* was almost always used until quite recently as a word of praise and as a synonym for *contemporary,* a growing sense is now evidenced that we can and should leave modernity behind—in fact, that we *must* if we are to avoid destroying ourselves and most of the life on our planet.

Modernity, rather than being regarded as the norm for human society toward which all history has been aiming and into which all societies should be ushered—forcibly if necessary—is instead increasingly seen as an aberration. A new respect for the wisdom of traditional societies is growing as we realize that they have endured for thousands of years and that, by contrast, the existence of modern society for even another century seems doubtful. Likewise, *modernism* as a worldview is less and less seen as The Final Truth, in comparison with which all divergent worldviews are automatically regarded as "superstitious." The modern worldview is increasingly relativized to the status of one among many, useful for some purposes, inadequate for others.

Although there have been antimodern movements before, beginning perhaps near the outset of the nineteenth century with the Romanticists and the Luddites, the rapidity with which the term *postmodern* has become widespread in our time suggests that the antimodern sentiment is more extensive and intense than before, and also that it includes the sense that modernity can be successfully overcome only by going beyond it, not by attempting to return to a premodern form of existence. Insofar as a common element is found in the various ways in which the term is used, *postmodernism* refers to a diffuse sentiment rather than to any common set of doctrines—the sentiment that humanity can and must go beyond the modern.

Beyond connoting this sentiment, the term *postmodern* is used in a confusing variety of ways, some of them contradictory to others. In artistic and literary circles, for example, postmodernism shares in this general sentiment but also involves a specific reaction against "modernism" in the narrow sense of a movement in artistic-literary circles in the late nineteenth and early twentieth centuries. Postmodern architecture is very different from postmodern literary criticism. In some circles, the term *postmodern* is used in reference to that potpourri of ideas and systems sometimes called *new age metaphysics,* although many of these ideas and systems are more premodern than postmodern. Even in philosophical and theological circles, the term *postmodern* refers to two quite different positions, one of which is reflected in this series. Each position seeks to transcend both *modernism* in the sense of the worldview that has developed out of the seventeenth-century Galilean-Cartesian-Baconian-Newtonian science, and *modernity* in the sense of the world order that both conditioned and was conditioned by this worldview. But the two positions seek to transcend the modern in different ways.

Closely related to literary-artistic postmodernism is a philosophical postmodernism inspired variously by pragmatism, physicalism, Ludwig Wittgenstein, Martin Heidegger, and Jacques Derrida and other recent French thinkers. By the use of terms that arise out of particular segments of this movement, it can be called *deconstructive* or *eliminative postmodernism.* It overcomes the modern worldview through an anti-worldview: it deconstructs or eliminates the ingredients necessary for a worldview, such as God, self, purpose, meaning, a real world, and truth as correspondence. While motivated in some cases by the ethical concern to forestall totalitarian systems, this type of postmodern thought issues in relativism, even nihilism. It could also be called *ultramodernism,* in that its eliminations result from carrying modern premises to their logical conclusions.

The postmodernism of this series can, by contrast, be called *constructive* or *revisionary.* It seeks to overcome the modern worldview not by eliminating the possibility of worldviews as such, but by constructing a postmodern worldview through a revision of modern premises and traditional concepts. This constructive or revisionary postmodernism involves a new unity of scientific, ethical, aesthetic, and religious intuitions. It rejects not science as such but only that scientism in which the data of the modern natural sciences are alone allowed to contribute to the construction of our worldview.

The constructive activity of this type of postmodern thought is not limited to a revised worldview; it is equally concerned with a postmodern world that will support and be supported by the new worldview. A postmodern world will involve postmodern persons, with a postmodern spirituality, on the one hand, and a postmodern society, ultimately a postmodern global order, on the other. Going beyond the modern world will involve transcending its individualism, anthropocentrism, patriarchy, mechanization, economism, consumerism, nationalism, and militarism. Constructive postmodern thought provides support for the ecology, peace, feminist, and other emancipatory movements of our time, while stressing that the inclusive emancipation must be from modernity itself. The term *postmodern,* however, by contrast with *premodern,* emphasizes that the modern world has produced unparalleled advances that must not be lost in a general revulsion against its negative features.

From the point of view of deconstructive postmodernists, this constructive postmodernism is still hopelessly wedded to outdated concepts, because it wishes to salvage a positive meaning not only for the notions of the human self, historical meaning, and truth as correspondence, which were central to modernity, but also for premodern notions of a divine reality, cosmic meaning, and an enchanted nature. From the point of view of its advocates, however, this revisionary postmodernism is not only more adequate to our experience but also more genuinely postmodern. It does not simply carry the premises of modernity through to their logical conclusions, but criticizes and revises those premises. Through its return to organicism and its acceptance of nonsensory perception, it opens itself to the recovery of truths and values from various forms of premodern thought and practice that had been dogmatically rejected by modernity. This constructive, revisionary postmodernism involves a creative synthesis of modern and premodern truths and values.

This series does not seek to create a movement so much as to help shape and support an already existing movement convinced that modernity can and must be transcended. But those antimodern movements which arose in the past failed to deflect or even retard the onslaught of modernity. What reasons can we have to expect the current movement to be more successful? First, the previous antimodern movements were primarily calls to return to a premodern form of life and thought rather than calls to advance, and the human spirit does not rally to calls to turn back. Second, the previous antimodern movements either rejected modern science, reduced it to a description of mere appearances, or assumed its adequacy in principle; therefore, they could base their calls only on the negative social and spiritual effects of modernity. The current movement draws on natural science itself as a witness against the adequacy of the modern worldview. In the third place, the present movement has even more evidence than did previous movements of the ways in which modernity and its worldview *are* socially and spiritually destructive. The fourth and probably most decisive difference is that the present movement is based on the awareness that *the continuation of modernity threatens the very survival of life on our planet.* This awareness, combined with the growing knowledge of the interdependence of the modern worldview and the militarism, nuclearism, and ecological devastation of the modern world, is providing an unprecedented impetus for people to see the evidence for a postmodern worldview and to envisage postmodern ways of relating to each other, the rest of nature, and the cosmos as a whole. For these reasons, the failure of the previous antimodern movements says little about the possible success of the current movement.

Advocates of this movement do not hold the naively utopian belief that the success of this movement would bring about a global society of universal and lasting peace, harmony, and happiness, in which all spiritual problems, social conflicts, ecological destruction, and hard choices would vanish. There is, after all, surely a deep truth in the testimony of the world's religions to the presence of a transcultural proclivity to evil deep within the human heart, which no new paradigm, combined with a new economic order, new child-rearing practices, or any other social arrangements, will suddenly eliminate. Furthermore, it has correctly been said that "life is robbery": a strong element of competition is inherent within finite existence, which no social-political-economic-ecological order can overcome. These two truths, especially when contemplated together, should caution us against unrealistic hopes.

However, no such appeal to "universal constants" should reconcile us to the present order, as if this order were thereby uniquely legitimated. The human proclivity to evil in general, and to conflictual competition and ecological destruction in particular, can be greatly exacerbated or greatly mitigated by a world order and its worldview. Modernity exacerbates it about as much as imaginable. We can therefore envision, without being naively utopian, a far better world order, with a far less dangerous trajectory, than the one we now have.

This series, making no pretense of neutrality, is dedicated to the success of this movement toward a postmodern world.

David Ray Griffin
Series Editor

Contents

Introduction

The historic upheavals in the Soviet Union and Eastern Europe in 1989–90 are ample evidence that communism, or at least a particular version of it, has failed. We have yet to admit that Western capitalism has failed as well. Our failures are still being concealed by bad book-keeping (both fiscal and ecological), dishonest rhetoric, and wishful thinking. But the day of reckoning is not far off. The two worlds built on the thought of Galileo, Descartes, Newton, Marx, and Smith are in ruin. The world does not work mechanically, it is not without limits. And humans are not themselves mechanical things or even "human resources." If communism has failed on this score, so too has capitalism. Communism has all but collapsed because it could not produce enough; capitalism is failing because it produces too much and shares too little. Communism imposed an ascetic morality on its subjects, while capitalism has permitted the collapse of morality itself. Neither system is sustainable in either human or ecological terms. We now face the task of rebuilding something different, a postmodern world that protects individual rights while protecting the larger interests of the planet and our children who will live on it.

The essays in this volume were written between 1984 and 1989 for different audiences and for different purposes. They represent an extended reflection on the crisis of sustainability now looming before the modern world, and what this portends for the theory and practice of education. The transition to modernity, in David Griffin's words, is associated with "individualism, anthropocentrism, patriarchy, mechanization, economism, consumerism, nationalism, and militarism."[1] The alternative, postmodern society, described in this series, "provides support for the ecology, peace, feminist and other emancipatory movements of our time, while stressing that the inclusive emancipation must be from modernity itself."[2] This enterprise is "constructive" in the sense that it aims not to discard the baby with the bathwater. Not all of the modern world can be or should be condemned as some propose. Still, in Griffin's concise statement of the problem we can envision a long, difficult, and risky transition to a world we can barely see. The path of history now leads along a perilous route. The transition to a postmodern world, a world that is sustainable, at peace, just, and democratic, will require unprecedented creativity, moral leadership, foresight, and wisdom. But to our descendents, the choices that now appear to us to be so difficult will seem merely obvious.

The word "sustainable" is now used as an adjective preceding any number of nouns, hence sustainable agriculture, forestry, economics, growth, development, etc. I have even seen an advertisement that ran "woman, mid-30s seeking sustainable male mid-40s." I do not know how her search turned out, but it occurred to me that the time had arrived to determine where the term legitimately applies and where it does not. Chapters 1–4 accordingly, were written to clarify the concept and implications of sustainability.

The essays in Part 2 were written between 1985 and 1990 as part of an attempt to think through issues of curriculum and pedagogy (a word that sounds like a foot disease) for a small nonprofit environmental education organization. Nearly all discussions about the transition to a sustainable society have to do with what governments, corporations, and individuals must do. But one thing that these have in common are people who were educated in public schools, colleges, and universities. We may infer from the mismanagement of the environment throughout the century that most emerged from their association with these various educational institutions as ecological illiterates, with little knowledge of how their subsequent actions would disrupt the earth. The essays in Section 2 originate in the conviction that the ecological crisis represents, in large measure, a failure of education. Said differently, educational institutions represent a major and largely ignored leverage point to move us toward sustainability.

My primary concern in Part 2 is with the role education must play in the journey to a postmodern world. Education in the modern world was designed to further the conquest of nature and the industrialization of the planet. It tended to produce unbalanced, underdimensioned people tailored to fit the modern economy. Postmodern education must have a different agenda, one designed to heal, connect, liberate, empower, create, and celebrate. Postmodern education must be life-centered.

For the sake of clarity some distinctions are in order. "Schooling" is what happens in school and colleges. "Training," the inculcation of rote habit, is how one instructs an animal. "Learning" is what can happen throughout life for those willing to risk it. Schooling should not be confused with learning. The difference is apparent in what appears at first to be the anomaly we have all observed between the highly schooled and heavily degreed fool, and a person lacking intellectual pedigree who lives with dignity, skill, intelligence, and magnanimity, qualities, that strictly speaking, cannot be taught or measured. Schooling may or may not increase intelligence. For those so inclined, it can provide some of the tools helpful to subsequent learning. Real learning on the other hand, always increases intelligence, by which I mean the ability to call things by their right names.

Schooling has to do with the ability to master basic functions that can be measured by tests. Learning has to do with matters of judgment, and with living responsibly and artfully, which cannot be measured so easily. Schooling is carried out between certain hours of the day on certain days of the month, and in certain months of the year, during a certain portion of a life. When it's over one has either dropped out—an increasingly popular career choice—or is suitably certified. For the alert, however, learning goes on until closure from senility, death, or election to Congress. It is possible, as Walker Percy once noted, to get all A's in school and flunk life. Postmodern education has to do with the integration of schooling and active learning, a juncture that has occurred under modern conditions less often then one might suppose or wish.

The shortcomings of education reflect a deeper problem having to do with the way we define knowledge. "Research" has come to be the central focus and primary justification for the modern university. Some research is vital to our prospects, some of it is utterly trivial. Some of it may produce results that, given our present state of collective wisdom, is dangerous. A sizeable part of it is motivated by the fantasy of making an end run around constraints of time, space, nature, and human nature. It is, in short, part of the old project of dominating nature at whatever cost. Such distinctions are seldom made or even discussed. I happen to believe that our prospects depend more on the cultivation of political wisdom, moral virtue, and clear headed self-knowledge than on gadgets. In any event, it is time to ask what we need to know to live humanely, peacefully, and responsibly on the earth and to set research priorities accordingly.

The essays in the third section were written in varying states of disenchantment with the university, corporate, and government research establishment. My specific targets are the Social Science Research Council, the United States Department of Agriculture, and those who presume that we can manage the planet as if it were a giant corporation. Each presumes that the crisis can be fixed by one economic or

technological means or another in accord with their particular professional advantage.

These essays reflect my vantage point on the 1980s which was a
small and lovely valley astride Meadowcreek three miles west of Fox,
Arkansas. It was an agreeable, if remote, catbird seat. The *New York
Times*, my primary window on the world, arrived not less than four
days late. I did not find this, all things considered, a disadvantage as its
tardiness saves me a certain amount of hyperventilation. Knowing the
front-page news is already stale and that even worse may have already
happened is strangely calming. I learned to begin reading about page
eight where I imagined today's headlines, or those of next year, began.
Since television reception in the valley was poor, even on a good day,
I was deprived of a sizeable portion of the chatter of the 1980s. This is
sometimes a disadvantage in filling empty spaces in certain conversa-
tions, but not otherwise. The void in my life was filled with news of a
more immediate and practical sort. Rural life tends to alter what one
finds to be important.

The essays bear the imprint of my involvement in an effort over
the past decade to create a fifteen-hundred-acre laboratory for the
study of environmentally sound means of agriculture, forestry, renewable energy systems, architectural design, and livelihood. The initial
motivation for the Meadowcreek Project, reminiscent of Thoreau's, was
to drive some of the problems of sustainable living into a corner where
they might be studied more thoroughly. I have come to believe that
good thinking is inseparable from the breadth and the friction between
an alert mind with well-conceived experience. These essays all origi-
nated in one way or another as an effort to help me clarify how these
are joined.

Finally, these essays reflect some of the larger forces of our time.
They are in no small measure a reaction to the Reagan–Bush–Quayle
years. This time will not be regarded as our finest, except by those
who profited greatly and the perverse. On the contrary, its historians
will most likely remark on the equanimity and poise with which those
who presided over the affairs of state sold off our national assets and
bankrupted the nation, while dutifully enriching their friends. They did
so throughout with a degree of self-assurance, patriotic fervor, and
even self-righteousness that is quite extraordinary, even for politicians
of the extreme right. Such matters, however, may well come to be
appreciated as the lesser part of their contribution to our national for-
tunes. They brought a similar degree of public rectitude, equanimity,
even somnambulance to their stewardship of the nation's environment
and natural resources. By the end of the decade they had inadvertently

clarified four issues beyond any shadow of a doubt: looting the public treasury is not an entirely adequate public philosophy; nor is neglect, studied ignorance, and greed an entirely adequate foundation for the stewardship of the environment; public tolerance of such malfeasances, while considerable, is not an inexhaustible resource; and time to set things right is running short. What is to be done?

I began by noting changes in the Soviet Union and Eastern Europe. We stand to learn from the honesty and forthrightness with which Mikhail Gorbachev admitted the shortcomings of a failed system and proceeded to dismantle it. We need a similar candor and directness in addressing the roots of our own malfeasances and shortcomings, which are traceable in one way or another to how we think, and how poorly we think about some things of long-term importance. This failure is reflected in that portion of our sciences, humanities, and social sciences that deal with (or ignore) the relation between humanity and the earth. Ultimately, the failure can be traced to our schools and to our proudest universities.

David W. Orr
Oberlin, Ohio

Part One

The Issue of Sustainability

INTRODUCTION

The four essays in Section 1 attempt to define the scope and depth of the crisis of sustainability. Chapter 1 describes the causes of our plight ranging from social traps to those that are inescapable parts of the human condition. To avoid appearing to be impractical or unreasonable, we often fail to penetrate below the surface of things to deeper causes. As a result we offer aspirin-level solutions to potentially terminal illnesses. Until we see the crisis of sustainability as one with roots that extend from public policies and technology down into our assumptions about science, nature, culture, and human nature, we are not likely to extend our prospects much.

The second essay examines two contrasting approaches to sustainability. One of these is set out by the Brundtland Commission in its remarkable document, *Our Common Future* (Oxford: Oxford University Press, 1987). The other approach is derived from an eclectic group of scholars, scientists, and activists. The primary differences between the two have to do with assumptions about future growth, the scale of economic activity, the balance between top-down and grass-roots activism, the kinds of technology, and the relationship between communities and larger political and economic structures. Without anyone saying as much, the former approach reinforces a tendency toward a global technocracy and a continuation along the present path of development, albeit more efficiently. The other view requires a rejuvenation of civic culture and the rise of an ecologically literate and ecologically competent citizenry who understand global issues, but who also know how to live well in their places.

1

Unless we learn how to manage problems of global security, sustainability anywhere for any length of time will be moot. The third chapter, accordingly, focuses on the relationship between the international system of sovereign nation-states and the biosphere. The former system must now be conformed to the imperatives of the latter. This will mean redefining security to include threats to well-being from environmental mismanagement as well as ending international economic rivalries based on perpetual economic growth.

The fourth chapter addresses three strategies for change, leaving another, education, for the following section. There is no shortage of books about "paradigm shifts" and "new ages," which regard change as inevitable and inevitably a good thing. Likewise, there is now a substantial literature on the use of market incentives for change. Neither of these, however, represent a strategy of change that can come only from a political process and from an active, informed citizenry. Environmental degradation and the decay in our concept of citizenship occurred simultaneously and as mutually reinforcing trends. The final section of Chapter 4 is an argument that sustainability, citizenship, and real democracy are linked.

The Problem of Sustainability

If today is a typical day on planet earth, humans will add fifteen million tons of carbon to the atmosphere, destroy 115 square miles of tropical rainforest, create seventy-two square miles of desert, eliminate between forty to one hundred species, erode seventy-one million tons of topsoil, add twenty-seven hundred tons of CFCs to the stratosphere, and increase their population by 263,000. Yesterday, today, and tomorrow. By year's end the total numbers will be staggering: an area of tropical rainforest the size of the state of Kansas lost; seven to ten billion tons of carbon added to the atmosphere; a total population increase of ninety million. Looking further into the future, three crises are looming. The first is a food crisis evident in two curves that intersect in the not too distant future: one showing worldwide soil losses of twenty-four billion tons, the other a rapidly rising world population. The second crisis on the horizon is that caused by the end of the era of cheap energy. We are in a race between the exhaustion of fossil fuels, global warming, and the transition to a new era based on efficiency and solar energy. The third crisis, perhaps best symbolized by the looming prospect of a global climate change, has to do with ecological thresholds and the limits of natural systems. We can no longer assume that nature will be either bountiful or stable or that the earth will remain hospitable to civilization as we know it. These three crises feed upon each other. They are interactive in ways that we cannot fully anticipate. Together they constitute the first planetary crisis, one that will either spur humans to a much higher state or cause our demise. It is not too much to say that the decisions about how or whether life will be lived in the next century are being made now. We have a decade or two in which we must make unprecedented changes in the way we relate to each other and to nature.

In historical perspective, the crisis of sustainability appeared with unprecedented speed. Very little before the 1960s prepared us to understand the dynamics of complex, interactive systems and the force of exponential growth. A few prescient voices, including those of George Perkins Marsh, John Muir, Paul Sears, Fairfield Osborn, Aldo Leopold, William Vogt, and Rachel Carson, warned of resource shortages and the misuse of nature. But their warnings went largely unheard. Technological optimism, economic growth, and national power are deeply embedded in the modern psyche.[1] The result is an enormous momentum in human affairs without as yet any good end in sight.

The crisis is unique in its range and scope including energy, resource use, climate, waste management, technology, cities, agriculture, water, biological resilience, international security, politics, and human values. Above all else it is a crisis of spirit and spiritual resources. We have it on high authority that without vision people perish. We need a new vision, a new story, as theologian Thomas Berry puts it,[2] that links us to the planet in more life-centered ways. The causes of the crisis are related to those described by Marx, Weber, Durkheim, Dostoevsky, Freud, and Gandhi. But they dealt principally with the social effects of industrialization, not with its biophysical prospects. Even if these prospects were unclouded, we would have reason to question the human and societal effects of our present course. The anomie, rootlessness, and alienation of the modern world are part of a larger system of values, technologies, culture, and institutions which also produce acid rain, climate change, toxic wastes, terrorism, and nuclear bombs.

Differences exist whether these collectively represent a set of problems, which by definition are solvable with enough money, the right policies, and technology, or dilemmas for which there can be no purely technical solution. Put differently, can the values, institutions, and thrust of modern civilization be adapted to biophysical limits, or must we begin the task of consciously creating a postmodern world? These questions have to do with the causes of unsustainability. Where and how did we go wrong? What problems are we attempting to solve? How do these mesh with different policies, technologies, and behavior now proposed as solutions?

Five possibilities stand out. The crisis can be interpreted as a result of one or more social traps; it may stem from flaws in our understanding of the relation between the economy and the earth; it could be a result of the drive to dominate nature evident in our science and technology; it may have deeper roots that can be traced to wrong turns in our evolution; or finally, it may be due to sheer human perversity. I am inclined to believe that any full explanation of the causes of our plight would implicate all five. They are like the layers of an onion, peel one off and you discover yet another below. In the intellectual peeling, asking "why?" leads to the next layer and deeper levels of causation. I will consider these from the "outside in," from the most apparent and, I think, least problematic causes to deeper ones that become harder to define and more difficult to resolve.

THE CRISIS AS A SOCIAL TRAP

The crisis of sustainability is in part the result of rational behavior in "situation(s) characterized by multiple but conflicting rewards.... Social traps draw their victims into certain patterns of behavior with promises of immediate rewards and then confront them with consequences that the victims would rather avoid."[3] Arms races, traffic jams, cigarette smoking, population explosions, and overconsumption are all traps in which individually rational behavior in the near term traps victims into long-term destructive outcomes. With each decision, players are lured into behavior that eventually undermines the health and stability of the system. In Garrett Hardin's essay "The Tragedy of the Commons," the villager rationally decides to graze an additional cow on an already overgrazed commons because the system rewards him for doing so.[4] He can ignore the costs to others and eventually to himself, because payoffs reward irresponsibility. Similarly, in the name of national security, the Pentagon deploys a new weapon only to be matched or overmatched by others, which raises the costs of deadlock and increases the risks of ultimate catastrophe. In both cases the rewards are short-term (profit and prestige) and costs are long-term and paid by all.

To the extent that the crisis of sustainability is a product of social traps in the way we use fossil energy, land, water, forests, minerals, and biological diversity, the solutions must in one way or another change the timing of payoffs so that long-term costs are paid up front as part of the "purchase price." This is the rationale behind bottle bills and proposals for life-cycle or full costing. Hardin's villager would be deterred from grazing another cow by having to pay the full cost of additional damage to the commons. The Pentagon's weapons addiction might be reversed by something like a tax on all weapons that could be used offensively in direct proportion to their potential destructiveness. In these and other instances, honest bookkeeping would deter entry into social traps.

The theory is entirely plausible. No rational decisionmaker willingly pays higher costs for no net gain, and no rational society rewards members to undermine its existence. To the contrary, rational societies would reward decisions that lead to long-term collective benefits and punish the contrary. A sustainable society, then, will result from the calculus of self-interest. This approach requires minimal change in existing values, and fits most of our assumptions about human behavior derived from economics.

The theory is vulnerable, however, to some of the same criticisms made of market economics. Do we have, or can we acquire, full information about the long-term costs of our actions? In some important cases the answer is "No." Consumers who used freon-charged spray cans in the 1960s, thereby contributing to ozone depletion, could not be charged because no one knew the long-term costs involved. Given the dynamism of technology and the complexity of most human/environment interactions, it is not likely that many costs can be predicted in advance and assigned prices to effect decisions in a timely way. Some may not even be calculable in hindsight. But assuming complete information, would we willingly agree to pay full costs rather than defer costs to the future and/or to others? There is a peculiar recalcitrance in human affairs known to advertisers, theologians, and some historians. It has the common aspect of preference for self-aggrandizement in the short term, devil take the hindmost in the long term. People who choose to smoke or who refuse to wear seatbelts persist, not because they are rational, but because they can rationalize. Some who risk life and livelihood for others do so not because these represent "rational" choices, as that word is commonly understood, but because of some higher motivation (I remain unconvinced by arguments to the contrary made by sociobiologists).

Efforts to build a sustainable society on assumptions of human rationality must be regarded as partial solutions and first steps. Acknowledgement of social traps and designing policies to avoid them in the first place would, however, constitute important steps in building a sustainable society. Why we fall into social traps and generally find it difficult to acknowledge their existence—that is, to behave rationally—leads to the consideration of deeper causes.

THE CRISIS AS A CONSEQUENCE OF ECONOMIC GROWTH

A second and related cause of the crisis of sustainability has to do with the propensity of all industrial societies to grow beyond the limits of natural systems. Economic growth is commonly regarded as the best measure of government performance. It has come to be the central mission of all developed and developing societies. In political scientist Henry Teune's words: "An individually based secular morality cannot accept a world without growth."[5] (Since sooner or later we will have to accept such a world, perhaps Professor Teune has unwittingly sounded the death knell for an "individually based secular morality.") Growth, he asserts, is necessary for social order, economic efficiency, equitable distribution, environmental quality, and freedom of choice. In the course of his argument we are instructed that agribusiness is more efficient than family farms, which is not true, that forests are doing fine, which is not true, and that we are all beneficiaries of nuclear power, which deserves no comment. Nowhere does Teune acknowledge the dependence of the economy on the larger economy of nature, or the unavoidable limits set by that larger economy. For example, humans now use directly and indirectly forty percent of the net primary productivity of terrestrial ecosystems on the planet,[6] thus changing climate, exterminating species, and toxifying ecosystems. How much more of nature can we coopt without undermining the biophysical basis of civilization, not to mention growth? Professor Teune does not say.

The most striking aspect of arguments for unending growth is the presumption that it is the normal state of things. Nothing could be further from the truth. The growth economy along with much of the modern world is, in a larger view, an aberration. For perspective, if we compare the evolutionary history of the planet to a week's time, as David Brower proposes, the industrial revolution occurred just 1/40th of a second before midnight on the seventh day, and the explosive economic growth since 1945 occurred in the last 1/500th of a second before midnight. In the words of historian Walter Prescott Webb, the years between 1500 and 1900 were "a boom such as the world had never known before and probably never can know again."[7] The discovery of a "vast body of wealth without proprietors" in the new world radically altered ratios of resources to people. But by the time Frederick Jackson Turner announced the closing of the American frontier in 1893, these ratios were once again what they had been in the year 1500. Technology, for Webb, offered no way out: "On the broad flat plain of monotonous living [he was from Texas] we see the distorted images of our desires glimmering on the horizons of the future; we press on toward them only to have them disappear completely or reappear in a different form in another direction."[8] Webb would not have been surprised either by the frantic expectations raised by the prospect of cold fusion, or by its rapid demise. For him, the inexorable facts were the ratios of people to land and resources.

Twenty-two years later, a team of systems scientists at MIT armed with computer models came to similar conclusions.[9] Their results showed that population and resource use could not continue to grow exponentially without catastrophic collapse within a century. Marked increases in resource efficiency and pollution control did not appreciably alter the results. Catastrophe in exponentially growing systems is not necessarily evident until it is too late to avert.

The assumption of perpetual growth raises fundamental questions about the theoretical foundations of modern economics. Growth does not happen without cause. It is in large part the result of a body of ideas and theories that inform, motivate, and justify economic behavior. The world economy has expanded by thirteen hundred percent in the twentieth century. Can this expansion continue indefinitely? Mainstream economists are evidently still in agreement with conclusions reached by Harold Barnett and Chandler Morse in 1963:

> Advances in fundamental science have made it possible to take advantage of the uniformity of matter/energy—a uniformity that makes it feasible, without preassignable limit, to escape the quantitative constraints imposed by the character of the earth's crust.... Science, by making the resource base more homogeneous, erases the restrictions once thought to reside in the lack of homogeneity. In a neo-Ricardian world, it seems, the particular resources with which one starts increasingly become a matter of indifference. The reservation of particular resources for later use, therefore, may contribute little to the welfare of future generations.[10]

Or as Harvard economist Robert Solow once said: "The world can, in effect, get along without natural resources."[11] For Julian Simon, resources "are not finite in any economic sense."[12] Human ingenuity is "the ultimate resource" (the title of Simon's book) and will enable us to overcome constraints that are merely biophysical.

Outside the mainstream, a postmodern economics is emerging.[13] It begins with the fact that the economic process is governed by the laws of thermodynamics: "The economic process consists of a continuous transformation of low entropy into high entropy, that is, into irrevocable waste."[14] The laws of thermodynamics (that is, we can neither create nor destroy energy and matter; and the process goes from ordered matter or "low entropy" to waste or "high entropy") set irrevocable limits to economic processes. We burn a lump of coal, low entropy, and create ashes and heat, high entropy. Faster economic growth only increases the rate at which we create high entropy in the form of waste, heat, garbage, and disorder. The destiny of the human species, according to Georgescu-Roegen, "is to choose a truly great, but brief, not a long and dull, career."[15]

Economic growth is the sum total of what individual people do. And at the heart of conventional growth economics one meets a theoretical construct that economists have named "economic man," a proudly defiant moral disaster programmed to maximize his utility, which is whatever he is willing to pay for. By all accounts this includes a great many things and services that used to be freely included as a part of the fabric of life in societies with village greens, front porches, good neighbors, sympathetic saloon keepers, and competent people. Economic man knows no limits of discipline, or obligation, or satiation, which may explain why the growth economy has no logical stopping point, and perhaps why good neighbors are becoming harder to find. Psychologists identify this kind of behavior in humans as "infantile self-gratification." When this kind of behavior is manifested by entire societies, economists describe it as "mature capitalism."

In a notable book in 1977, economist Fred Hirsch described other limits to growth that were inherently social.[16] As the economy grows, the goods and services available to everyone theoretically increase, except for those that are limited, like organizational directorships and lakeside homes, which Hirsch calls "positional goods." After basic biological and physical needs are met, an increasing portion of consumption is valued because it raises one's status in society. But, "If everyone in a crowd stands on tiptoe," as Hirsch puts it, "no one sees better." Rising levels of consumption do not necessarily increase one's status. Consumption of positional goods, however, gives some the power to stand on a ladder. The rest are not necessarily worse off physically, but are decidedly worse off psychologically. The attendant effects on economic psychology "become an increasing brake" on economic growth. Growing numbers of people whose appetites have been whetted by the promise of growth find only social congestion that limits leadership opportunities and status. As Hirsch puts it:

> The locus of instability is the divergence between what is possible for the individual and what is possible for all individuals. Increased material resources enlarge the demand for positional goods, a demand that can be satisfied for some only by frustrating demand by others.[17]

The results, which he describes as the "economics of bad neighbors," include a decline in friendliness, the loss of altruism and mutual obligation, increased time pressures, and indifference to public welfare. Moreover, the pursuit of private and individual satisfaction by corporations and consumers undermines the very moral underpinnings—honesty, frugality, hard work, craftsmanship, and cooperation—necessary for the system to function. In short, after basic biological needs are met, further growth both "fails to deliver its full promise" and "under-mines its social foundations." [18]

The economist Joseph Schumpeter once made a similar argument. Capitalism, he thought, would ultimately undermine the noncapitalist attitudes and morale necessary to its stability. "There is in the capitalist system," he wrote in 1942, "a tendency for self-destruction."[19] Robert Heilbroner argues similarly that business civilization will decline not only because of pollution and "obstacles of nature," but also because of the "erosion of the 'spirit' of capitalism."[20] A business civilization inevitably becomes more "hollow" as material goods fail to satisfy deep-er needs, including those for truth and meaningful work. Its demise will result from the "vitiation of the spirit that is sapping business civilization from within."[21] At the very time that the system needs the loyalty of its participants most, they will be indifferent or hostile to it.

If the evidence suggest that economic growth is ecologically destructive, and soon to be constrained by biophysical and/or social limits, why do most economists want even more of it? A common answer is that growth is necessary to improve the situation of the poor. But this has not happened as promised. The rapid growth of the 1980s increased the concentration of wealth in the United States: the top one percent now control 34.3 percent of the wealth.[22] The same pattern is evident worldwide, as the gap between the richest and poorest has widened from 3:1 in 1800 to 25:1 at present. Within poor countries, the benefits of growth go to the wealthiest, not to those who need them most. The importance of growth to the modern economy cannot be justified empirically on the grounds that it creates equity. Growth serves other functions, one of which is the avoidance of having to face the issue of fair distribution. As long as the total pie is growing, abso-lute but not relative wealth can be increased. If growth stops for any reason, the questions of distribution become acute. Political scientist Volkmar Lauber has made a good case that "the main motivation of growth...is not the pursuit of material gratification by the masses but the pursuit of power by elites."[23] His case rests in part on analysis of public opinion polls in Europe and the United States showing only indifferent support for economic growth and much stronger support for quality of life improvements. In other words, economic growth occurs not because people demand it, but because elites do. Growth makes the wealthy more so, but it also gives substantial power to gov-ernment and corporate elites who manage the economy, its technolo-gy, and all of its side effects.

From the perspective of physics and ecology, the flaws in main-stream economics are fundamental and numerous. First, the discipline lacks a concept of optimal size, which is a polite way of saying that it has confused bloatedness with prosperity. Second, it mistakenly regards an increasing gross national product as an achievement, rather than as a cost required to maintain a given level of population and arti- facts. Third, it lacks an ecologically and morally defensible model of the "reasonable person," helping to create the behavior it purports only to describe. Fourth, growth economics has radically misconceived nature as a stock to be used up. The faster a growing volume of mate- rials flows from mines, wells, forests farms, and oceans through the economic pipeline into dumps and sinks the better. Depletion at both ends of this stream explains what Wendell Berry calls the "ever-increas- ing hurry of research and exploration" driven by the "desperation that naturally and logically accompanies gluttony."[24] Fifth, growth eco- nomics assumes that the human economy is independent of the larger economy of nature with its cycles and ecological interdependencies, and of the laws of physics that govern the flow of energy.

The prominence of the economy in the modern world, and that of growth economics in the conduct of public affairs explains, I think, a great deal of the propensity for social traps. The cultivation of mass consumption through advertising promotes the psychology of instant gratification and easy consumer credit, which create pressures that lead to risky technological fixes, perhaps the biggest trap of all. The disci- pline of economics has taught us little or nothing of the discipline imposed on us by physics and by natural systems. To the contrary, these are regarded as minor impediments to be overcome by substitu- tion of materials and by the laws of supply and demand. But eco- nomics is, in turn, a part of a larger enterprise to dominate nature through science and technology.

THE CRISIS AS THE RESULT OF THE URGE
TO DOMINATE NATURE

At a deeper level, then, the crisis of sustainability can be traced to a drive to dominate nature that is evident in Western science and tech- nology. But what is the source of that urge? One possibility, according to historian Lynn White, is that the drive to dominate nature is inherent in Judaic-Christian values.[25] The writers of Genesis commanded us to be fruitful, multiply, and to have dominion over the earth and its crea- tures. We have done as instructed. And this, according to White, is the source of our problems. But the Bible says many things, some of which are ecologically sound. Even if it did not, there is a long time

between the writing of Genesis and the onset of the problems of sustainability. An even larger gap may exist between biblical commandments generally and human behavior. We are enjoined, for example, to
love our enemies, but as yet without comparable results. Something
beyond faith seems to be at work. That something is perhaps found in
more proximate causes: capitalism, the cult of instrumental reason, and
industrial culture.[26]

Lewis Mumford attributes the urge to dominate nature to the
founders of modern science: Bacon, Galileo, Newton, and Descartes.
Each, in Mumford's words, "lost sight of both the significance of nature
and the nature of significance."[27] Each contributed to the destruction of
an organic world view and to the development of a mechanical world
that traded the "totality of human experience...for that minute portion
which can be observed within a limited time span and interpreted in
terms of mass and motion."[28]

Similar themes are found earlier in writings of Martin Heidigger
and Alfred North Whitehead, and in the recent work of Carolyn Merchant, William Leiss, Morris Berman, Jacques Ellul, and nearly all critics
of technology.[29] With varying emphases, all argue that modern science
has fundamentally misconceived the world by fragmenting reality, separating observer from observed, portraying the world as a mechanism,
and dismissing nonobjective factors, all in the service of the domination of nature. The result is a radical miscarriage of human purposes
and a distortion of reality under the guise of objectivity. Beneath the
guise, however, lurks a crisis of rationality in which means are confused with ends and the domination of nature leads to the domination
of other persons. In C. S. Lewis's words:

> At the moment, then, of man's victory over nature, we find the whole
> human race subjected to some individual men, and individuals sub-
> jected to that in themselves which is purely 'natural'—to their irra-
> tional impulses. Nature, untrammelled by values, rules the Condition-
> ers and, through them, all humanity.[30]

The crisis of rationality of which Lewis wrote is becoming acute
with the advent of nuclear weapons and genetic engineering. In a
remarkable article entitled "The Presumptions of Science" in the journal
Daedalus in 1978, biologist Robert Sinsheimer asked: "Can there be forbidden or inopportune knowledge?"[31] *Frankenstein* was Mary Shelley's
way of asking a similar question one hundred sixty years earlier: Is there
knowledge for which we are unwilling or unable to take responsibility?
Thoroughly modern humans believe quite fervently that all knowledge
is good and its embodiment in technology unproblematic. These articles

of faith rest, as Sinsheimer notes, on the belief that "nature does not set traps for unwary species," and that our social institutions are sufficiently resilient to contain the political and economic results of continual technological change. He recommends that "we forgo certain technologies, even certain lines of inquiry where the likely application is incompatible with the maintenance of other freedoms."

The idea that science and technology should be limited on grounds of ecological prudence or morality apparently struck too close to the presumptions of establishment science for comfort. Sinsheimer's article was met with a thundering silence. Science and technology have become sanctified in Western culture. Research, adding to society's total inventory of undigested bits of knowledge, is now perhaps as holy a calling as saving the heathen was in other times. Yet the evidence mounts that unfettered scientific exploration, now mostly conducted in large, well-funded government or corporate laboratories, compounds the difficulties of building a sustainable society. Weapons labs create continual upward pressures on the arms race independent of political and policy considerations. The same is true in the economy where production technologies displace workers, threaten the economies of whole regions, and introduce a constant stream of environment-threatening changes (for example, ten thousand new chemicals introduced each year; synthetic fabrics substituted for cotton and wool; plastics for leather and cellulose; detergents for soap; chemical fertilizers for manure fossil; or nuclear energy for human, natural, or animal energy). In each case, the reason for the change has to do with economic pressures and technological opportunities. In historian Donald Worster's words, the problem posed by science and technology lies "in that complex and ambitious brain of Homo sapiens, in our unmatched capacity to experiment and explain, in our tendency to let reason outrun the constraints of love and stewardship..."[32] For Worster, as for Sinsheimer, we need "the most stringent controls over research."

On the other side of the issue is the overwhelming majority of scientists, engineers, and their employers who regard science and technological innovation as inherently good and essential either to surmount natural constraints (the cornucopians) or to the development of energy and resource efficiency necessary for sustainability. These two positions differ not on the importance of knowledge, but over the kind of knowledge necessary. On the minority side are those seeking "old and solid knowledge," which used to be called wisdom.[33] It has less to do with specialized learning and the cleverness of means than with broad, integrative understanding and the careful selection of ends. Such knowledge, in Wendell Berry's phrase, "solves for pattern."[34] It does not result, for example, in the expenditure of millions of federal research dollars to develop genetically derived ways to increase milk production at the same time that the U.S. Department of Agriculture is spending millions to slaughter dairy herds because of a milk glut.

No one, of course, is against wisdom. But while we mass-produce technological cleverness in research universities, we assume that wisdom can take care of itself. The results of technical research are evident and most often profitable. Wisdom is not so easy—what passes for wisdom may be only eloquent foolishness. Real wisdom may not be particularly useful. The search for integrative knowledge would probably not contribute much to the gross national product, or to the list of our technological achievements, and certainly not to our capacity to destroy. As often as not, it might lead us to stop doing a lot of things that we are now doing, and to reflect more on what we ought to do.

But for those who advocate controls on scientific inquiry and technology, three major problems arise. The first is that of separating the baby from the bathwater. Research needs to be done, and appropriate technologies will be important building blocks of a sustainable world. In this category, I would include research into energy efficiency and solar technologies, materials efficiency, the restoration of damaged ecosystems, the knowledge of how to build healthy cities and to revitalize rural areas, how to grow food in an environmentally sound manner, and research on the conditions of peace. These are things on which our survival, health, peace, and peace of mind depend. Without much effort, we could assemble another list of research that works in the opposite direction. The challenge before us is to learn how to make distinctions between knowledge that we need from that which we do not need, including that which we cannot control. This distinction will not always be clear in advance, nor can it be enforced at all times. What is possible, however, is to clarify the relationship between technology, knowledge, and the goals of sustainability, and to use that knowledge to shift public R and D expenditures accordingly.

A second problem is the real possibility that controls will undermine freedom of inquiry and first-amendment guarantees. Sinsheimer argues that freedom of inquiry be balanced against other freedoms and values. Freedom of inquiry, in short, is not an absolute, but must be weighed against other values, including the safety and survival of the system that makes inquiry possible in the first place. A third concern is the effectiveness of any system of controls. Sinsheimer proposes that limits be placed on funding and access to instruments, while admitting that past efforts to control science have given license to bigots and charlatans. Part of the difficulty lies in our inability to predict the consequences of research and technological change. Most early research is probably innocent enough, and becomes dangerous only later when converted into weapons, reactors, PCBs, and production systems. Even these cannot automatically be regarded as bad without reference to their larger social, political, economic, and ecological context. If one society successfully limits potentially dangerous scientific inquiry, however, work by scientists elsewhere continues unless similarly proscribed. The logic of the system of research and technological development operates by the same dynamics evident in arms races or Hardin's tragedy of the commons. Failure to pursue technological developments, regardless of their side effects, places a corporation or government at a potential disadvantage in a system where competitiveness and survival are believed to be synonymous.

There are no easy answers to issues posed by technology and science, but there is no escape from their consequences. At every turn the prospects for sustainability hinge on the resolution of problems and dilemmas posed by that double-edged sword of unfettered human ingenuity. At the point where we choose to confront the effects of science and technology, we will discover no adequate philosophy of technology to light our path. Technology has expanded so rapidly and initially with so much promise that few thought to ask elementary questions about its relation to human purposes and prospects. Intoxication replaced prudence.

There is another way to see the problem. Perhaps much of our technology is not taking us where we want to go anyway. The thrust of technology has almost always been to make the world more effortless and efficient. The logical end of technological progress, as George Orwell once put it, was to "reduce the human being to something resembling a brain in a bottle...to make the world safe for little fat men."[35] Our goal, Orwell thought, should be to "make life simpler and harder instead of softer and more complex." Making life simpler, ecologically sustainable, more friendly, and more conducive to human growth requires only a fraction of the technology now available.

Technological extravagance is most often justified because it makes our economy more competitive, that is, it enables us to grow faster than other economies. In doing so, however, we find ourselves locked into behavior patterns that impose long-term costs for short-term gains. Beyond social traps, growth economics, and the drive to dominate nature are more distant causes having to do with human evolution and the human condition.

THE CRISIS AS THE RESULT OF AN
EVOLUTIONARY WRONG TURN

Perhaps in the transition from hunter-gatherer societies to agricultural and urban cultures we took the wrong fork in the road. That primitive hunter-gatherer societies more often than not lived in some stable harmony with the natural world is of some embarrassment to the defenders of the faith in progress, as is the fact that they did so at a high quality of life, with ample leisure time for cultural pursuits and with high levels of equality.[36] The designation of hunter-gatherers as "primitive" is a useful rationalization for cultural, political, and economic domination. In spite of vast evidence to the contrary, we insist that Western civilization should be the model for everyone else, but for most anthropologists there is no such thing as a superior culture, hence none that can rightly be labeled as primitive. Colin Turnbull concluded in *The Human Cycle* that in many respects hunter-gatherer tribes handled various life stages better than contemporary societies. In Stanley Diamond's words, the reason "springs from the very center of civilization, not from too much knowledge but from too little wisdom. What primitives possess—the immediate and ramifying sense of the person, and...an existential humanity—we have largely lost."[37]

If civilization represents a mistaken evolutionary path, what can we do? Paul Shepard proposes a radical program of cultural restructuring that would combine elements of hunter-gatherer cultures with high technology and the wholesale redesign of contemporary civilization.[38] Recently, he has proposed a more modest course that requires rethinking the conduct of childhood and the need to connect the psyche with the earth in the earliest years. Contact with earth, soil, wildlife, trees, and animals, he believes, is the substrate that orients adult thought and behavior to life. Without this contact with nature, maturity is spurious, resulting in "childish adults" with "the world's flimsiest identity structures."[39]

For all of the difficulty in translating the work of Sahlins, Diamond, Shepard, and others into a coherent strategy for change, they offer three perspectives important for thinking about sustainability. First, from their work we know more about the range of possible human institutions and economies. In many respects, the modern world suffers by comparison with earlier cultures from a lack of complexity, if not complicatedness. This is not to argue for a simple-minded return to some mythical Eden, but an acknowledgment that earlier cultures were not entirely unsuccessful in wrestling with the problems of life, nor we entirely successful. Second, from their work, we know that aggressiveness, greed, violence, sexism, and alienation are in large part cultural artifacts not inherent in the human psyche. Earlier cultures did not engender these traits nearly as much as mass-industrial societies have. Riane Eisler, in reinterpreting much of the prehistorical record, concludes that the norm prior to the year 5000 was peaceful societies that were neither matriarchal nor patriarchal.[40] Third, the study of other cultures offers a tantalizing glimpse of how culture can be linked to nature through ritual, myth, and social organization. Our alienation from the natural world is unprecedented. Healing this division is a large part of the difference between survival and extinction. If difficult to embody in a programmatic way, anthropology suggests something of lost possibilities and future potentials. A fifth possibility remains to be considered having to do with the wellsprings of human behavior.

THE CRISIS OF SUSTAINABILITY AND THE HUMAN CONDITION

In considering the causes of the crisis of sustainability, there is a tendency to sidestep the possibility that we are a flawed, cantankerous, willful, perhaps fallen, but certainly not entirely planet-broken, race. These traits, however, may explain evolutionary wrong turns, flaws in our culture and science, and an affinity for social traps. It's us. Philosophers call this the 'human condition'. In Ernest Becker's words: "We are doomed to live in an overwhelmingly tragic and demonic world."[41] The demonic is found in our insatiable restlessness, greed, passions, and urge to dominate whether fueled by eros, thanatos, fear of death, or the echoes of our ancient reptilian brain. At the collective level, there may be what John Livingston calls "species ambition" that stems from our chronic insecurity. "The harder we struggle toward immortality," he writes, "the fiercer becomes the suffocating vise of alienation."[42] We are caught between the drive for Promethean immortality, which takes us to extinction, and what appears to be a meaningless survival in the recognition that we are only a part of a larger web of life. Caught between the prospect of a brief, exciting career and a long, dull one, the anxious animal chooses the former. In this statement of the problem we can recognize a variant of Bateson's double bind from which there is no purely logical escape.

Can we build a sustainable society without seeking first the Kingdom of God or some reasonable facsimile thereof? Put differently, is cleverness enough, or will we have to be good in both the moral and ecological sense of the word? And if so, what does goodness mean in an ecological perspective? The best answer to this question I believe was given by Aldo Leopold: "A thing is right when it tends to preserve the integrity, stability, and beauty of the biotic community. It is wrong when it tends otherwise."[43] The essence of Leopold's Land Ethic is "respect for his fellow members, and also respect for the (biotic) community as such."[44] Respect implies a sense of limits, things one does not do, not because they cannot be done but because they should not be done. But the idea of limits, or even community, runs counter to the Promethean mentality of technological civilization and the individualism of *laissez faire* economics. At the heart of both, David Ehrenfeld argues, is an overblown faith in our ability "to rearrange the world of nature and the affairs of men and women." But "In no important instance," he writes, "have we been able to demonstrate comprehensive successful management of our world, nor do we understand it well enough to be able to manage it in theory."[45] Even if we could do so, we could never outrun all of the ghosts and fears that haunt Promethean men.

All theological explanations, then, lead to proposals for a change in consciousness and deeper self-knowledge that recognize the limits of human rationality. In Carl Jung's words: "We cannot and ought not to repudiate reason, but equally we must cling to the hope that instinct will hasten to our aid."[46] The importance of theological perspectives in the dialogue about sustainability lies in their explicit recognition of persistent and otherwise inexplicable tragedy and suffering in history, and in history to come—even in a world that is otherwise sustainable. This realism can provide deeper insight into human motives and potentials, and an antidote to giddy and breathless talk of new ages and paradigm shifts. Whatever a sustainable society may be, it must be built on the most realistic view of the human condition possible. Whatever the perspectives of its founders, it must be resilient enough to tolerate the stresses of human recalcitrance. Theological perspectives may also alert us to the physics of goodness in the certainty that a sustainable society will require a great deal of it. They also alert us to the desirability of scratching where we itch. If we can fulfill all of our consumer needs, desires, and fantasies, as cornucopians like Julian Simon or devotees of technology and efficiency predict, there may be other nightmares ahead of the sort envisioned by Huxley in *Brave New World* or that which afflicted King Midas. There is good reason not to get everything we want, and some reason to believe that in the act of consumption and fantasy fulfillment we are scratching in the wrong place. But it is difficult to link these insights into a program for change, indeed the two may be antithetical. Jung, for one, dismissed the hyperintellectuality found in most rational schemes in favor of the process of metanoia arising from the collective unconscious. After a lifetime of reflection on these problems, Lewis Mumford could only propose grass-roots efforts toward a decentralized, "organic" society based on "biotechnics," and "something like a spontaneous religious conversion...that will replace the mechanical world picture with an organic world picture."[47]

CONCLUSION: CAUSATION IN HISTORICAL
PERSPECTIVE

The crisis of sustainability is without precedent, as is the concept of a sustainable society. In attempting to build a durable social order we must acknowledge that efforts to change society for the better have a dismal history. Societies change continually, but seldom in directions hoped for, for reasons that we fully understand, and with consequences that are anticipated. Nor, to my knowledge, has any society planned and successfully moved toward greater sustainability on a willing basis. To the contrary, the historical pattern is, in Chateaubriand's words, for "forests to precede civilization, deserts to follow." The normal response to crises of carrying capacity has not been to develop a carefully calibrated response meshing environmental demands with what the ecosystem can sustain over the long run. Rather, the record reveals either the collapse of the offending culture, or technological adaptation that opens new land (new sources of carbon), water, or energy (including slave labor to contemporary use of fossil fuels). Economic development has largely been a crisis-driven process that occurs when a society outgrows its resource base.[48]

The argument, then, that humankind has always triumphed over adversity in the past, and will therefore automatically meet the challenges of the future, has the distinction of being at once bad history and irrelevant. Optimists of the "ultimate resource" genre neglect the fact that history is a tale written by the winners. The losers, including those who violated the commandments of carrying capacity, disappeared mostly without writing much. We know of their demise in part through painstaking archeological reconstruction that reveals telltale signs of overpopulation, desertification, deforestation, famine, and social breakdown—what ecologists call "overshoot."

Even if humankind had always triumphed over challenges, the present crisis of sustainability is qualitatively different, without any historical precedent. It is the first truly global crisis. It is also unprecedented in its sheer complexity.[49] Whether by economics, policy, passion, education, moral suasion, or some combination of the above, advocates of sustainability propose to remake the human role in nature, substantially altering much that we have come to take for granted from Galileo and Adam Smith to the present. Most advocates of sustainability recognize that it will also require sweeping changes in the relations between people, societies, and generations. And all of these must, by definition, have a high degree of permanence. In their range, number, and urgency, these are not modest goals.

Still, history may provide important parallels and perspectives, beginning with the humbling awareness that we live on a planet littered with ruins that testify to the fallibility of our past judgments and foresight. Human folly will undoubtedly accompany us on the journey toward sustainability, which further suggests something about how that journey should be made. This will be a long journey. The poet Gary Snyder writes of a thousand-year process. Economists frequently write as if several decades will do. Between the poet's millennia and the economist's decades, I think it is reasonable to expect a transition of several centuries. But the major actions to stabilize the vital signs of earth and stop the hemorrhaging of life must be made within the next decade or two.

History, however, gives many examples of change that did not occur, and of other changes that were perverted. The Enlightenment faith in reason to solve human problems ended in the bloody excesses of the French Revolution. In historian Peter Gay's words:

> The world has not turned out the way the philosophes wished and half expected that it would. Old fanaticisms have been more intractable, irrational forces more inventive than the philosophes were ready to conjecture in their darkest moments. Problems of race, of class, of nationalism, of boredom and despair in the midst of plenty have emerged almost in defiance of the philosophes' philosophy. We have known horrors, and may know horrors, that the men of the Enlightenment did not see in their nightmares.[50]

To the extent that the faith in reason survives, it is applied to narrow issues of technology. The difference, in Leo Marx's words, "turns on the apparent loss of interest in, or unwillingness to name, the social ends for which the scientific and technological instruments of power are to be used."[51] Similarly, Karl Marx's vision of a humane society became the nightmare of Stalin's Gulags.

In our own history, progressive reforms far more modest than those necessary for sustainability have run aground on the shoals of corporate politics. The high democratic ideals of late nineteenth-century populism gave way to a less noble reality. In one historian's words:

A consensus thus came to be silently ratified: reform politics need not concern itself with structural alteration of the economic customs of the society. This conclusion , of course, had the effect of removing from mainstream reform politics the idea of people in an industrial society gaining significant degrees of autonomy in the structure of their own lives.... Rather,...the citizenry is persuaded to accept the system as 'democratic'—even as the private lives of millions become more deferential, anxiety-ridden, and less free.[52]

A similar process is apparent in the decline of the reforms of the 1960s, which began with the high hopes of building "participatory democracy" described in the Port Huron Statement, only to tragically fall apart in chaos, camp, racism, assassinations, domestic violence, FBI surveillance, and a war that never should have been fought.[53]

History is a record of many things, most of which were not planned or foreseen. And in the same century as Auschwitz, Hiroshima, and the H-bomb, we know that at best it is only partially a record of progress. It is easy at this point to throw up one's hands and conclude with the Kentucky farmer who informed the lost traveler that "you can't get there from here." That conclusion, however, breeds self-fulfilling prophecies, fatalism, and resignation—perhaps in the face of opportunities, but certainly in the face of an overwhelming need to act. We also have the historical examples of Gandhi, Martin Luther King, and Alfred Schweitzer suggesting a different social dynamic, one that places less emphasis on confrontation, revolution, and slogans, and more on patience, courage, moral energy, humility, and nonpolarizing means of struggle. And we have the wisdom of E. F. Schumacher's admonition to avoid asking whether we will succeed or not and instead to "leave these perplexities behind us and get down to work."[54]

Finally, the word 'crisis', based on a medical analogy, misleads us into thinking that after the fever breaks things will revert to normal. This is not so. As long as anything like our present civilization lasts it must monitor and restrain human demands against the biosphere. This will require an unprecedented vigilance and the institutionalization (or ritualization) of restraints through some combination of law, coercion, education, religion, social structure, myth, taboo, and market forces. History offers little help, since there is no example of a society that was or is both technologically dynamic and environmentally sustainable. It remains to be seen how and whether these two can be harmonized.

Two Meanings of Sustainability

A sustainable society, as commonly understood, does not undermine the resource base and biotic stocks on which its future prosperity depends. In the words of Lester Brown, Christopher Flavin, and Sandra Postel, "A sustainable society is one that satisfies its needs without jeopardizing the prospects of future generations."[1] To be sustainable means living on income, not capital. The word "sustainable," however, conceals as much as it reveals. Hidden beneath the rhetoric are assumptions about growth, technology, democracy, public participation, and human values. The term entered wide public use with Lester Brown's book *Building a Sustainable Society,* and with the International Union on the Conservation of Nature's *World Conservation Strategy,* both of which appeared in 1980.[2] In 1987, the Brundtland Commission adopted "sustainable development" as the pivotal concept in its report *Our Common Future.* As defined by the Brundtland Commission, development is sustainable if it "meets the needs of the present without compromising the ability of future generations to meet their own needs."[3] Sustainable development requires "more rapid economic growth in both industrial and developing countries."[4] The commission, therefore, politely appeased both sides of the debate. The word "sustainable" pacifies environmentalists, while "development" has a similar effect on businessmen and bankers.

The phrase "sustainable development" raises as many questions as it answers. It presumes that we know, or can discover, levels and thresholds of environmental carrying capacity, which is to say what is sustainable and what is not. But a society could be sustainable in a number of technology, population, and resource configurations. To be sustainable, for example, a larger population would have to live with less of almost everything per capita than a smaller society drawing on the same resource base. The phrase also deflects consideration about the sustainability and resilience of political and economic institutions, which certainly have their own limits. Third, the phrase seems to imply social engineering on an unlikely scale. Finally, the phrase suggests agreement about the causes of unsustainability, which does not exist. The dialogue about environment and development is mostly centered on discussion about policy adjustments or technological fixes of one sort or another. The deeper causes discussed in the previous chapter are seldom mentioned perhaps because they raise the possibility that we are in much more dire straits than most care to believe.

In effect, the commission hedged its bets between two versions of sustainability, the first of which I will call "technological sustainability," the second, "ecological sustainability." In the most general terms, the difference is whether a society can become sustainable within the modern paradigm[5] through better technologies and more accurate prices, or whether sustainability requires the transition to a postmodern world that transcends, in David Griffin's words quoted in the introduction: "individualism, anthropocentrism, patriarchy, mechanization, economism, consumerism, nationalism, and militarism."[6] If regarded as successive stages, these are not necessarily mutually exclusive. To the contrary, I consider both to be necessary parts of a sustainable world. To use a medical analogy, the vital signs of the heart attack victim must be stabilized first or all else is moot. Afterward comes the longer-term process of dealing with the causes of the trauma which have to do with diet and life-style. If these are not corrected, however, the patient's long-term prospects are bleak. Similarly, technological sustainability is about stabilizing planetary vital signs. Ecological sustainability is the task of finding alternatives to the practices that got us in trouble in the first place; it is necessary to rethink agriculture, shelter, energy use, urban design, transportation, economics, community patterns, resource use, forestry, the importance of wilderness, and our central values. These two perspectives are partly complementary, but their practitioners tend to have very different views about the extent of our plight, technology, centralized power, economics and economic growth, social change and how it occurs, the role of public participation, the importance of value changes, and ultimately very different visions of a sustainable society.

TECHNOLOGICAL SUSTAINABILITY

Advocates of technological sustainability tend to believe that every problem has either a technological answer or a market solution. There are no dilemmas to be avoided, no domains where angels fear to tread. Resource scarcity will be solved by materials substitution, or genetic engineering. Energy shortages will be solved by more efficiency improvements and, for some, by nuclear fusion. The belief in techno-logical sustainability rests on the following beliefs.

A. The first and most important of these is, in Herman Kahn's words, the belief that humans should "everywhere be numerous, rich, and in control of the forces of nature."[7] The goal of sustainable develop-ment in this sense is familiar to devout readers of the dominion passage in Genesis, and to acolytes of Francis Bacon. From Bacon we found jus-tification for the union of science and power that, in his words, would "command nature in action." Bacon sought not truth as such, but a par-ticular kind of truth that would lend itself to specific outcomes. His means of "vexing" nature were aimed to "squeeze and mould" *her* in ways more desirable to her interrogators and molders. Bacon's legacy is found in the continuing belief that nature can be "managed" by under-standing and manipulating natural processes. Economist Robert Repetto, for example, seeks a "strategy that manages all assets, natural resources, and human resources...for increasing long-term wealth and well-being."[8] This assumes a great deal about human management abilities. For advocates of technological sustainability, ecology provides the sci-entific underpinnings for a system of planetary management. Techno-logical sustainability is the total domination of nature plus population control. It is Gifford Pinchot with high technology.[9]

B. Advocates of technological sustainability believe that humans are best described by the model of economic man, who knows no limits of sufficiency, satiation, or appropriateness. Economic man maximizes gains and minimizes losses according to an internal schedule of preferences that does not distinguish between right and wrong. These assumptions are familiar to students of sociobiology and behaviorist psychology. In varying ways both assume that humans are products of their neurological structure, conditioning, genes, and appetites not free choice informed by considerations of ethics and morality. This view, in Clifford Geertz's words, "is the moral equivalent of fast food, not so much artlessly neutral as skillfully impoverished."[10] The issue is not whether people are capable of being greedy or selfish—they most certainly are—but whether human nature makes them inescapably so, and whether society rewards such behavior or not. After reviewing what passes for scientific literature about human nature drawn from economics, sociobiology, and behavioral psy-chology, psychologist Barry Schwartz concludes that:

> Each discipline is importantly incomplete or inaccurate even within its own relatively narrowly defined domain.... Even if we accept what

the disciplines have to say within their own domains, there is no reason to accept their principles as a general account of what people
are.[11]

The society created in the belief that people are incapable of rising
above narrow self-interest will differ from one in which other assumptions prevail. In other words, our beliefs about our nature become self-
fulfilling prophecies which produce the behavior they purport only to
describe.

Arguments for technological sustainability rest heavily on beliefs
that humans as economic maximizers are incapable of the discipline
implied by limits even though they are somehow capable of the wisdom and good judgment necessary to manage all of the earth's
resources in perpetuity. This deeply pessimistic view of human potentials assumes that we cannot control our appetites, act for the common
good, or wisely direct our collective energies.

C. Advocates of technological sustainability believe that economic
growth is essential. The World Commission on Environment and
Development, for example, calls for a "new era of growth," by which
they mean "more rapid economic growth in both industrial and developing countries, freer market access for the products of developing
countries, lower interest rates, greater technology transfer, and significantly larger capital flows."[12] The Commission plainly regards growth
as the engine for sustainable development everywhere. James Gustave
Speth, President of the World Resources Institute, in a more resigned
fashion believes that "economic growth has its imperatives; it will
occur." He cites a projection of a "five-fold expansion in world economic activity."[13] Instead of the radical disbelief such numbers should
elicit, he is "excited" by the prospects for "greening" technology, as he
puts it, and for the transformation of industry, eventually permeating
"the core of the economies of the world" with ecological good sense.

This view raises several questions. First, since growth and environmental deterioration have occurred in tandem, how could they now be
disassociated? It is not easy to envision sustainable growth in the main
sectors of the industrial economy—energy, chemicals, automobiles,
and the extractive industries. Newer parts of the economy, such as
genetic engineering, remain unproven; they may spawn entirely new
threats to the habitability of the planet. They will also lead to vast new
concentrations of wealth with all that portends for democracy. And
growth in the industrial world has not contributed consistently to Third
World development; to the contrary, the gap between the richest and
the poorest is mostly widening. Why would growth in the developed
world in even more precarious times lead to different results?

Second, advocates of technological sustainability are not clear on what it is that is being sustained: development, a new concept, or growth as more of the same with greater efficiency. The Brundtland Commission compounded the confusion by defining sustainable development as economic growth. Sustainable growth, in Herman Daly's words, "implies an eventual impossibility" of unlimited growth in a finite system.[14] Sustainable development, implying qualitative change, not quantitative enlargement, might be sustainable. The distinction is fundamental and usually overlooked. Because growth cannot be sustained in a universe governed by the laws of thermodynamics, we must confront issues of scale and sufficiency. "We need something like a Plimsoll line," Daly writes, "to keep the economic scale within ecological carrying capacity."[15] Carrying capacity, the total population times resource-use level that a given ecosystem can maintain, cannot be specified with precision. But neither can we be absolutely clear about other concepts in economic theory, such as time and money. Daly proposes three criteria to determine optimal scale: (1) it must be sustainable over the long term; (2) human appropriation of global net primary productivity, which is now twenty-five percent or forty percent of terrestrial primary productivity (see Chapter 1, note 6); and—from the work of Charles Perrings—(3) "that the economy be small enough to avoid generating feedbacks from the ecosystem that are so novel and surprising as to render economic calculation impossible."

A related ambiguity concerns the relationships between developed and less-developed economies. For example, growth in the developed economies depends on a steady flow of food, energy, and raw materials from the less-developed world. The acres from which such food, timber, minerals, and materials are extracted and on which industrial economies depend constitute "ghost acreage," the land and resources outside national boundaries which supply the difference between consumption and resources. The use of ghost acres creates two problems. First, an imbalance is created by the price differential between exports of raw materials and imports of finished goods. Second, sellers of raw materials are highly vulnerable to price fluctuations and materials substitution. Together, they give ample reason for developing countries to selectively disengage from the global economy and chart alternative strategies for meeting basic needs.[16] For theorists of sustainability, they raise practical and ethical questions. To what extent must population and resource use stay within the limits of regional or national carrying capacity? What level of imports of which commodities constitutes unsustainability? The Japanese, for example, have preserved their remaining forests at the expense of those in Alaska, Brazil, and Southeast Asia. In Daly's words, "A single country may substitute man-made for natural capital to a very high degree if it can import the products of natural capital from other countries which have retained their natural capital to a greater degree."[17] Either some must agree to remain undeveloped while others develop, or the structural disparity between developed economies and less developed economies must be rectified.

D. Advocates of technological sustainability often assume that the causes of unsustainability are those of inaccurate pricing and poor technology. Sustainability merely means "finding and using the (right) policy levers,"[18] adjusting prices to reflect true scarcity and real costs, and developing greater efficiency in the use of energy and resources. And who will do this? For advocates of technological sustainability, the answer is policymakers, scientists, corporate executives, banks, and international agencies. Advocates rarely mention citizens, citizen groups, or grass-roots efforts around the world.[19] This perspective perhaps explains why the poor are often regarded as the cause of problems. The authors of the World Resources Institute's study of tropical deforestation, for example, state that "it is the rural poor themselves who are the primary agents of destruction,"[20] none of whom were included as "task force members." Not surprisingly, those who control decisions about land tenure, or those who have systematically uprooted and undermined village economies that were once sustainable were not mentioned.[21] This perspective may reflect an inordinate desire to appear "reasonable," or it may come from the parochialism that enfogs (a new word) too many conferences in expensive settings that exclude people with calloused hands. Technological sustainability is largely portrayed as a painless, rational process managed by economists and policy experts sitting in the control room of the fully modern, totally computerized society cooly pulling levers and pushing buttons. There is little evidence that its proponents understand democratic process, or comprehend the power of an active, engaged, and sometimes enraged citizenry. This may also explain the near total neglect of environmental education in the Brundtland Commission report and other policy reports coming regularly from Washington think tanks.[22] If sustainability is a top-down process, then an active, ecologically competent citizenry is irrelevant, and the effort to create such a citizenry through education is a diversion of scarce funds.

ECOLOGICAL SUSTAINABILITY

A second approach to the issues of sustainability holds that we will not get off so easily. Wendell Berry, for example, writes that, "We must achieve the character and acquire the skills to live much poorer than we do. We must waste less, we must do more for ourselves and each other."[23] This, however, has less to do with "policy levers" than it does with general moral improvement in society, which may not otherwise care to find policy levers. Ivan Illich similarly regards the goals of development as a fundamental mistake:

> The concept implies the replacement of widespread, unquestioned competence at subsistence activities by the use and consumption of commodities; the monopoly of wage labor over all other kinds of work; redefinition of needs in terms of goods and services mass-produced according to expert design; finally, the rearrangement of the environment in such fashion that space, time, materials and design favor production and consumption while they degrade or paralyze use-value oriented activities that satisfy needs directly.[24]

According to Wolfgang Sachs, "Eco-developers"—his term for advocates of technological sustainability—"transform ecological politics from a call for new public virtues into a set of managerial strategies." Without questioning the economic worldview, Sachs argues, one cannot question the "notion that the world's cultures converge in a steady march toward more material production."[25] The alternative he proposes is one that regards development as a cultural process in which needs and their satisfaction arise from a vernacular culture. Ecological sustainability can be portrayed in terms of six characteristics.

A. First, humans they argue are limited, fallible creatures. Wendell Berry, for example, writes:

> We only do what humans can do, and our machines, however they may appear to enlarge our possibilities, are invariably infected with our limitations.... The mechanical means by which we propose to escape the human condition only extend it.[26]

And further:

> No amount of education can overcome the innate limits of human intelligence and responsibility. We are not smart enough or conscious enough or alert enough to work responsibly on a gigantic scale.[27]

Berry describes two different kinds of limits: those on our ability to coordinate and comprehend things beyond some scale; and those inherent in our nature as creatures with a limited sense of the good and willingness to do it. Even if the first could be overcome, the second limit would remain to infect the results. In other words, we cannot escape our creaturehood, and we can compound our plight many times over in the attempt to do so.

B. A second component of ecological sustainability has to do with the role of the citizen in the creation of a sustainable future. The modern world is one in which the corporation and the state are dominant over the small enterprise and the community. People in the modern world have become increasingly passive in their roles as consumers and employees. Sustainability in the postmodern world will rest on different foundations that require an active, competent citizenry. Lewis Mumford, writing in 1938, described this task, or what he called "regional development," in these words:

> We must create in every region people who will be accustomed, from school onward, to humanist attitudes, co-operative methods, rational controls. These people will know in detail where they live and how they live: they will be united by a common feeling for their landscape, their literature and language, their local ways, and out of their own self-respect they will have a sympathetic understanding with other regions and different local peculiarities.[28]

His approach to regional planning was based on the need to "educate citizens: to give them the tools of action, to make ready a background for action, and to suggest socially significant tasks to serve as goals."[29] Political scientist John Friedmann has recently proposed a similar "escape" from our plight which involves the

> re-centering of political power in civil society, mobilizing from below the countervailing actions of citizens and recovering the energies for a political community that will transform both the state and the corporate economy from within.[30]

His approach to "radical planning" is premised on the belief that:

> The great strength of American radicals is the self-organizing capacity of the American people on a local level, and the bastion of the national state is too powerful and too remote from the centers of radical practice to become an arena in its own right. This is not to say that the struggle cannot occasionally be carried to Washington, but in this huge country, America, the political life that holds promise is, *for the time being,* better concentrated in the diversity of its many local communities and the fifty states of the Union.[31]

Friedmann proposes to center the political life of the community on "restructured households that have shed their passivity and embraced the 'production of life' as their central concern."[32] While acknowledging that the interdependent global economy will not unravel anytime soon, Friedmann, along with Daly and Cobb and Dieter Senghaas, proposes a selective delinking of the economics and politics of local communities from those of the larger world.[33] It is important to note that none of these advocate a return to parochial and closed communities or nations. Rather, they propose a process of rebuilding from the bottom up, seeing an active and competent citizenry as the foundation for a world *appropriately* linked.

Wendell Berry's comments about the "futility of global thinking" must be understood in this context. For Berry, global problems begin in the realm of culture and character, for which there can be no national or international solutions separate from those that begin with competent, caring, and disciplined people living artfully in particular localities. Biologist Garrett Hardin similarly argues that most "global problems" are, in fact, aggregations of national or local problems, for which effective solutions can only occur at the same level.[34] Even if this were not the case, top-down solutions are often inflexible, destructive, and unworkable. Even if this were not true, the best policies in the world will not save ecologically slovenly, self-indulgent people who are not likely to tolerate such policies in any case. In other words, the constituency for global change must be created in local communities, neighborhoods, and households from people who have been taught to be faithful first in little things.

Proponents of ecological sustainability, then, aim to restore civic virtue, a high degree of ecological literacy, and ecological competence throughout the population. This, in contrast to the Hollywood conservatism of the 1980s, begins by conserving people, communities, energy, resources, and wildlife. It is rooted in the Jeffersonian tradition of an active, informed, competent citizenry. A citizenry capable of conservation is a product of good homes, good farms, good communities, good churches and synagogues, good schools, and good livelihood. There is a synergy between an active, competent citizenry and visionary leadership. A country made up of good communities will tend to foster and support leadership, and real leaders will empower citizens and communities.

C. Third, ecological sustainability is rooted as much in past practices, folkways, and traditions as in the creation of new knowledge. Michael Redclift, for example, writes that "if we want to know how ecological practices can be designed which are more compatible with social systems, we need to embrace the epistemologies of indigenous people, including their ways of organizing their knowledge of their environment."[35] One of the conceits of modern science is the belief that it can be applied everywhere in the same manner. Traditional knowledge, as economist Richard Norgaard puts it, "is location specific and only arrived at through a unique coevolution between specific social and ecological systems."[36] Traditional knowledge is rooted in a local culture.

It is a source of community cohesion, a framework that explains the origins of things (cosmology), and provides the basis for preserving fertility, controlling pests, and conserving biological diversity and genetic variability. Knowledge is not separated from the multiple tasks of living well in a specific place over a long period of time. The crisis of sustainability has occurred only when and where this union between knowledge, livelihood, and living has been broken and knowledge is used for the single purpose of increasing productivity. It may be, as Redclift says, that the "question is whether 'we' [the "developed" nations] are prepared for the cultural adaptation that is required of us."[37] For the most part, we have systematically uprooted both the kind of traditional knowledge of this sort and the people who created and preserved it.

The loss of traditional knowledge, Norgaard argues, is directly related to increased species extinction and the risks inherent in the rise of a single knowledge-economic system controlling agriculture worldwide. From a systems perspective, Norgaard writes,

> the patchwork quilt of traditional agroeconomies consisted of social
> and ecological patches loosely linked together. The connections
> between beliefs, social organization, technology, and the ecological
> system were many and strong within each patch for these things coe
> volved together. Between patches, however, linkages were few,
> weak, and frequently only random. The global agroeconomy, on the
> other hand, is tightly connected through common technologies, and
> international crop, fertilizer and pesticide, and capital markets.[38]

For the present system, any failure of knowledge, technology, research, capital markets, or weather can prove highly destabilizing or fatal. Disruptions of any sort ripple throughout the system. Not so for traditional agroeconomic systems. A failure of one did not threaten others.

Finally, Norgaard points out, the "global exchange economy" treats all parts of the world the same regardless of varying ecological conditions. Since "the diversity of the ecological system is intimately linked to the diversity of economic decisions people make," there is a steady reduction of biological diversity.[39] Biological diversity is a factor in social risks, since "agroeconomic systems with many components have more options for tinkering and happening upon a stable combination or for learning and systematically selecting combinations with stabilizing negative feedbacks."[40]

Ecological sustainability will require a patient and systematic effort to restore and preserve traditional knowledge of the land and its functions.[41] This is knowledge of specific places and their peculiar traits of soils, microclimate, wildlife, and vegetation, as well as the history and the cultural practices that work in each particular setting. Sustainability will not come primarily from homogenized top-down approaches but from the careful adaptation of people to particular places. This is as much a process of *re*discovery as it is of research.

D. Fourth, proponents of ecological sustainabilty regard nature not just as a set of limits but as a model for the design of housing, cities, neighborhoods, farms, technologies, and regional economies. Sustainability depends upon replicating the structure and function of natural systems. John and Nancy Todd, for example, propose nine design precepts:

1. The living world is the matrix for all design
2. Design should follow the laws of life
3. Biological equity must determine design
4. Design must reflect bioregionality
5. Projects should be based on renewable energy sources
6. Design should integrate living systems
7. Design should be co-evolutionary
8. Building and design should heal the planet
9. Design should follow a sacred ecology.[42]

Ecology is the basis for their work on the design of bioshelters (houses that recycle waste, heat and cool themselves, and grow a significant portion of the occupants' food needs), the design of ocean arks, and currently in the design and construction of solar aquatic systems for purifying water. In the design of solar aquatic waste systems, John Todd asked how nature would deal with organic wastes. The answer, he believes, lies in the creation of "living machines," ensembles of plants that perform specific functions necessary to remove human wastes, heavy metals, and toxics from water. Three working models confirm the theory at costs and performance levels superior to standard waste systems that require great amounts of energy and chemicals. In Todd's words, living machines

> are engineered with the same design principles used by nature to build and regulate its great ecologies in forests, lakes, prairies, or estuaries. Their primary energy source is sunlight. Like the planet they have hydrological and mineral cycles.[43]

Todd sees the world as a "vast repository of...biological strategies" and components that might be integrated into a more coherent science and into "economies wrapped in the wisdom of the natural world."[44]

Amory and Hunter Lovins, founders of the Rocky Mountain Institute, similarly draw on ecology for the design of resilient technological systems. Resilience implies the capacity of technological systems to withstand external disturbances and internal malfunctions. Resilient systems absorb shock more gracefully and forgive human error, malfeasance, or acts of God. Resilience does not imply a static condition, but rather flexibility that permits a system "to survive unexpected stress; not that it achieve the greatest possible efficiency all the time, but that it achieve the deeper efficiency of avoiding failures so catastrophic that afterwards there is no function left to be efficient."[45] Resilient systems exhibit certain qualities, including:

1. Modular, dispersed structure
2. Multiple interconnections between components
3. Short linkages
4. Redundancy
5. Simplicity
6. Loose coupling of components in a hierarchy.

Like the process of evolution, designers of resilient systems tend to follow the old precepts such as: KISS (keep it simple stupid); If it ain't broke, don't fix it; You don't put all your eggs in one basket; and, If anything can go wrong, it will, so plan accordingly! Resilience implies small, locally adaptable, resource-conserving, culturally suitable, and technologically elegant solutions whose failure does not jeopardize much else.

Wes and Dana Jackson use the prairie as a model for ecologically complex farms that do not rely on tillage and chemical fertilizers. Ecologically and aesthetically, they would resemble the original prairie that once dominated the great plains. For Wes Jackson, "The patterns and processes discernible in natural ecosystems still remain the most appropriate standard available to sustainable agriculture.... what is needed are countless elegant solutions keyed to particular places."[46] The Jacksons' work follows that of Sir Albert Howard, who once proposed the forest as the model for agriculture:

> Mother earth never attempts to farm without livestock; she always raises mixed crops; great pains are taken to preserve the soil and to prevent erosion; the mixed vegetable and animal wastes are converted into humus; there is no waste; the processes of growth and the processes of decay balance one another; ample provision is made to maintain large reserves of fertility; the greatest care is taken to store the rainfall; both plants and animals are left to protect themselves against disease.[47]

The case for regarding nature as a model for farms, housing, cities, technologies, and economies rests on three beliefs. First, the biosphere is a catalogue recorded over millions of years of what works and what does not, including life-forms and biological processes. The sudden intrusion of new technologies, chemicals, and other massive human impacts disrupts established patterns and introduces novel elements for which nature has no adaptive experience. In other words, human activity will be disruptive unless it is designed to fit within ecological processes and the carrying capacity of natural systems.

Second, ecosystems are the only systems capable of stability in a world governed by the laws of thermodynamics. The energy efficiency, closed loops, redundancy, and decentralization characteristic of ecosystems allow them to swim upstream against the force of entropy. Industrial systems, on the contrary, assume linearity, perpetual growth, and progress which increase entropy and decrease stability.

A third argument has overtones of mysticism and theories of vitalism. The Todds' "sacred ecology," for example, reflects the belief in an underlying structure which connects "the human and natural worlds in an unknowable 'metapattern'."[48] Similar interpretations are often made of the biosphere as portrayed in the Gaia hypothesis of James Lovelock, and of Teilhard de Chardin's "noosphere" in which human intelligence and communications technology are presumed to be something like a planetary nervous system in the making.

Advocates of ecological sustainability use nature as a model, but they do not necessarily agree on the use of that model. Does sustainable development require the restoration of natural systems as authentically as possible, or only the imitation of their structure and ecological processes? Restoration ecology is the best example of the former,[49] while Wes Jackson's efforts to breed perennial polycultures that resemble prairies exemplifies the latter. Attempts to mimic nature and ecological processes may in time come to resemble Baconian science with its goal of total mastery. If, on the other hand, sustainability is interpreted to mean the restoration (and/or preservation) of natural systems as authentically as possible, letting natural selection do most of the work, then its advocates must develop a clear understanding of what is natural, what is not, and why the difference is important.[50]

E. Among the most important implications of using nature as a model for human systems are issues of scale and centralization. If ecology is the model, should society be more decentralized? Surface-to-volume ratios limit the size of biological organisms and physical structures. Are there similar principles of optimum size for cities, nations, corporations, and technologies? Leopold Kohr, E. F. Schumacher, and other proponents of decentralization supported decentralization and appropriate scale on three grounds.[51] The first has to do with human limits to understand and manage complex systems. Wendell Berry similarly argues, for example, that the ecological knowledge and level of attention necessary to good farming limits the size of farms. Beyond that limit, the "eyes to acres" ratio is insufficient for land husbandry. At some larger scale it becomes harder to detect subtle differences in soil types, changes in plant communities and wildlife habitat, and variations in topography and microclimate. The memory of past events like floods and droughts fades. As scale increases, the farmer becomes a manager who must simplify complexity and homogenize differences in order to control. Beyond some threshold, control requires power not stewardship. Grand scale creates islands of ignorance, small things that go unnoticed, and costs that go unpaid.

Is the same true of things other than farms? I think so, even if we cannot prescribe the ideal size of a city or corporation any more than we can define the exact number of acres one person can farm responsibly. To know the optimum farm size requires that we know the farmer's intelligence, skill, depth of motivation, energy level, age, state of his or her marriage, the type of land, and so forth. Appropriate scale is not an absolute but a continuum, bounded by the limits of nature and those of the mind. Disorder, breakdown, ugliness, and disease suggest that these limits have been transgressed. In the transition from Plato's ideal polis of five thousand to a Mexico City of twenty million, neighborhoods unravel, pollution overwhelms local ecosystems, public health deteriorates, transportation becomes congested, civility declines, crime increases. But not all of these things happen at once. As scale increases, good things happen as well. Growing cities support symphony orchestras, but when they continue to grow people are mugged leaving the symphony and acid rain dissolves the exterior marble of the civic auditorium. So we can speak only of a ratio of good to bad that gradually or precipitously declines as scale crosses some threshold.

When obscure place names—Seveso, Bhopal, Three Mile Island, Chernobyl, Love Canal, Times Beach, Prince William Sound—become synonymous with disasters, a similar dynamic is at work in technological systems. In each case, large scale, complexity, improbability and human error, led in due time to what Charles Perrow describes as "normal accidents," that is, events which are predictable given enough time.[52]

The thread connecting all questions of appropriate scale from farms to technological systems, then, has to do, first, with the human limits to comprehend and manage beyond some threshold of scale and complexity. Increasing scale increases the number of things that must be attended to and the number of interactions between components. Rising scale also increases the costs of carelessness. Preoccupation with quantity replaces the concern for quality: the farm becomes an agribusiness, the city become a megalopolis, the shop becomes a corporation, tools become complicated technologies, the legitimate concern for livelihood becomes an obsession with growth, and weapons become instruments of total destruction.

The second ground for proposing decentralization and appropriate scale is that centralization and large scale undermine the potential for ethical action and increase the potential for mischief. As scale increases it becomes easier to separate costs and benefits, creating winners and losers who are mostly strangers to each other. Ethical responsibility means paying the full costs for one's actions, or mutually agreed compensation to those who do. Ethical behavior seems most likely when the decisionmaker's own hide is at stake. It still works fairly well if costs are levied against friends, neighbors, and relatives encountered face to face. The likelihood of ethical behavior, however, decreases with distance in time and space between beneficiaries and losers.

Scale can also make it difficult to assign responsibility. Whom can we blame for acid rain? For CO_2-induced climate change? For species extinction? For Chernobyl? In each case the costs are widely distributed in the form of increased cancer rates and the generalized costs of ecological changes. Responsibility is diffused among political leaders, utilities, corporations, government agencies, and the consuming public.

Leopold Kohr argues, third, that large scale, whether in nations or social organizations, provides the impetus for imperialism, war, and aggression: "For whenever a nation becomes large enough to accumulate the critical mass of power...it will become an aggressor."[53] He draws the conclusion that wickedness derives from bigness, and that "no misery on earth can be handled, *except* on a small scale."[54] Smallness is nature's principle of health; bigness the principal cause of disease.[55]

F. The paradigm of ecological sustainability has evolved an epistemology of sorts around the concept of interrelatedness. This epistemology involves what Gregory Bateson called the "pattern that connects."[56] This pattern always includes both observer and observed, subject and object. "We are not outside the ecology for which we plan," he says, "we are always and inevitably a part of it." The search for interrelatedness is a revolt from Cartesian logic, reductionism, and the fragmentation characteristic of modern science, conventional economics, and even some of modern ecology.[57] It also recognizes that the world is paradoxical and that our understanding will always be incomplete. We are makers and participants in reality, not just observers. Where science has dismantled nature, we must study whole systems, linkages, processes, patterns, context, and emergent properties at higher systems levels. "Holistic science" cannot be conducted through the reductionist methods characteristic of much science.[58] We cannot reach valid knowledge of nature simply by taking it apart and studying the pieces any more than we could understand human behavior from the study of anatomy.

The recognition of interrelatedness leads to equally radical changes in the conduct of human affairs. Conflict has often been essential to the existence of nations, churches, movements, and ideologies that identify themselves in opposition to something else. The tendency is to presume one's side to be the sole possessor of truth, a useful tool with which to bludgeon infidels into submission. The truth is no less uncertain, incomplete, relative, and paradoxical in human affairs than it is in the physical world described by Heisenberg or Einstein. An ancient insight, ignored by ideologists of all kinds, states that we become that which we hate. Life is a dance of opposites, each necessary to the other. "Truth," in William Irwin Thompson's words, "cannot be expressed except in relationships of opposites."[59] We cannot fathom the unconscious drives and purposes which create irony and counterintuitive effects; anything like total truth is beyond our comprehension. We intend one thing and do the opposite. From this we can learn humility in the fact of unfathomable mystery and paradox. Second, we can make no absolute distinctions between the self and the world. Treating others as we would have them treat us isn't just good for them, it's also in our own self-interest. Goodness, mercy, justice, and ecological prudence have both survival value and spiritual rewards. Before rushing out to do good, however, we might reflect on how much of the world's misery began with good intentions. Competence in doing good is still an underdeveloped art.

THE LIMITS OF METAPHORS

As with all concepts and metaphors, we must ask where that of ecological sustainability applies and where it does not. Two categories are particularly problematic. Cities will always be something of an exception to the model of natural systems. Under the best conditions, large urban areas will import substantial amounts of food, energy, water, and materials, and they will export roughly equivalent amounts of sewage, garbage, pollution, and heat. Many of these impacts could be reduced by better mass transit, careful urban planning that includes parks, systematic use of solar energy, urban-regional agriculture, urban reforestation, laws (like bottle bills) reducing material flows, and biological treatment of organic wastes. Nevertheless, although these measures significantly reduce environmental damage, they do not make cities "sustainable" such that the net environmental impact of urban concentrations is within the absorptive and healing capacities of the surrounding natural systems. The sheer concentration of large numbers of people will reduce environmental resilience, encroach on wildlife habitat, and impose significant ecological costs elsewhere. Urban concentrations must be justified on their contributions to intellectual, economic, and cultural life, not their sustainability. I do not think that cities have to be as ugly, formless, inhuman, and inefficient as we have made them. But given that we have urbanized badly, and cannot quickly undo what we have done, urban conglomerations cannot easily be made a harmonious part of a sustainable society. This is not an argument against cities, but rather one against megapolitan areas without plan or form. It is also one for "green cities" with greenbelts, urban parks, urban agriculture, and urban wilderness preserves.[60]

Another and increasingly problematic area is that of technology. The cumulative effects of technology extend human power over nature so that we can transcend the limits of gravity, space, time, biology, and now, with computers, those of mind. In the process, we remove ourselves further and further from the natural conditions, both good and bad, that previously constrained human development. In a society that worships technology, questions of this sort are heresy. Technology is our declaration of independence from nature. As a user of airplanes, automobiles, computers, telephones, tractors, and digital equipment, I am a cosigner. These things allow me to avoid a great many things about nature that I do not like. But this may be a Pyrrhic victory of convenience over substance. It may also reflect the domination of technology over free choice since many of the technologies I use I do so out of necessity. I would much prefer to travel by train, for example, but the rail service has been allowed to deteriorate. I would like to ride a bicycle, but without risking my life. Whether technology is beyond human control[61] there can be no question that it is now the preeminent fact in modern societies. Whether it can be controlled and harnessed to the long-term benefit of humanity is *the* question of our civilization. If so, the goal of a sustainable society based on the model of natural systems is not necessarily antithetical to technology. The question then becomes what kind of technology, at what scale, and for what purposes. In thinking about issues of this sort, we lack a philosophy of technology that could help us decide the most important issues on the human agenda. Without such clarity, we are prone to what Langdon Winner has called "technological somnambulism, a willing sleepwalk," a passive acceptance of whatever technologies are thrust upon us by whomever for whatever purposes. Because artifacts do have politics, in

Winner's words, any decent philosophy of technology will be a political philosophy that clarifies the effects of technology on the distribution of power and control in society.[62] It will also be a philosophy of
nature because technological choices often have sweeping effects on
ecosystems.

An alternative, postmodern technology, in Frederick Ferre's view,
would aim to optimize rather than maximize, to cultivate rather than
manipulate, and to differentiate rather than centralize.[63] The beginnings
of postmodern technology are evident in solar technologies, in the
development of regenerative farming practices, and in computers.
Future advances in postmodern technology will combine ecology and
technology in subtle and ingenious ways. The model for John Todd's
"solar aquatic" system is that of a marsh. The "technology" includes
plants, aquatic animals, computers, and space-age materials. Todd's
genius lay in recognizing nature as an effective and benign partner
with human artifice.[64]

Postmodern technology is only in its infancy. Nonetheless, I
believe that we know enough of its potential promise for housing,
energy, food, transportation, and waste cycling to say that it represents
a radically new departure that is neither a rejection of technology, nor
a sleepwalk along the edge of catastrophe.

CONCLUSION

The modern world has failed; a postmodern world is still to be
born. Transitions such as this are times of both promise and peril. The
promise comes from the necessity (read opportunity) to reconsider,
rethink, reform, restore and rebuild our world and worldviews. This
process raises old issues, and some new ones, having to do with the
balance between centralization and decentralization, urban and rural,
freedom and order, individual and community, sacred and secular,
organic and mechanical. The peril comes from both the urgency and
scope of our plight and the resulting pressures that could cause us to
make the transition badly. The nightmare hanging over humanity is
that we will lack the intellectual clarity, good will, and moral power
needed to make wise choices with all that this portends for whether
and how humanity survives.

A Tale of Two Systems: Sustainability in International Perspective

The modern international system was created when the world's population was five hundred million, the fastest speed attainable was by horse, and the most destructive weapon was a naval gun that could hurl an eight-pound iron ball several hundred yards. The system ratified at the Treaty of Westphalia in 1648 acknowledged the territorial state as the arbiter of the issues of war and peace. From that time until quite recently, territory has been the primary issue on the international agenda. The present, much longer agenda is dominated by issues that in one way or another have to do with adaptation to the limits of the earth.

Nearly a century and a half after the establishment of the Westphalian system, an English parson, Gilbert White, published *The Natural History of Selbourne*. The book is notable, not only because is has gone through more than one hundred editions since it was first published in 1789, but also because it marks the beginning of the modern study of natural history and ecology. From White to the contemporary work of James Lovelock, we have progressively discovered a world of interdependent parts, no one of which can be said to be sovereign. The world of nature, in contrast to the international system, functions as a community in which the welfare of the individual and the species is bound to the health of the larger system.

Ecological interdependence was largely unknown to the statesmen of 1648. It is now the predominant global fact. At some future time, the death of the modern Westphalian system and the beginning of a postmodern consciousness may be given as 1926, the year in which the Russian ecologist Vladimir Vernadsky published *The Biosphere*.[1] Although few noticed, the implications of a planetary system of life, which Vernadsky called the biosphere, foreshadowed the end of the nation-state system predicated upon absolute sovereignty and the threat of violence. International sovereignty and the reality of the biosphere were on a collision course.

THE INTERNATIONAL SYSTEM

The system of European international relations ratified at West-phalia assumed no higher authority than the nation-state. The world of nations was and has remained an "anarchical society."[2] Order in the system has been largely imposed by the dominant military and economic powers. The Westphalian system is now a global system, not just a system of European states. Its structure has shifted from the classical balance of power of the nineteenth century to the post-1945 bipolar world, and now to the more complex world structure of the late twentieth century. The dominant military powers of the present are no longer the most dynamic economies. Both the Soviet Union and the United States have lost their competitiveness to the Japanese and European economies which are not great military powers. But the notion of military self-help in an anarchical system, if weakened, has survived as the keystone of a system which rests as before on the pillars of military and economic power. Great powers, as Yale University historian Paul Kennedy states, must "simultaneously provide military security (and)...ensure sustained growth."[3] These in turn have required an increasing level of technology.

At the core of the Westphalian system is the conceptual muddle of "national security." For a concept cited so often and with such gravity, it is remarkably vague. As conventionally defined, it implies the safety of a nation from hostile attack or coercion detrimental to its "national interests," a term of equal clarity. Both terms have reflected the megalomania of reigning elites. As these come and go, the definition of national security and national interest has shifted accordingly. For militarists in Japan in the 1930s, both national interest and security required conquest to build a "co-prosperity sphere." Since 1945, their successors have become much richer than their militaristic forebears at a fraction of the effort and risk by selling automobiles and VCRs to the rest of the world.

For slow learners, however, the means to security in the Westphalian order are still military predominance and alliances. Even before the present era, these were imperfect means to protect nations from real and imagined adversaries. In the present era they are increasingly counterproductive. Even the most ardent chauvinist must wonder what was gotten for the $2.13 trillion spent on weapons in the years between 1980 and 1988, or the $8.4 trillion spent between 1960 and 1987. Crash-proof coffee machines, the glories and medals of Grenada and Panama, and our occupation of the Persian Gulf may not represent a proper return on investment. In lucid moments, he or she may also have noticed that in the event of any respectable nuclear war, New Zealand's prospects for survival are considerably better than our own. One of the less celebrated accomplishments of our Department of "Defense" is that it has made the United States the world's most prominent bull's-eye.

While the traditionalist, armed with doctrines of national security, scans the horizon for signs of threats, other threats are emerging from ecological malfeasance and mismanagement of resources that do not fit old theories of national security. The situation is not unlike that of a man who arms himself to the point of bankruptcy to keep robbers from his home while letting termites, gas leaks, and faulty wiring go unnoticed. The United States and the Soviet Union have together amassed an unholy array of weapons in the name of security while letting their national households deteriorate. The same is glaringly true as well in the highly militarized parts of the underdeveloped world.

For reasons its founders could not have foreseen, the Westphalian system no longer works as intended. First, the system has failed to limit conflict. The twentieth century has been a period of unparalleled bloodshed, with some two hundred million deaths due to war. In the 1980s, twenty-two wars were fought, with no clear winners.[4] The Westphalian system worked best between 1815 and 1890 in the limited geographic area of Europe when: (a) the major actors were all nation-states of roughly similar size and structure; (b) the heads of state were in agreement about the rules of the system; and (c) they could perceive a common enemy in radicalism. The disintegration of that order has been a function of the reverse of these in the twentieth century: (a) the system is now a world system consisting of many political systems, cultures, and nonstate actors ranging from the Red Cross to the Hezbollah; (b) rules of state behavior are not universally agreed upon; and (c) conflicts and issues cut across the lines of race, region, ideology, and economics. Without an effective system of conflict control, enforcement, and dispute resolution, the system of sovereign nation-states has become increasingly destructive. The steady march of weapons technology will only make it more so.

The second reason the Westphalian system no longer works is that it now confronts the consequences of a greater complexity, speed, and volume of political events. The interaction of technological, economic, political, social, and military forces that produce change are poorly understood or undiagnosed altogether. Compared to the world of 1648, the sheer volume of events and interactions in the world system has risen by orders of magnitude. Revolutions in communications and transportation have increased the rate of change. A far more complex world system moves ever more rapidly. In political scientist Andrew Scott's words:

> For the global system to work tolerably well, a large number of sub-systems must function effectively without letup. The failure, or imperfect functioning, of any of them will create problems. Peril is therefore built into the system and would exist even if all actors were to abandon hostility to one another in favor of unremitting cooperation.[5]

The international system now generates problems faster than it is creating solutions. The only good response, in Scott's view, involves "an increasing amount of cooperation and coordination." Nations "will need to focus less on state-centered interests and more on system-centered interests."[6] Cooperation, however, runs against the key assumption of the Westphalian order: self-help in an anarchical system.

Third, the costs of resorting to or preparing for violence are undermining the Westphalian system of military self-help. Political economist Robert Gilpin asserts that there is a "law of the increasing cost of war."[7] Every weapons system is becoming more expensive than its counterparts of past decades. An aircraft carrier of World War II vintage cost several millions, while a present one costs several billions. Since 1945, military weapons have increased in cost 105 times compared with a price inflation of 6.5 times.[8] Ironically, the costs of Armageddon have fallen sharply since nuclear weapons are relatively cheap. All else—delivery systems, research, conventional weapons—has become exponentially more costly. Global military expenditures since 1960 are in excess of sixteen trillion dollars.[9] Of this amount the United States has spent some $8.4 trillion. War has become prohibitively destructive, and preparation for war has become prohibitively expensive.

The direct costs, however, do not tell the full story. The real costs of militarism must include "opportunity costs," all of those things not done because money is drained away by military expenditures. Gold-plated military systems contrast markedly with declining cities, crumbling infrastructure, and growing poverty. For the cost of one Trident submarine we could immunize all the children in the Third World against six diseases, saving one million lives a year. For the cost of one aircraft carrier we could feed twenty million undernourished people in the United States for six months. The Star Wars research budget would provide elementary education in Latin America for 1.4 million children. Fuel consumed by the Pentagon in a year would run all U.S. public transportation for twenty-two years. Evidence from a number of studies shows that dollars spent on weapons produce fewer jobs than those in most other sectors. Military spending is a drag on the rest of the economy, no longer offset by purported "spinoff" benefits from weapons research.[10]

Militarization imposes more subtle costs. The secrecy which is drawn around the process of weapons acquisition has promoted corruption of the most venal sort, as well as monumental incompetence evident in large cost overruns. Beyond public scrutiny, weapons contractors and generals alike have not infrequently proven themselves to be of negotiable honesty and patriotism, proving over and over again what the warriors of the free market hold as gospel: the lack of competition begets waste, incompetence, and dependence on public charity. It also undermines democracy.[11] The use of "national secrecy" as a veil to conceal corruption and justify the harassment and surveillance of critics undermines the democratic process in the most blatant and fundamental ways.

A fourth factor undermining the Westphalian system is that it has become ecologically implausible. War, the ultimate expression of sovereignty, has become too destructive for victor and vanquished alike. Even small nuclear wars would be utterly catastrophic, triggering nuclear winter and probably other as yet unforeseen ecological consequences.[12] They would certainly devastate complex industrial societies beyond any recovery. Even beyond physical recovery, the effects of limited nuclear war on the survivors' morale and their capacity to restore a humane society are mostly ignored by military analysts. Many assume that people would clean up the rubble and life would go on as before, not unlike the rebuilding of Europe after 1945. But the suddenness, totality, and global effects of nuclear war would not only destroy completely by blast and radiation, they would crush the spirit of any survivors in ways previous wars did not.

Conventional war is also becoming prohibitively destructive and indecisive. The ecological effects of U.S. bombing on Vietnam will take decades or longer to restore. Bomb craters have altered water flow and provided habitat for noxious insects. Effects of defoliants, and the destruction of vegetation and wildlife, in some cases cannot be restored.[13] The government of Vietnam reports significantly higher rates of disease and cancer in areas where defoliants were used. As yet, no good studies have been done on the ecological effects of war in the

Middle East. But prolonged warfare in fragile environments would impose severe damage to plant and animal communities, disrupt watercourses, and contribute to soil loss.

Projections of the future of the war system mostly fall along two lines. One school of thought holds that it will die a natural, if not entirely honorable, death as it comes to be seen as wasteful, counterproductive, and generally unfashionable. Political scientist John Mueller, for example, argues that war has become obsolete and is now widely regarded as morally repulsive. "It may not be obvious," he writes, "that an accepted, time-honored institution that serves an urgent social purpose can become obsolescent and then die out because a lot of people come to find it obnoxious."[14] In fact something like this, he argues, has been happening to the institution of war. No longer do we hear anyone of discernible sanity say that war is good as a character-building exercise, or that we could survive a nuclear conflict. Yet not long ago these attitudes were widely held. Recent history provides some evidence that attitudes toward war are changing, at least in the nations of the northern hemisphere who hold the records for futile carnage. The American experience in Vietnam and that of the Soviet Union in Afghanistan may in historical perspective be watersheds. The militarization of recent years, in his view, is similar to the brilliance of a sunset marking the end of the day. The war system then fades away as societies "learn" to handle conflicts in better ways.[15]

In *The Parable of the Tribes,* Andrew Bard Schmookler exemplifies the second major school of thought, in which peace requires the resolution of the paradox of security. Power, according to Schmookler, is like a virus in a body.[16] Once introduced to human history, no tribe or society wishing to survive could avoid developing its own power to the maximum. Power thus introduced into human affairs has tragically deflected human development from more benign paths. The results ripple outward through history and through societies:

> Anarchy dictates that a chronic contest of wills afflicts the whole system of civilization. The people wounded in this contest make wounded parents. Unable to exercise their right as human beings to a say in their destiny, adults may compensate by being tyrants with their children. What is strangled in the macrocosm pours forth with a fury in the microcosm of the home. Thus is the disease spread from generation to generation, from chicken to egg and back again.[17]

Schmookler makes no assumptions about human evil. To the contrary, power directs the system according to its own logic. In the modern world, the pursuit of power has led to greater centralization of control, societies permanently mobilized for war, and the technologies necessary to harness nature to the state's ends. Humane values, culture, and ecosystems are sacrificed for the sake of maintaining and preserving power within a pitiless international system.

Schmookler concludes that "Where the parable of the tribes is the root, the problem of man's power over nature can be solved only by solving first the problem of power among people."[18] We are accustomed to thinking of environment and security as two mostly unrelated problems. Schmookler argues that the pursuit of power in the international system has been a major cause of the decline in environmental quality. By the same logic, sustainability will depend on the evolution of a system of world order that neutralizes power.

The logic of the parable is similar to that described by Rousseau in the Stag Hunt, or that of the game theoreticians' Prisoners' Dilemma. In all three, cooperative behavior is penalized in the short term. The system creates strong incentives to maximize individual short-term self-interest with the real likelihood of disaster in the long haul. No evil intentions are necessary for catastrophe, only the remorseless workings of the logic of self-interest. How are we to solve the paradox?

In his sequel, *Out of Weakness,* Schmookler concludes with the need for a "new, overarching order that fosters harmony and wholeness," and which is necessary to "make the world safe for the consciousness that transcends boundary." In other words, the paradox has no logical answer short of moral improvement, which according to the logic of the parable, must occur everywhere simultaneously.[19] He calls this system "the bio-civisphere." Civilization has engendered a "sick consciousness," which must be replaced with "a consciousness of a very different sort." The ingredients he proposes for this state of consciousness include humility, tolerance, transcendence, love, forgiveness, and reconciliation. If we are open to the cosmic process, "the weeds of our historical fears (can) give way to a garden of love."[20]

Robert Axelrod suggests another not totally unrelated way out of the paradox of power. Over a number of simulations of the Prisoners' Dilemma, the best course was what Axelrod calls a "tit-for-tat" strategy that resembles an arms race in reverse. To work, the process must be mutual, beginning with relatively small steps that are easily reciprocated and gradually move to more substantial issues. The strategy does not require major agreements, at least in the beginning. Axelrod's advice to national leaders is: "Don't be envious, don't be the first to defect, reciprocate both cooperation and defection, and don't be too clever."[21] The effect of the strategy is to build trust by small reciprocal steps and trial and error.[22]

Efforts to stabilize the earth's vital signs and to build sustainable societies cannot wait until the paradox of power is resolved. But both the Prisoner's Dilemma and *The Parable of the Tribes* suggests that steps to build a sustainable society will always be tentative in an international system in which fear undermines good intentions and power tempts. Is there another way? Mikhail Gorbachev suggests another possibility, one not unlike Alexander the Great's response to the Gordian knot. Faced with the perplexities of a decaying system of corrupt power, an arms race without end, and a stagnant economy, Gorbachev acted with boldness and decisiveness to exit Afghanistan, cut military spending, open the Soviet economy, dismantle one-party rule, end the Cold War, and liberate Eastern Europe. Whatever the lasting effects of these stunning changes, Gorbachev stands as an example of the power of decisive, visionary leaders to cut through seemingly intractable dilemmas.

THE BIOSPHERE

The international system is a human creation and an expression of the human condition. It exists, however, within another and larger system, the biosphere, which operates independently of human volition. Until recent years, statesmen could assume the stability of this larger system. Indeed, most remained quite blissfully ignorant of it. But assumptions of ecological stability which underlay the Westphalian system no longer hold. For example, hidden in the logic of international politics are unstated beliefs that:

1. Climate would remain stable within historic limits and the biosphere would absorb human and industrial wastes
2. Human population could be fed, housed, clothed
3. Science provided an adequate basis for managing nature
4. Energy would be cheap and abundant.

In other words, it was assumed that the ecological and biospheric foundations of political, social, and economic systems were secure. But expanding knowledge of the natural world has been Janus-like. On the one hand, we have learned to create new materials and life-forms, things the alchemists only dreamed of doing. On the other hand, at the level of ecosystems and the biosphere, the consequences of unfettered human creativity and procreativity have been anything but benign. Knowledge of these consequences, however, has developed more slowly than the reductionist knowledge necessary to tinker with the pieces. As it does, we have discovered that each of the above unstated beliefs was wrong. In other words, we have discovered the following limits of which we were previously unaware.

The limits of the earth. The idea that the planet is alive in some sense probably predates human records. But the scientific study of the planet as a living system began with Vernadsky and more seriously with James Lovelock, author of the Gaia hypothesis, which is that: "the temperature, oxidation state, acidity and certain aspects of the rocks and waters are at any time kept constant, and that this homeostasis is maintained by active feedback processes operated automatically and unconsciously by the biota."[23] In other words, life has played an active role in creating and maintaining the conditions necessary for its perpetuation. The Gaia hypothesis raises a number of questions about the role of micro flora and fauna in the larger biogeochemical cycles of earth. Whether subsequently confirmed in detail or not, it is clear to many observers that life is not simply a passive hitchhiker on the earth. It is also clear that the biosphere, whether operating in a Gaian fashion or not, has limits. In Lovelock's words, "If the world is made unfit by what we do, there is the probability of a change in regime to one that will be better for life but not necessarily better for us."[24]

Humans are now the dominant force on the planet, equivalent to that of previous geologic upheavals. Agriculture, energy use, and manufacturing lie at the heart of the human global impacts. Since 1850, nine million square kilometers have been converted into permanent cropland. Energy use has risen by a factor of eighty, disrupting geochemical cycles of carbon, nitrogen, and sulphur. Industrial production is up more than ten thousand percent. Since 1700, the decline in forested area is larger than Europe. Sediment loads in major rivers has increased by three hundred percent, and in smaller rivers by as much as eight hundred percent. Increased water use in the same period is roughly equal to the volume of Lake Huron. Methane in the atmosphere has doubled. Heavy metals and toxics now exist everywhere in measurable quantities. Humans are causing a biological holocaust that is destroying life ten thousand times more rapidly than the natural rate of extinction. The rate of change since 1945 is staggering and is still accelerating.[25]

Among these trends, the most serious is global warming caused by the release of heat trapping gases including CO_2 from the combustion of fossil fuels and deforestation, methane from anaerobic decay, and industrial chemicals such as the CFC compounds, bromine, and halons.[26] As a result, the earth has warmed by .5 to .7 C since 1860, and six of the warmest years on record have been in the 1980s.[27] Data on the rate of CO_2 accumulation show a rise beginning in 1987 from 1.5 parts per million (ppm) to 2.4 ppm. One explanation for the increasing rate is the effect of warmer temperatures on the rates of plant decay and respiration. The effects of planetary warming will be irreversible, cause substantial changes in rainfall, flood low coastal areas, and initiate rapid, perhaps devastating, changes in forests and whole bioregions. The appropriate responses are also equally clear, including a reduction of combustion of fossil fuels through energy efficiency and the development of renewable sources, reversing the deforestation of the tropics, and large-scale reforestation nearly everywhere.[28] Each of these steps would be beneficial for other reasons as well.[29]

Depletion of planetary ozone is closely related. The primary culprit is a family of chemicals known as CFCs.[30] Since their discovery in the 1930s, they have been used widely in many industries as solvents, propellants, and cleaners, and in products ranging from computer chips to insulation. They do not break down quickly and, once released, they accumulate in the stratosphere where their decomposition releases chlorine which destroys ozone. Each day we release some twenty-seven hundred tons of CFCs to the atmosphere. The results are an ozone "hole" over the South Pole which covers the Antarctic and extends now over Australia, the beginnings of the same condition over the North Pole, and a general thinning throughout the mid-latitudes. Even with an immediate ban on CFCs we may expect a significant decline in ozone levels over the next 30 years.[31] Warming and ozone depletion may also be linked. As the lower portion of the atmosphere warms, the upper layers cool forming ice crystals which also destroy ozone.

Several conclusions are beyond contention. First, we are crossing critical planetary thresholds, or will soon do so. Second, we are woefully ignorant of the critical causal linkages between complex systems and the effects of human actions. Third, we do not have readily available data about the "vital signs" of the planet comparable, say, to the Dow Jones index. Fourth, most research is still directed toward manipulation of the natural world, not toward understanding the impacts of doing so, or to the development of low-impact alternatives. It is a fact of no small importance that key parts of the evidence were gathered by freelance scientists operating outside the normal channels of large, well-funded scientific organizations.

Population limits. World population reached one billion sometime around the year 1800; two billion after 1900; 2.5 billion in 1950; four billion by 1975, and five billion in 1987. The United Nations Population Division estimates that world population in the year 2025 will reach 8.5 billion.[32] Given existing fertility rates and the momentum built into the age structure, we will add one billion people to the planet in each of the next three decades. Ninety-five percent of the growth will be in the poorest countries, which can least afford more mouths to feed.

While disagreement exists about the total population that the earth can support, three conclusions can be drawn from these numbers. First, population growth is exerting great pressure on ecosystems nearly everywhere. In developed nations, these impacts are compounded many times over by high rates of resource consumption. In poor nations, the effects of growing population are evident in soil erosion, desertification, and deforestation. Second, between ten to twenty percent of the present population is malnourished. Although distribution and the decline in local subsistence farming are primarily to blame, these figures cast doubt about how well we might do with a much larger population in coming decades. Third, the race between population growth and food production will become more difficult as effects of climate change, ozone depletion, and acid rain become evident.

Reverend Thomas Malthus was among the first to recognize that population tended to increase exponentially while food supply grew only arithmetically. If history proved Malthus wrong, as is commonly believed, it did so only partially and only temporarily. Population has continued to increase exponentially, and it is true that the food supply has increased as well, much more than Malthus could have known. The reasons, however, had to do with the availability of land for agriculture and cheap energy. "Green revolutions" work only with large inputs of fertilizer, pesticides, herbicides, and machinery, all of which depend on a stable supply of low-cost oil. U.S. agriculture, for example, uses about ten calories of fossil fuel energy to put one calorie on the plate.[33] Farm energy costs are roughly thirty percent of the total energy use, and are rising. Conventional agriculture, dependent on chemical solutions for fertility and pest control, is requiring more to reach the same level of productivity. Cornell University scientist David Pimentel reports that losses to insects have nearly doubled since 1945 while the use of insecticides increased tenfold in the same period.[34] Insects are becoming resistent to pesticides that formerly proved fatal to ninety-nine percent of their species.[35] World soil loss due to poor farm practices is now estimated to be twenty-four billion tons per year.[36] The intersection of these two curves suggests that the specter of famine raised by Malthus continues to stalk many nations of Africa and Asia. At least one study shows that it may also visit developed countries as fossil energy supplies dwindle and prices for inputs rise.[37]

Climate change is now the joker in the deck. Projections made by the Environmental Protection Agency and the National Center for

Atmospheric Research indicate that the grainbelt in the Midwest will become both hotter and drier, shifting the prime growing area northward into Canada.[38] Early studies on the effects of increasing ultraviolet radiation (which results from stratospheric ozone depletion) show that it suppresses biotic activity markedly.[39] Air pollution, particularly in the form of ground-level ozone, reduces crop productivity as well. Acid rain has similar effects.

We have not escaped the trap Malthus described. In fact, by delaying it we may only have made it a much larger trap. Technology, dependent on fossil fuels, has increased carrying capacity for a time. Whether this represents a permanent or temporary increase depends now on a level of technological heroism that Malthus could never have imagined. The two "inputs" that have allowed us to avoid the starvation Malthus predicted are cheap energy and land. If feeding the world continues to depend on an energy input/output ratio of ten to one, Malthus will have the last groan. Additions to farmable land will also be much more difficult in the future. In fact, with the expected global warming we will lose land to rising oceans. In places like Bangladesh, flooding would be utterly catastrophic. Climate change will be no less catastrophic in the United States, with the nearly certain shift in rainfall making the Southeast and Midwest much hotter and drier, while draining away capital to dike the east and gulf coasts from rising sea levels.

The limits of ecosystems.   As our knowledge of the natural world has grown, other limits have become apparent. George Perkins Marsh gave us the first systematic analysis of these and of the human impact on the natural world. He was not optimistic. "Man," he wrote in 1864, "is everywhere a disturbing agent. Wherever he plants his foot, the harmonies of nature are turned to discords."[40] Everything we have learned in the century and a quarter since has made Marsh's pessimism sound like understatement. Human impacts on the biosphere have increased markedly, while our land wisdom creeps forward. Knowledge of how to manipulate nature outruns our understanding of the impacts. As a result, our approach to agriculture, grazing lands, wildlife, and forests has been almost invariably manipulative, shortsighted, and destructive.

Since 1945, mainstream agriculture—by which I mean that espoused by agronomy departments in land-grant universities, the United States Department of Agriculture, and major farm organizations—has pursued a model of agriculture based on the industrial metaphor. Its goal has been to join land, labor, and capital in ways that maximize productivity. Farming is regarded not as a way of life but as a business. Like other businesses, it has led to highly specialized farms that grow one or two crops, or raise thousands of animals in automated confinement facilities. Like other businesses, agribusiness invested heavily in technology, became dependent on "inputs" of chemicals, fertilizer, feed, and energy, and went heavily into debt to finance it all. Farmers were advised to plow fence row to fence row, buy out their less-efficient neighbors, substitute monoculture for crop diversity, cut down windbreaks, and replace people with machinery. The results are there for all to see. The ongoing farm crisis of the 1980s suggests that it did not work economically (except for those who learned how to farm the tax code).[41] From dying rural towns across the United States one can infer that it did not work socially. And neither does it work ecologically.

In the meantime, an alternative agriculture is being developed in places like Santa Cruz, California, Emmaus, Pennsylvania, and Salina, Kansas.[42] Based on the ideas of Albert Howard, J. Russell Smith, and Edward Faulkner, among others, sustainable agriculture stresses soil conservation, perennialism, crop diversity, natural pest controls, small scale, tree cropping, local marketing, and the economics of good neighbors.[43] Its metaphor is ecological, not industrial. Its goal is to preserve the health of the land and the people who live on it.[44] Sustainable agriculture involves both the rediscovery of older patterns of farming that worked for centuries and research into new methods.

There is as yet no comparable field of sustainable forestry. If and when there is, one of its founders will be Chris Maser, a former U.S. Forest Service forester and author of *The Redesigned Forest*.[45] Maser's research suggests that contemporary forest practices contravene ecological requisites of healthy forests. Like mainstream agriculture, forestry schools, forest products companies, and the U.S. Forest Service have applied the industrial metaphor to forests, aiming to increase productivity regardless of the consequences. Maser argues that the removal of trees inevitably lowers long-term productivity. The upshot of his work is that we will have to use forests much more sparingly and efficiently. Logging practices and the removal of timber removes vital nutrients and trace elements essential to subsequent forest growth. Like Howard's work in agriculture, Maser traces the sustainability of forests back to the health of the soil. And like Howard, Maser proposes a model of forestry management that begins with a thorough understanding of forest ecology over the long run.

The work of Alan Savory on semiarid lands (what he calls "fragile") represents a third example of ecological management.[46] Grazing lands in the United States and elsewhere are rapidly desertifying, often without being overgrazed. In *Holistic Resource Management,* Savory has argued that existing theories of land management are wrong and has developed a new approach. In contrast to the conventional wisdom, Savory's "holistic management" involves grazing lands intensively but for shorter periods in ways that mimic the behavior of herding animals. Accordingly, holistic resource management is largely based on a model of the way herding animals interact with the land in its wild state and replicating these in a controlled setting.

These three ecosystem management strategies, dealing with agriculture, forestry, and rangeland, have several traits in common. First, they agree that the present pace of resource extraction, whether food, timber, or flesh, is higher than can be sustained over the long term. Second, the model for each approach is that of natural systems. Third, the knowledge required in each case is considerably greater than that required for industrial methods. In each case, sustainable practices begin with a thorough knowledge of soils and ecological factors.

Many of the same conclusions apply in other areas of applied ecology. Aldo Leopold's research in wildlife management, for example, caused him to see the land as an organism in which all parts, including those without explicit economic value, were important.[47] More than any previous thinker, Leopold laid the basis for an ethically solvent human ecology. In his later writings, collected in *A Sand County Almanac,* he was not optimistic. Like Marsh, Leopold saw human energies working at cross-purposes to those of the land. "One of the penalties of an ecological education," he wrote, "is that one lives alone in a world of wounds.... An ecologist must be the doctor who sees the marks of death in a community that believes itself well and does not want to be told otherwise."[48]

Rachel Carson's book *Silent Spring* (1962) brought the concept of the web of life into public prominence, and with it the effects of chemicals at the ecosystem level. With rare decisiveness, history has proven that Carson was right, but in the years since *Silent Spring* pesticide use has continued to increase. Slightly more than five hundred million pounds of pesticides were used in 1962. By 1985, the figure had risen to more than one billion pounds. As Carson predicted, pest resistance also increased, and with it crop losses. In 1945, thirty-two percent of crops were lost to pests. In 1984, the figure was thirty-seven percent.[49] With the increase in pesticide use came increased environmental damage to wildlife, streams, soil biota, aquifers, and inevitably to Homo sapiens sitting atop the food chain. The lesson that Carson tried to teach was that of caution in dealing with natural systems. The application of chemicals for which nature has had no time to adjust has undermined a billion years of evolution.

Almost without exception, research on the effects of human activity at the ecosystem level has revealed limits to natural systems that were previously unknown. Present methods of agriculture, forestry, land management, and game management are jeopardizing future productivity for the sake of present consumption. In matters of applied ecology, we lack a system of full-cost accounting based on the long-term health of biotic stocks. And we lack a system of checks to limit exploitation where we are largely ignorant of the effects of our actions.

Limits of energy. The rate and volume of fossil fuel use is the most distinctive feature of the modern world. The ability to burn fuels at a time and rate of our choosing has allowed the vast increase in human population, the rise of large urban concentrations, and the growth of industry. Without fossil fuels, the present world in anything like its present form and scale simply could not have been created. The enormous increases in industrial and agricultural production are the result of our ability to substitute energy for labor. Given our dependence and vulnerability, it is curious why we have been so slow to develop a clear understanding of the energy foundations of modern society.

Low energy prices in the late 1980s created a sense of unwarranted complacency. The price of oil has now (November 1990) passed the 1985 levels of thirty dollars a barrel. At the same time, the Department of Energy expects an increase in oil demand by developing countries of some 2.5 million barrels a day.[50] More ominously, a decade of increasing efficiency in the United States levelled out in 1986 and demand once again increased. The United States is now importing more oil than it produces.[51] Oil production peaked in 1970 and began its long descent. Despite huge outlays for exploration, proven U.S. reserves of oil have declined from thirty-two billion barrels in 1977 to twenty-seven billion barrels in 1989.[52] Experts give no hope that this decline can be stopped. We are simply running out and will be increasingly dependent on imported oil.

More importantly, all U.S. energy sources, according to Charles Hall, Cutler Cleveland, and Robert Kaufman in *Energy and Resource Quality,* have declining "energy return on investment" (EROI), which is the "gross amount of fuel extracted in the energy transformation process to the economic energy required to make that fuel available to society."[53] EROI, or net energy, is a much more important figure than total reserves available. They tell us how much energy it costs to deliver a given quantity of fuel. When it costs a barrel of oil to deliver a barrel of oil we have reached an EROI of zero. By this measure, fossil fuels have a declining return on investment. For example, one study of selected Louisiana oil fields indicates that the break-even point will be reached in the late 1990s. When that point is reached, it is irrelevant whether there is still oil in the ground or not. There will be no good reason to remove oil with an EROI of zero or less. In this perspective, efficiency gains in the use of energy would sooner or later be offset by declining energy return on investment resulting in economic decline.

Fossil energy has shaped the modern world, and that fact now poses the most extreme jeopardy. Combustion of fossil fuels is the primary cause of global warming and acid rain. The geopolitics of oil make all of the oil-importing industrial economies hostage to the politics of an unstable region. Finally, world oil production will peak in the first quarter of the next century. From the standpoint of supply, climate effects, and environmental costs associated with the combustion of fossil fuels, there is good reason to investigate alternatives such as hydrogen.[54]

The decline of the fossil fuel era will be traumatic unless timely measures are taken to build a transition to another era based on efficiency and renewable sources. These will not be cheap, only cheaper than the alternatives. The good news about energy is that efficiency improvements now technically feasible could substantially reduce consumption of all energy forms. A Department of Energy study shows that U.S. energy consumption could be reduced by fifty percent with present technologies, and with a net positive economic impact.[55] New technologies on the horizon would create even greater savings.

Nuclear power does not constitute a viable alternative. The problem of energy scarcity has to do with liquid fossil fuels used primarily in transportation and heating, not in electricity. Moreover, aside from well-known problems of waste disposal, the security and safety of the nuclear fuel cycle, waste disposal, and proliferation, nuclear energy also suffers from a low-to-negative EROI, when all costs are included, such as those of decommissioning plants after their useful lifetime.[56] Gregory Kats and William Keepin in a definitive study have shown that, even under the most optimistic assumptions, dollars spent in conservation in effect remove seven times more carbon than those spent on nuclear power.[57] Nuclear power is not an answer either to the global warming crisis or to the impending shortage of liquid fossil fuels.

From a policy perspective, we will have to depend upon one or more of three broad courses of action: (1) economic policies that rely on heroic technological breakthroughs to increase energy supplies in the face of declining rates of EROI; (2) efficiency improvements that more than offset declining EROI; and/or (3) slower economic growth or even economic contraction. The wager, like that of Pascal, depends on asking of each course: Can this be done in time? At what cost? And what happens if the underlying assumptions turn out to be wrong?

Some mildly heroic technologies, such as solar electricity and hydrogen fuels, now appear to be feasible. Given its costs and engineering uncertainties, fusion power, however, does not appear to be a good alternative. Efficiency improvements are available now, and with attractive payback times. Economic growth, meaning the increase in quantity, must begin to give way to economic development, implying qualitative improvements for reasons discussed in Chapter 2.

CONCLUSION

The Westphalian system of political economy and the biosphere are in conflict because they work in fundamentally different ways.

The logic of evolution versus the logic of power. The two systems work according to different dynamics. The biosphere works by processes of evolution and ecology. The "machinery of nature" (Paul Ehrlich's words) is not, of course, machinery at all but a vast interconnected web of relationships, biogeochemical cycles, and energy flows. Its "logic" is evolutionary, adaptive, co-evolving. It is as dependent upon cooperation—mutualism, commensalism, symbiosis—as on competition. Predator-prey relationships are seldom "zero-sum" games at the species level. James Lovelock believes that evolution legitimately applies to the planet more than to separate species.[58] There is no natural counterpart in Gaia to the absolutisms that lead humans to commit genocide or demand unconditional surrender in the name of the most fleeting passions.

By contrast, the war system is driven by the logic of power. The resort to force is most typically played as a zero-sum game: winners win it all. As the Westphalian order grew into the global war system, the driving force became technological. In the words of Solly Zuckerman: "The momentum of the arms race is undoubtedly fuelled by the technicians in governmental laboratories and in the industries which produce the armaments."[59] The technological revolution in warfare now exceeds the capacities of the biosphere, and the capacities of humans to manage. The result is a widening "gap between mechanical intelligence and human intent."[60] We are nearing the point where weapons systems are "passing out of human control." Behind the technological momentum are worst-case fears institutionalized in defense bureaucracies, greed, and the dark side of human ingenuity. There is no apparent counterpart in natural systems for the dynamic behind the arms race. Nature plays out its role in a more tentative, cautious, purposive way.

Ecological time versus technological time.   Natural evolution has occurred over millions of years. Life in all its manifestations is obviously in no hurry.

By contrast, the human political economy has been speeding up decade by decade for the past two centuries. Seen in perspective, the economic growth of the post-1945 era has been more of an eruption than an evolution. Computers and instantaneous communication throughout the planet have changed the clock speed at which humans think, work, and live.[61] The revolution in military technology now means that decisions about the fate of 2.5 billion years of evolution will be made in minutes and seconds! The result is a disjunction between the rhythms of nature measured in geologic, evolutionary, and ecological time, and technological time measured in days, hours, minutes, seconds, and nanoseconds. As technological time is superimposed on older patterns of day and night and changing seasons, human behavior is increasingly disoriented in ways that suggest that speed has become an addiction.

Maintenance versus unlimited growth.   The two systems also have different goals. Natural evolution at the ecosystem level leads toward increasing diversity, ecological complexity, stability, and balance. Left to itself, nature evolves in ways that tend to create systems that are stable over long periods of time within relatively narrow limits. As systems "mature," nutrient cycles become tighter, and more energy goes into maintenance rather than into growth. Life at the planetary level, according to Lovelock, is an active agent in maintaining the climate and temperature conditions appropriate to more life. Gaia is a vast system including bacteria that controls levels of atmospheric gases. As conditions move away from those suitable for life, biological organisms act to restore the balance.[62]

Modern societies, by contrast, seem to have adopted the purpose of growing to their maximum extent. Having eliminated most or all of their natural competitors, humans now face no limits other than those imposed by the planet or the perverse consequences of their own actions. Evolution has equipped humans with no instinct that tells us when enough is enough.

Diversity and redundancy versus homogenization and fragility. Finally, the two systems differ in structure. Natural systems are organized as a kind of loose hierarchy with a great deal of redundancy and diversity. Species fit together in a complex tangle of relationships, niches, and trophic levels governed by how efficiently they use available energy. The whole operates as a kind of fail-safe system so that the demise of any one life-form has little effect on the whole system. Evolution has equipped ecosystems with spare parts, backup systems, and, at the genetic level, lots of information about what to do in emergencies. At the planetary level, Lovelock has made a convincing case that the system has evolved to include feedback between the biota and the atmosphere sufficient to maintain atmospheric stability for the past two billion years.

The structure of human society, by contrast, is increasingly homogeneous. The great diversity of human cultures is being rapidly destroyed by the global force of modernization. Humans are now being congealed into one great megaexperiment. (It is as if Gaia were to have wagered it all by attempting to place rain forests throughout the entire planet.) The system in its entirety is extremely fragile. If there are any flaws in the logic, science, technology, and/or adaptability underlying this great wager, the entire system is in jeopardy. If the resources and energy on which the world system depends run short, the system will collapse catastrophically. In the past, cultural diversity, like diversity in natural systems, provided a margin for error. Not so long ago, human societies constituted hundreds of experiments with the problems of living in different settings. But the failure of any one did not pose a problem for others. The rise of a global civilization, for all of its benefits, has no such margin. What margin it does have is based on a planetary wager that the human mind can create and implement solutions faster than it creates problems.

From the perspective of human survival, however, there is a disturbing lack of accurate feedback between policy and the results of our behavior. Adaptation of natural systems to changing conditions has worked well for millions of years. But adaptation to changing circumstances in the war system, operating at a different clock speed, are excruciatingly slow. The war system operates to a great extent on information that is erroneous. Images of the enemy, strategies, definitions of security, national slogans having to do with "threat," "commitments," national honor, and falling dominoes tend to remain frozen long after they cease to describe reality. And weapons continue to be piled on top of weapons to levels of absurd redundancy and danger.

Fragments of Strategy

A cartoon that once appeared in *American Scientist* showed a white-frocked scientist standing before a chalkboard with the equation [x] + [y] + [then a miracle occurs] = z. Most strategies of social change have similar dependence on the miraculous, and for good reason. Barring miracles, how might we think about the transition to a world that is peaceful, just, and sustainable? If two hundred years from now we have achieved such a world, how might the transition appear to its historians? What events, trends, processes, actions, and policies will be credited? What changes of knowledge or outlook occurred? What industrial illusions and technological fantasies were jettisoned along the way? To what extent did the transition occur because of bold leadership or because of a social movement? Who were the heroes and heroines of what surely would have been humankind's finest hour? And what will cause us to act in time?

Some believe that our best prospect is for a global catastrophe large enough to get our attention, but small enough to recover from. This prospect presumes that the causes of any such event would be correctly diagnosed, the proper conclusions drawn, and wise actions result. But it is not difficult to see this chain interrupted by the complexity of events, political pressures, shortsightedness, nationalism, and irrationality.

That problem aside, we cannot count on having a catastrophe just the right size. More likely we will have to contend with processes that are not sufficiently shocking until it is too late to do anything about them. Frogs, I am told, will continue to sit calmly in water brought slowly to a boil. Cumulative processes of climate change, soil erosion, deforestation, species extinction, and acid rain are slowly bringing our water to a boil. Someone, somewhere, may be watching to see if we jump in time.

Conjecturing as we must from this side of the transition, these choices are yet to be made or ignored, opportunities to be seized or lost, miracles or nightmares yet to happen. From our vantage point we must unavoidably wrestle with the revolutionist's query: "What is to be done?" The question lands us squarely in the realm of praxis, which is the study of efficient action. We begin, however, knowing that humanitarian visions can all too easily become gulags. Praxis leads us to ask, first, about the quality of the solutions that we propose. Perhaps the best thought about solutions is that of Wendell Berry:

> A bad solution is bad because it acts destructively upon the larger patterns in which it is contained. It acts destructively upon those patterns, most likely, because it is formed in ignorance or disregard of them.[1]

A solution is good, on the contrary, "because it is in harmony with those larger patterns." Good solutions, he states:

1. Accept given limits
2. Accept the limits of discipline
3. Improve the balances, symmetries, or harmonies within a pattern
4. Solve more than one problem
5. Will satisfy a whole range of criteria
6. Embody a clear distinction between the biological and the mechanical
7. Have wide margins
8. Answer the question of "How much is enough"
9. Should be cheap and should not enrich one person by the distress or impoverishment of another
10. Exist in proof
11. Imitate the structure of natural systems
12. Are good for all parts of a system
13. Preserve the integrity and pattern that contains it
14. Are in harmony with good character, cultural value, and moral law.[2]

What strategies produce solutions with these characteristics? Broadly speaking, we have only four choices: (1) those strategies that regard change as inevitable and strategy as a kind of midwifery; (2) those that rely on markets and economic self-interest; (3) those that rely on public policy, government power, and regulation; and (4) those aiming to change values through education. In this chapter, I will focus on the first three, considering education in greater detail in Part 2.

CHANGE AS INEVITABLE,
STRATEGY AS MIDWIFERY

It has been fashionable to portray change at particularly turbulent periods of history as a matter of destiny or historical inevitability. Orthodox Marxists, for example, assumed that the crisis of capitalism and the Communist revolution would occur automatically. Since the revolution was inevitable but difficult, whatever one did to help it along was justifiable. The expenditure of great effort and blood in the service of the inevitable is only one of the lesser ironies of communism. The more important ones have to do with why things did not work out as predicted. Marxist revolutions have occurred only in backward agrarian societies, not advanced industrial countries as Marx predicted. And now, even there it is in retreat. Not surprisingly, Marx was a better analyst of nineteenth-century capitalism than he was a prophet of its future.

The fate of Marxism may cast light on more recent theories of inevitable (but easy) change, such as those that anticipate a "New Age." Advocates of a new age assume that considerable change in human behavior is now possible, and that if realized it would be for the better. Marilyn Ferguson, author of *The Aquarian Conspiracy*, for example, describes the human potential in these terms:

> You can break through old limits, past inertia and fear, to levels of fulfillment that once seemed impossible...to richness of choice, freedom, human closeness. You can be more productive, confident, comfortable with insecurity. Problems can be experienced as challenges, a chance for renewal, rather than stress. Habitual defensiveness and worry can fall away. It can all be otherwise."[3]

The road to salvation? Not a revolution but a paradigm shift based on a combination of Eastern mysticism, new science, transformation psychology, and the recognition that, "For the first time in history, humankind has come upon the control panel of change—an understanding of how transformation occurs."[4] And how does transformation occur? Through the recognition that "we are not victims, not pawns, *not limited by conditions or conditioning*" (emphasis added). Ferguson writes a great deal about openness, creativity, holism, wholeness, flow, spirituality, asserting that "the old forms of relationship are inappropriate to the demands of the transformative journey"[5] (words that sound remarkably like those of some nineteenth-century radical revolutionaries). Ferguson suggests a process of change, that is more like a mass awakening or, as she puts it, a "spiritual adventure." It seems also to include a great deal of network-

ing and jetting about to spread the new gospel. Her book appeared in
the same year that Americans elected Ronald Reagan to the presidency.
Their popularity and simultaneously that of right-wing electronic evan-
gelicals, of Shirley MacLaine, and of Harmonic Convergences suggest a
widespread hunger for meaning and certainty, and the easier the better.
Like Marxist theories of inevitable revolution, each of these assumes that
if enough people get enlightened, get right with God, hold hands, hum
OM on key, or wear designer jeans, things will be just fine. In a way, of
course, this is true with exactly the same sturdy logic that undergirded
the 1960s query: "What happens if they hold a war and no one shows
up?" After the militarization of the 1980s, Rambo, and the war with Iraq,
we know that lots of folks will show up, and lots of others will drop out
of Aquarian Conspiracies and new-age movements when they discover
something that makes them feel even better.

For whatever the visionary merits of new-age thinking (what
Richard Falk calls "Disneyland Postmodernism"), strategies of change
that produce real results must be of sterner stuff. To bring about real
change they must, in Falk's words:

> engag(e) concrete sources of resistance, including human depravity
> and greed...moral concern is serious only if it includes active partici-
> pation in ongoing struggles against injustice and suffering.[6]

The problem is not so much new-age goals, but with naivete about the
persistence of human evil and wishful thinking about how mass
change comes about. And when it does, it is not always for the better.
As an antidote to mental hyperventilation, I propose that the use of the
phrase "new age" either be outlawed or preceded by a detailed explanation of how the Germany of Goethe became that of Hitler, in ten
thousand words or more.

MARKET STRATEGIES

Adam Smith once described a second strategy of change in these
words:

> As every individual, therefore, endeavors as much as he can both to
> employ his capital in the support of domestic industry and so to
> direct that industry that its produce may be of the greatest value...he
> intends only his own gain, and he is in this, as in many other cases,
> led by an invisible hand to promote an end which was no part of his
> intention.... By pursuing his own interest he frequently promotes that
> of the society more effectually than when he really intends to pro-
> mote it.[7]

In other words, as individuals pursue private interests they create wealth, part of which circulates in the larger society, becoming available for others. By arguing that the pursuit of selfish interests would promote the common good, Smith turned Christian ethics upside down. He may have turned some of reality upside down as well. Herman Daly points out that instead of some "invisible hand" directing private actions toward public good, there is "an invisible foot [that] leads private self-interest to kick the common good to prices."[8]

The advantages of economic strategies are clear. They require no leap of consciousness, no Aquarian Conspiracies, and no quick paradigm shifts. And they make no heroic assumptions about our moral possibilities. Does the same logic hold if sustainability, not economic expansion or private accumulation, is the goal? To what extent can rational economic self-interest be harnessed to control its earlier excesses?

Amory and Hunter Lovins maintain that there is a convergence between economically rational "least-cost" energy choices and longer-term collective benefits. By purchasing the most efficient energy consuming/generating technologies, consumers and utilities can lower costs while conserving resources. It is cheaper and less risky by far to weatherize houses than it is to maintain a military presence in the Persian Gulf at a cost of one billion dollars or more each month. Their research suggests that the same may hold true for other resource areas as well.

Their reasoning is clear. First, efficient means to whatever ends lead to outcomes in which everyone is better off, or what economists call Pareto optimality. Second, careful analysis of end use may lead us to more efficient solutions. For example, our goal is not the consumption of energy, but the use of energy services such as light, heat, and mobility. Third, least-cost approaches to energy and resource decisions will entail conservation rather than an increase in supply. Fourth, these choices will also generally be the best ethical choices.[9]

As a strategy of change, the least-cost approach promises four major benefits. First, it is aimed to take us as far down the road to greater energy and resource efficiency as possible. By all evidence this will be a long way. Second, by steadily wringing inefficiency out of the economy, the strategy buys us time that could be put to good use in rethinking longer-term goals. Third, it harnesses the powerful engine of economic self-interest to the cause of lowering energy/resource use per dollar of GNP and therefore lowers environmental impacts. Fourth, by identifying win/win options, the strategy avoids unnecessary conflicts. The strategy they propose is one of enlightened self-interest which combines economic rationality with ecological virtue.

Adam Smith only proposed that the pursuit of self-interest would increase total economic benefits. But the Lovins go further, maintaining that least-cost decisions in energy and other resources converge with ethical decisions that promote long-term collective welfare, broadly defined. This is close to an adequate definition of morality. Careful end-use analysis (not necessarily analysis of ends, however) may also lead to broader perceptions of self-interest. In other words, if we knew enough about the interconnections between our well-being and that of others (and other life-forms) we would act with greater prudence and altruism, but at least partly for reasons of self-interest. Individual self-interest at some point becomes indistinguishable from the collective interest.

Since there can be no good case for waste, least-cost approaches that promote efficiency are to a point beyond reproach. We should go as far as they take us. But they do not take us far enough. Economic self-interest, as a strategy, has four drawbacks.

First, the driving force of rational self-interest begins in a tautology. We have no choice but to be self-interested, but how people describe their self-interest, or what economists call utility, defies clear definition. Utility is whatever people define as valuable; the fact that they value it is proof of utility. But as every advertiser knows, efficiency and lower costs are only one motivation among many. Others include conspicuous consumption and waste. In other words, economic rationality and private utility do not always converge on least-cost choices.

Second, even if we assume that people consistently seek out economically rational, least-cost options, by definition they will not act if costs are high or rates of marginal return low. Their potential for good is limited to those cases where least-cost choices and ethics converge. There are reasons to think that they may not converge as often as one might hope, and that in some cases self-interested people might keep them from converging. One reason is that economically rational, self-interested people will know that least cost is not always the same as true cost. Food prices, for example, do not include the loss of topsoil, groundwater depletion or contamination, stream destruction, health costs to farmers and farm workers, or subsidies for public water in the West, or transportation. Nor do we pay a depletion tax on nonrenewable resources or disposal costs for our trash, including toxics and radioactive waste. If we did pay the true costs of consumption, prices would be considerably higher. But willingness to pay full costs, especially for no immediate gain, has very little to do with rational behavior as economists use the term and everything to do with ethical behavior that comes from a sense of responsibility and obligation. All of this underscores the persistent conflict between rationality applied to means (economics) and that applied to ends (theology).

Third, least-cost approaches work only as long as the process of technological innovation continues to lower resource/energy use per unit of output. The strategy relies on technology to help us avoid choices about limits that are fundamentally ecological, political, and ethical. Abdication in this instance only postpones difficult choices while leaving us vulnerable to anything that slows or ends technological innovation. It is a measure of how much we take for granted that even this possibility seems inconceivable. But like most social processes, technological innovation carries with it built-in limits.

Fourth, the equation implicit in least-cost strategies, which says that self-interest leads to least-cost decisions which leads to the collective good, is not just economic; it is deeply theological. It suggests that ethics is a by-product of good economic choices. In other words, it suggests that we can become good in the process of acting efficiently. The key to economic rationality is accurate information about the cheapest options. If we only do what is rational, the collective welfare will take care of itself. Accordingly, we do not have to distinguish between right and wrong, only between efficient and inefficient defined in economic terms. This argument comes close to the position that evil results from ignorance of the higher good, not from malice. If we only had more complete knowledge we would act ethically. In other words, there are no real conflicts, only misunderstandings, and no evil, only the lack of information. It is possible to hear in such arguments echoes of the Enlightenment faith in human reason that must reverberate oddly across the battlefields and human carnage of the twentieth century.

None of this is intended as an argument against economic rationality in the realm to which it legitimately applies. I do intend to argue, however, that thoroughly rational economic behavior, which implies the willingness to analyze ends *and* end uses, ironically depends on an ethical perspective and a larger vision that transcends self-interest. Strategies that are based on the priority of economic reasoning over ethics will sooner or later founder on the shoals of human recalcitrance or technological malfeasance. They give economics an undeserved priority over ethical reasoning and reasons on the premise that we can only sell sustainability on "practical" grounds of self-interest and that these exist independent of moral considerations, or at least of moral considerations that we openly profess. When we have exhausted all of those instances where ethics and economics converge and face more costly choices, it will matter a great deal whether or not we remember how to distinguish right from wrong and to act accordingly.

POLITICS AND THE STRATEGY OF CHANGE

A third set of strategies for change focuses on democratic politics, public policy, and the role of government as a catalyst for change through legislation and regulation. From this perspective, environmental deterioration represents a political failure in the way we make decisions, the distribution of power and wealth, and in leadership at all levels. The environmental crisis reflects a prior crisis in the political community: a failure to manage and protect our commonwealth. Our tendency to seek market and technological remedies first is doomed to fail. Economic and technological choices will, in the main, reflect the distribution of power in society. If power is distributed unfairly, if power is corrupt, if power is capricious and shortsighted, there is no other remedy. Both Marx and Ellul were wrong; politics is more basic than either economics or technology.

But what kind of politics and political institutions will we need? Political scientist William Ophuls argues that "liberal democracy as we know it...is doomed by ecological scarcity."[10] He proposes a "completely new political philosophy and set of political institutions." Robert Paehlke, on the contrary, proposes that environmentalism "be seen as a third wave of progressivism" that fits well within the existing political paradigm. At issue are questions of public attitudes toward the environment, the relative centralization of power, geographic scale, the potential for democratic renewal, and the definition and role of leadership. We will consider these in turn.

Public opinion. Americans take environmental issues more seriously in 1990 than they did in 1970 or 1980. When asked in 1976, for example, whether we must sacrifice environmental quality for economic growth, the public said "No" by thirty-eight percent to twenty-one percent. By 1986, the public favored environmental quality over economic growth by a fifty-eight percent to nineteen percent margin. Proenvironment responses to a CBS/*New York Times* question whether environmental standards could be too high and whether environmental improvements should be pursued regardless of cost have steadily risen from forty-five percent in 1981 to sixty-six percent in 1986. One observer concludes that "the available data consistently indicate a significant upturn in public concern for environmental quality during the Reagan presidency."[11] The drought and heat wave during the summer of 1988 raised public consciousness about the environment considerably. By 1990 pollster Lou Harris reported that environmental concern is higher than ever before.[12] *Time* and *Newsweek* have run regular cover stories on global environmental issues. Television coverage has been unprecedented.

At the same time, however, evidence from the presidential elections of 1976, 1980, 1984, and 1988 suggest that environmental issues, let alone those of long-term sustainability, are not very important in national elections. Ronald Reagan and George Bush, in spite of poor to abysmal environmental records, were able to win or neutralize the environmental vote. Their three Democratic opponents failed to raise the issue in any serious way. How can this apparent discrepancy between strong public support for environmental protection and its lack of impact on national politics be explained? Part of the answer, according to sociologist Riley Dunlap, is that environmental issues are only one among many that affect voters. The impact of environmental concerns is diluted by other fears and priorities. A second and related explanation is that public support for environmental quality, however widespread, is still not very intense. Perhaps both may be attributed to the fact that neither party has made any consistent effort to develop a coherent agenda on environmental issues. Why?

One answer is that issues of environment and those of sustainability are complex and long-term, while politics addresses more immediate issues like jobs and crime. Politicians who talk about complex issues and difficult choices do not win elections, or so we are told. Issues of environment and sustainability entail a far more radical critique of industrial societies than Marxism, but Americans are conservative and pragmatic. Environmental issues are complex, but our political process works incrementally, nibbling at the edges of the status quo. In the words of Walter Truett Anderson:

> The whole style of American politics is nonecological. Ecology is a comprehension of systems, interdependencies, webs of relationship, connections extending over space and time—and the very essence of our politics is to zero in on single causes.[13]

In other words, the electorate must be pandered to and spoonfed: politics of the lowest common denominator. Perhaps. But politicians who have used their offices as a pulpit to educate an electorate in ecological complexities have won in conservative states: Richard Lamm, former governor of Colorado, and in 1984 Jim Hightower, Agriculture Commissioner in Texas. The evidence indicates: (a) that environmental issues can be explained to the public if politicians care to do so; (b) the majority in the United States is strongly proenvironment; (c) that the resolution of environmental problems are rooted in the best of our Western, democratic, Judaic-Christian heritage; and (d) that money corrupts the political process and works against achievement of the common good.

Two other factors are involved in the paradox. The first is simply a lack of political courage to deal with uncomfortable and demanding issues. Great leaders did not emerge in the 1980s. With the exception of Prime Minister Gro Harlem Brundtland in Norway and ex-Chancellor Willy Brandt of the Federal Republic of Germany, the rest of the world's leaders have mostly watched in silence as the problems of the habitability of the earth reached crisis proportions. The decade of the 1980s may in hindsight appear to its historians like those before the U.S. Civil War or World War I. Those too were times of evasion, chauvinism, posturing, procrastination, and nickel leaders in dollar jobs. The difference between their times and ours is that we know the names of the catastrophes that followed their dereliction.

Dereliction in our time is due in part to the fact that issues of the environment have not yet been incorporated into our theories of politics, institutional habits, political language, and political symbols. The politics of the environment are complex, they do require a systems approach, they do challenge orthodoxy of all sorts, and they are long-term. We are baffled about how to get from here to there and fearful about what we may have to jettison in the transition. Most important, we lack a conception of ecological citizenship that joins place and planet. We will need to reinvent politics at the ecosystem level.[14] This need raises other issues.

The question of centralization. The first task of political reconstruction is to rediscover the proper role for various levels of government. On the one hand, national governments are too small to deal with issues that are genuinely global including planetary warming, ozone depletion, and protection of the common biological heritage of humankind. For these we need global institutions. On the other hand, national governments are often too large and cumbersome to effectively handle most other problems. Goldilocks confronted the same perplexities of matching problems with appropriately scaled solutions. During the transition to sustainability, the Goldilocks dilemma—the question of appropriate government scale—will grow more important and more divisive. Robert Heilbroner and others proposing the centralization of authority, on the one hand, and E. F. Schumacher and other decentralists on the other, could both agree that the ecological crisis is real while reaching opposite conclusions about its resolution. Heilbroner in *An Inquiry into the Human Prospect* wrote:

> I not only predict but I prescribe a centralization of power as the only means by which our threatened and dangerous civilization can make way for its successor.[15]

Similarly, William Ophuls, in *Ecology and the Politics of Scarcity*, argues that ecological scarcity will create "overwhelming pressures toward political systems that are frankly authoritarian."[16] Likewise, Garrett Hardin in "The Tragedy of the Commons" finds no solution other than "mutual coercion mutually agreed upon."[17] Each assumes that the crisis can be managed only by the increased centralization of government power. This is not a conclusion disagreeable to men of opposite bent such as nuclear physicist Alvin Weinberg who once proposed a "Faustian bargain" between physicists and society to solve the energy crisis.[18]

Underlying such proposals are unstated beliefs about the capabilities of large institutions. From very different perspectives, Heilbroner, Weinberg, and others of like mind believe that an authoritarian state can manage nature and uphold its end of Faustian bargains while coping with its own increased size and complexity, in perpetuity. This position, however, is badly supported by what we know about governments and large organizations. For many reasons, governments do not act single-mindedly, but as loosely coupled and competing fiefdoms, occasionally subservient to power and privilege. Nor are they above deceit and the bamboozlement of the gullible in the name of one national interest or another. Large private organizations manifest similar pathologies. One can only marvel at the greed, lethargy, and obesity of U.S. auto manufacturers whose advertisements continue to amaze us while we drive vehicles of other national origin. Even if we could believe that big governments or giant corporations could be effective, we have no reason to believe that this effectiveness might provide any long-term guarantee of sustainability. Having centralized authority and power over resources and the environment, it is only a matter of time before that authority is captured by others with no interest in sustainability. American history between 1980 and 1990 has provided us an object lesson in the tenuousness of such arrangements.

Decentralists, such as E. F. Schumacher and Leopold Kohr,[19] have a different response to the crisis of sustainability that begins with the belief that the centralization of power is a cause of the crisis, not its cure. Once centralized, power becomes more difficult to hold accountable. The transfer of power, authority, resources, talent, and capital from the countryside, towns, neighborhoods, and communities to the city, corporations, and national government has undermined in varying degrees responsibility, care, thrift, and social cohesion—qualities essential to sustainability. In contrast to Heilbroner and others, decentralists assume that people, given the chance, are capable of disciplined self-government. In this view, democracy has not failed; it has not been tried.

This is not a new debate. In some respects it continues that between

Hamilton and Jefferson at the founding of the United States. Hamilton envisioned an urban industrial society presided over by a powerful central government. His was a theory of an urban, manufacturing society fully engaged in the world traffic in goods and power. Jefferson's vision was that of a predominantly rural, agrarian, participatory society. Twentieth-century America is Hamilton's America, but Jefferson's vision continues to exert a powerful effect on our imagination of what it could have been and perhaps still might in some measure become.

In both eras we are caught between the harsh imperatives of authoritarian government, on the one hand, and mostly untried theories of decentralized participatory democracy, on the other. We have entered a new era and cannot responsibly avoid reexamination of political structures, institutions, and philosophies as the founders of this republic did two hundred years ago. Their task, however, was easier. They could draw on a century of brilliant political reflection by Locke, Montesquieu, Rousseau, Paine, and Jefferson among others. The writers of the Constitution could well assume that one of the primary tasks of government was to unleash human energies on an unlimited continent. We now know that it's easier to start things than it is to bring them under control once underway. Our task is more like taming an avalanche, and we labor under tighter, more demanding deadlines.

The reinvention of politics at the ecosystem level first requires clarity about what should be done locally and what can only be done at higher levels. Effective controls on carbon emmissions, for example, can only be accomplished at an international level. Energy conservation, the means of reducing energy use and thereby the release of CO_2, is best done by individuals, institutions, and local communities. The function of the federal government as conceived in the U.S. Constitution was to do those things in the common interest that could not happen at lower levels, such as the regulation of commerce, national security, and establishment of a postal service. In the transition to sustainability, the federal government must get the big things right, such as correcting market distortions that undervalue biotic resources, ensuring equity, establishing environmental standards, disseminating information, and cooperating in the establishment of global environmental institutions. At the same time, many things can and ought to be decentralized to a much greater extent for reasons of social resilience, environmental impacts, human scale, and true economy. Among these we can list agriculture, energy systems, population, property ownership, wealth, some aspects of governance, and certain technologies. Practically, this means stopping some things, such as subsidies for agribusiness and preferred tax treatment for large corporate enterprises, energy companies, utilities, and land speculators. On the other side, it means rebuilding the local communities, small towns, and neighborhoods that have suffered from decades of neglect.

The geography of power. Reinvention of politics at the ecosystem level will require a substantial disengagement from the global economy and the passivity and dependence it fosters. The ecological potential of the region must be integrated with its economy, culture, education, and governance. Bioregionalism is the name often given to the various attempts to make this juncture by rejuvenating regional and local institutions. At one level, bioregionalism celebrates the regional ecology and attempts to create a corresponding culture. At another level, it is an attempt to create economies, technologies, material flows, and educational systems appropriate to the bioregion. It is also a political strategy, which Kirkpatrick Sale in *Dwellers in the Land* describes in these words:

> It asks nothing of the Federal government, and needs no national legislation, no government regulation, no Presidential dispensation...only Federal obliviousness to permit it...nor does bioregionalism envision a takeover of the national government or a vast rearrangement of the national machinery...the task after all is to build power at the bottom not to take it from the top."[20]

The strategy has its roots in the nineteenth century anarchism of Peter Kropotkin and more recently in the thought of Lewis Mumford, who concluded *The Pentagon of Power* with the proposal that we withdraw from organized power in order to "quietly paralyze it."[21] What Sale, Mumford, and the bioregionalists advocate is slowly hollowing out national political structures through the development of bioregional institutions and economies. Bioregionalism represents a secession from major parts of the global economy to create regionally appropriate means of living and livelihood.[22] Its success will depend on the degree to which its advocates can create workable economies, technologies, material sources, and educational forms rooted in a particular bioregion.

There is no model of a bioregional economy that also incorporates high technology. But we are not without alternative ideas and models of other economies from which we might learn. Herman Daly, for example, has developed an outline of the macrodimensions of bioregional economies in which population and physical artifacts are held to a sustainable level by: (1) population controls; (2) resource depletion quotas; and (3) the redistribution of wealth. He also advocates placing restrictions on the mobility of capital to limit the vulnerability of local economies.

At the micro level, native economies frequently mirrored natural cycles by encouraging the free movement of property. In such "gift economies," private property was minimized and the attitudes supporting it were discouraged by cultural means, including humiliation of the greedy.[23] Social status was not tied to the quantity of possessions but the reverse: possessions were a sign of low status. Something similar operates to a lesser extent in present-day Amish economies.[24] Possession of cars, electronic devices, extravagant clothing, and other ego displays are strictly forbidden. Frugality, simplicity, discipline, hard work, and celebration are grounded in deep biblical convictions. E. F. Schumacher described similar patterns as "Buddhist Economics," the elegant calibration of "small means and extraordinarily satisfactory results."[25]

In recent years there has been a proliferation of ideas in alternative economics including the work of Hazel Henderson, papers published for the Alternative Economic Summit, the works brought together by Paul Ekins, those of Herman Daly and John Cobb cited previously, and those published in the *Human Economy Newsletter*.[26] These and other examples indicate that we are not without good ideas and workable bioregional alternatives to growth economics. In different ways each proposes: (a) rewards for good work and a right livelihood; (b) provision of basic needs for everyone; (c) the conservation of biotic resources; (d) inclusion of barter and gift relationships; (e) retention of wealth in the community; (f) subordination of economic to social relationships; and (g) the restoration of distinctive local culture. From their response to these concerns and to the work of Daly and Georgescu-Roegen in particular, I think it is clear that mainstream economists will not participate in the construction of a bioregional economy. For reasons Thomas Kuhn once explained, they will be engaged by events on the ramparts of crumbling paradigms. Perhaps this is good news. It means that noneconomists and plain citizens will have to roll up their sleeves and do the job of rebuilding the economy themselves. Many of the experts will be busy elsewhere.

The rejuvenation of local economies will also require the development of different forms of technology. These have been characterized over the years by terms such as "convivial," "alternative," "appropriate," and "soft." They share common traits of being smaller in scale, generally based on renewable energy, relatively less expensive, widely dispersed, locally owned and controlled, and environmentally benign. The discussion of alternative technology, pro and con, has tended to focus too much on tools and too little on materials and bioregionally appropriate designs and procedures that reduce the need for expensive and destructive technologies. Pliny Fiske in Austin, Texas has developed a catalogue of bioregionally available and cost-competitive build-ing materials, such as caliche and mesquite.[27] Similar inventories need to be done elsewhere as an alternative to importing expensive, envi-ronmentally damaging materials. We need similar catalogs of biore-gionally appropriate methods of forestry, land management, and agri-culture that minimize the need for energy and high technology.

The question of citizenship. The most glaring weakness of most proposals for reform is the omission of a concept of citizenship and par-ticipation in the process of change. Reinventing politics at the ecosystem level will require a process of civic renewal, or what Benjamin Barber calls "strong democracy."[28] It is roughly equivalent to rebuilding the crumbling foundation before trying to remodel the house. Despite our rhetoric about democracy, real democratic participation in the West is in decline, while undergoing a renaissance throughout much of Eastern Europe. Whether from apathy or disgust, half of the eligible population in the United States does not vote. Opportunities for participation have declined with the rise of megacorporations and public bureaucracies. People are losing control over the basic conditions of their lives. What Alexis de Tocqueville regarded as the roots of democracy—the civic association, the small town, the neighborhood, the workplace—are in disarray. In John Dewey's words: "Democracy must begin at home, and home is the neighborly community."[29] Restoration of the civic tradition depends on our ability to transcend, in the words of the authors of *Habits of the Heart,* "the language of individualism" to describe and sus-tain a political conversation on the important issues of our time.[30] The language of individualism is mainly about consumption and private interests. That of a renewed civic tradition must be about the responsi-ble use of shared power. Where a civic tradition has survived, public interests are in a continual David-and-Goliath struggle against huge blocks of power and money. Goliath ridicules ideas that preparations for Armageddon are wrong, or that Iowa topsoil ought to stay in Iowa, or that poisons do not belong in the environment.

Politics is the process by which we define the terms of our collec-tive existence. That existence is now in real jeopardy. Something is gravely wrong with those political processes, namely the widespread withdrawal from the political community by people who no longer see a relationship between their lives and the political life of the larger society. But there is no such thing as political noninvolvement. To avoid political matters is only to leave them to others. Democratic poli-tics is grounded in the faith that everyone is entitled to a voice in that process, and that no one, whether by circumstances of wealth or birth, is entitled to more. Representative democracy is an uneasy compromise between democracy and demography, with a touch of fear about mob rule. Strong democracy goes further, premised on the belief that people can and do act responsibly, given the opportunity, and that those opportunities can be nurtured in a mass society. Barber proposes several steps to this end, including:

1. A national system of neighborhood assemblies
2. A civic communications cooperative
3. A national initiative and referendum process
4. Electronic balloting
5. A lottery for local offices
6. Universal citizens service
7. Workplace democracy
8. A new architecture of civic space.[31]

Barber argues that strong democracy is the "only legitimate form of politics [and] constitutes the condition for the survival of all that is most dear to us."

I would add that strong democracy or some comparable program of civic renewal is a prerequisite for sustainability and real security as well. The connection is often missed. Significant mischief in human affairs most often begins behind closed doors, and concentrated power enables a few to close doors to the many. The usual arguments for oligarchy of any kind rest finally on the premise that the public is incompetent to decide matters of public concern. Behind Oliver North's efforts to create democracy in Nicaragua is the belief that it does not work here and so must be subverted by whatever means necessary. The case for technocracy is similar. Issues, we are told, are so complex that only experts can make intelligent choices. In the full light of day, such arguments can be seen for what they are: self-serving chicanery by people who have little or no sense of the public interest and little understanding of the democratic process, and a great deal to gain by remaining aloof from both.

We might dismiss the issue here except that the steady erosion of democratic participation also affects the prospects for sustainability and, I think, for peace. The centralization of power has removed many resource decisions from the public arena. Disposition of large tracts of land and resources including the use of common properties like air and water are made as if they were private decisions with wholly private consequences. The concentration of power deflected the development of technics away from tools toward the kind of machinery necessary for large-scale resource manipulation and extraction: the machines necessary to level mountains, divert rivers, split atoms, and alter genes.

The crisis of sustainability to a great extent results from centralization and scale operating unfettered by effective public constraints, citizen complaints, or private morality. These constraints were eroded as the independent shopkeeper, farmer, and small businessman became employees in enterprises over which they exerted no control. If dependence begets venality, as Jefferson once said, it also leads to demoralization and passivity in the face of wrongs. But frequently these wrongs occurred incrementally in quiet crises and in remote areas where few could see what was happening. In either case the institutions, attitudes, and independence necessary to resist were weakened at the source. Orwellian nightmares are no longer idle fantasies in a world of genetic engineering, computers, fusion reactors, and Star Wars technologies. Can anyone believe that sustainability will be taken seriously by technicians promoting one technical fix or another?

Civic renewal begins with the dispersion of power and the extension of the range of things decided by those affected. Participation is a way both to acknowledge those effects and to elevate public discourse. It is also a recognition, in Jefferson's words, that there is

> no safe depository of the ultimate powers of the society but the people themselves; and if we think them not enlightened enough to exercise their control with a wholesome discretion, the remedy is not to take it from them, but to inform their discretion.[32]

Informed public involvement is also a way to develop more prudent policy choices. Where an active citizenry is involved we may expect greater equity in the distribution of costs and benefits. We might also expect their vigilance to counter elite interests. As de Tocqueville, Dewey, and others have noted, civic education can only occur though participation in the neighborhood, community, and workplace decisions. Civic education for the sustainable management of food, energy, water, materials, and waste can only occur if people have a part in these decisions and understand their consequences.

The success of any program of civic renewal also depends on the reversal of two centuries of social atomization. Citizenship places common interests over self-interest. For people whose heroes are lonely cowboys or egotistical rock stars, this may be a difficult lesson, learned under duress of scarcity. The requirements of sustainability will also lead us to recognize that we are citizens of a larger community whose individual and collective well-being is tied to that of the larger fabric of life.

The issue of leadership. Having argued that Barber's case for strong democracy and civic renewal is a necessary condition for sustainability, I must still acknowledge a large gap of the "Then a miracle occurs" size. We live in an age of unprecedented transition, but as yet without transformative leaders. "The essence of leadership," James MacGregor Burns once wrote,

> is the recognition of real need, the uncovering and exploiting of con- tradictions among values and between values and practice, the realigning of values, the reorganization of institutions where neces- sary, and the governance of change...to induce people to be aware or conscious of what they feel...that they can be moved to purposeful action.[33]

The eruption of environmental awareness across the planet has occurred without significant national political leadership anywhere. Leaders of the stature of Gandhi, Roosevelt, and Martin Luther King, persons capable of defining, clarifying, and motivating people toward a sustainable future, have yet to appear at the national or international levels. But they are beginning to appear at state, local, and neighbor- hood levels nearly everywhere. In various ways, millions of people know that the earth is reaching its limits, that things are out of balance. Transformative leadership must first articulate what people feel in their bones, then translate this into a coherent agenda of reform and change within the context of familiar values of justice, fairness, peace, and democratic participation.

Throughout history, leadership has been equated mostly with bold, aggressive, militarily heroic men. Their role in ecological perspective has been to expand a particular society's niche, increasing opportuni- ties, geography, resources, population, and energy. They are revered historically to the degree that they did so. The task of leadership in coming decades will be the opposite, helping us to stabilize and con- tract our role in the natural world, but with as little trauma as possible. The challenge of adapting to planetary finiteness leads me to think what we will need to change in the kind of people that we accept as leaders. Military historian John Keegan, for one, believes that we need "post-heroic" leaders characterized by "modesty, prudence, and ratio- nality."[34] Said differently, we need leaders who exhibit a higher order of heroism, consisting of moral depth, intellectual clarity, farsighted- ness, personal integrity, and a commitment to global transformation.

Robert Greenleaf once proposed a model of "servant leader," one who is a servant first and leader second.[35] Greenleaf contrasts what he calls the "servant-first" type, who is motivated to serve, with the "leader- first" type, who leads because of innate drives for power, recognition, or wealth. To distinguish these, Greenleaf proposes the following test:

Do those served grow as persons? Do they, *while being served,* become healthier, wiser, freer, more autonomous, more likely themselves to become servants? *And,* what is the effect on the least privileged in society; will they benefit, or, at least, not be further deprived?"[36]

In contrast to the widespread assumption that leaders are first and foremost charismatic personalities, the servant leader emerges through a "long arduous discipline of learning to listen, first." In other words, qualities of character, integrity, and purity of motivation are the hallmarks of the kind of leaders Greenleaf describes. Servant leaders bear resemblance to the Taoist ideal: "Hesitant, he does not utter words lightly. When his task is accomplished and his work done the people all say, 'It happened to us naturally.'"

Joseph Campbell in *The Hero With a Thousand Faces* identified the task of leadership in our time as that of "questing to bring to light again the lost Atlantis of the co-ordinated soul." The problem for the modern hero is that of "rendering the modern world spiritually significant...making it possible for men and women to come to full human maturity."[37] In other words, modern heroes must help people grow up. Leaders in the United States in the decade just past pandered to and promoted fantasy, whim, caprice, indulgence, and the evasion of reality—the very antithesis of heroism. The hero in former times dealt with "the task of sharing wilderness with" the animal kingdom, resulting in half-human, half-animal mythical figures who served as tutors to humanity.[38] Having brought the animal and plant world under our control, these symbols have lost their potence. "Man himself," Campbell writes, "is now the crucial mystery." The contemporary hero will help us all cast off the "slough of pride, fear, rationalized avarice, and sanctified misunderstanding."[39]

Transformative leaders, then, will be people whose loyalties are rooted in a place but extend to the planet. They will not be dividers and hatemongers who can only appeal to fear and greed. They will be persons of a different sort, possessed of vision, spiritual depth, intellectual breadth, courage, and the drive to serve. The self-described "realists" have had their time. They are the makers and perpetuators of our present nightmares, able to offer no realistic blueprint or even reason for human survival. It is now time for visionaries: those able to dream, as did Gandhi and Martin Luther King, of people living in harmony and justice. Humans, as Campbell as shown, are creatures of symbols, and one of the tasks for a new generation of transformative servant leaders is to change the mythical symbols from ones for which we have fought and died to ones for which we can live. We will not build the con-

stituency for sustainable futures on mere logic alone. We must kindle
the moral energy that will ignite the actions necessary to build that
future. If sustainability implies, as I have argued, that we must do with
less, these constraints must be placed within a compelling moral vision.
"Humans," in Erazim Kohak's words, "can bear an incredible degree of
meaningful deprivation, but only very little meaningless affluence."[40]

There is no shortage of reasons for pessimism about the task of
political reconstruction. But after we have sorted through our political
traditions, ideas, and institutions, I think that we will have rediscovered
the value of thoroughly democratic institutions and the vibrant small
community. While we exalt private self-interest and free enterprise, our
best religious traditions and the ecological perspective tell us that our
prospects are connected. Our anemic concept of public interest would
have dismayed the Greeks, who would have regarded it as a sign of
derangement. An idiot, in their view, was the purely private person. In
our era, the confusion of individual freedom with the rights of vast corporations undermines our ability to define a genuine public interest
and to act on its behalf. Yet within our political heritage we can also
find the tradition of civic responsibility that attempted to balance the
rights of individuals within the larger civic order.[41] The challenge of
sustainability may lead us to rediscover, renew, and extend this tradition as a covenant with the land, with life, and with our children.

Part Two

Education

INTRODUCTION

The crisis of sustainability, the fit between humanity and its habitat, is manifest in varying ways and degrees everywhere on earth. It is not only a permanent feature on the public agenda; for all practical purposes it is *the* agenda. No other issue of politics, economics, and public policy will remain unaffected by the crisis of resources, population, climate change, species extinction, acid rain, deforestation, ozone depletion, and soil loss. Sustainability is about the terms and conditions of human survival, and yet we still educate at all levels as if no such crisis existed. The content of our curriculum and the process of education, with a few notable exceptions, has not changed. We have added computers to the scene, but mostly to do things we did before only faster. Whether this is a net gain for the advance of wisdom I do not know. What is apparent, however, is that we do not worry about what our children and young people learn and how well they learn it until a crisis happens along. When the Russians launched Sputnik in 1957 we worried that our children could not compete in science and math and that America would lose its preeminent position in world affairs. Now we are worried sick that our economy is no longer world dominant and that our children cannot compete with the Japanese or the Germans. But we have not yet begun to worry whether or not our children will know how to protect the biological resources upon which any economy ultimately depends.

The crisis cannot be solved by the same kind of education that helped create the problems. Against the test of sustainability, our ideas, theories, sciences, humanities, social sciences, pedagogy, and educational institutions have not measured up. Schools, colleges, and universities are part of the problem. What passes for environmental education is still mostly regarded as a frill to be cut when budgets get tight. Environmental education is done by teachers and faculty mostly on release

83

time or on their own as an overload. Environmental concerns and the issues raised by the challenge of sustainability are still blithely ignored in the mainstream of nearly all the disciplines represented in the catalogs of our proudest institutions. From a casual sampling of the various professional journals, one would have little idea that humanity had any problems beyond methodological esoterica.

The essays in Section 2 have to do with the question of what the limits of earth have to do with the content and process of education and with the way we define knowledge. They are written in the belief that educational institutions are potential leverage points for the transition to sustainability. Four themes from the essays in Section 1 are found throughout those in Section 2. First, as suggested in Chapter 1, I believe that education must acquaint students with deeper causes of the crises just ahead. This requires the active engagement of the humanities in particular. The problems of sustainability are rooted in the human condition and their resolution will require people of greater philosophical depth and perspective. Second, sustainability as described in Chapter 2 requires a different kind of curriculum that encourages the development of ecological competence throughout the population. Yes, we need experts, but not to the exclusion of a population that is both ecologically literate and competent. We will need farmers, businesspersons, writers, bureaucrats, builders, foresters, and workmen who are also ecologically literate and competent and who can build sustainable solutions from the bottom up. The goal of ecological competence implies a different kind of education and a different kind of educational experience that develops the practical art of living well in particular places.

Third, as argued in Chapter 4, ecological sustainability implies a recovery of civic competence. I see no prospect whatsoever for building a sustainable society without an active, engaged, informed, and competent citizenry. The environmental movement is almost without exception one in which citizens forced governments and large economic interests to do something they were otherwise not inclined to do. It is quite literally a democratic movement, but it will not necessarily remain such without an unwavering commitment by educational institutions to foster widespread civic competence.

The essays in Section 2 are based on a belief that a reformed education is an essential part of a solution to the crisis described in Section 1. Education, however, is not just about society, it is about persons. At the individual level, the goal is something like the Greek model of Paideia or that of the Renaissance person of wide understanding, competence, and commitment to the common good.

V

Ecological Literacy

Literacy is the ability to read. Numeracy is the ability to count. Ecological literacy, according to Garrett Hardin, is the ability to ask "What then?" Considerable attention is properly being given to our shortcomings in teaching the young to read, count, and compute, but not nearly enough to ecological literacy. Reading, after all, is an ancient skill. And for most of the twentieth century we have been busy adding, subtracting, multiplying, dividing, and now computing. But "What then?" questions have not come easy for us despite all of our formidable advances in other areas. Napoleon did not ask the question, I gather, until he had reached the outskirts of Moscow, by which time no one could give a good answer except "Let's go back home." If Custer asked the question, we have no record of it. His last known words at Little Big Horn were, "Hurrah, boys, now we have them," a stirring if dubious pronouncement. And economists, who are certainly both numerate and numerous, have not asked the question often enough. Asking "What then?" on the west side of the Niemen River, or at Fort Laramie, would have saved a lot of trouble. For the same reason, "What then?" is also an appropriate question to ask before the last rain forests disappear, before the growth economy consumes itself into oblivion, and before we have warmed the planet intolerably.

The failure to develop ecological literacy is a sin of omission and of commission. Not only are we failing to teach the basics about the earth and how it works, but we are in fact teaching a large amount of stuff that is simply wrong. By failing to include ecological perspectives in any number of subjects, students are taught that ecology is unimportant for history, politics, economics, society, and so forth. And through television they learn that the earth is theirs for the taking. The result is a generation of ecological yahoos without a clue why the color of the water in their rivers is related to their food supply, or why storms are becoming more severe as the planet warms. The same persons as adults will create businesses, vote, have families, and above all, consume. If they come to reflect on the discrepancy between the splendor of their private lives in a hotter, more toxic and violent world, as ecological illiterates they will have roughly the same success as one trying to balance a checkbook without knowing arithematic.

FORMATION OF ATTITUDES

To become ecologically literate one must certainly be able to read and, I think, even like to read. Ecological literacy also presumes an ability to use numbers, and the ability to know what is countable and what is not, which is to say the limits of numbers. But these are indoor skills. Ecological literacy also requires the more demanding capacity to observe nature with insight, a merger of landscape and mindscape. "The interior landscape," in Barry Lopez's words, "responds to the character and subtlety of an exterior landscape; the shape of the individual mind is affected by land as it is by genes."[1] The quality of thought is related to the ability to relate to "where on this earth one goes, what one touches, the patterns one observes in nature—the intricate history of one's life in the land, even a life in the city, where wind, the chirp of birds, the line of a falling leaf, are known." The fact that this kind of intimate knowledge of our landscapes is rapidly disappearing can only impoverish our mental landscapes as well. People who do not know the ground on which they stand miss one of the elements of good thinking which is the capacity to distinguish between health and disease in natural systems and their relation to health and disease in human ones.

If literacy is driven by the search for knowledge, ecological literacy is driven by the sense of wonder, the sheer delight in being alive in a beautiful, mysterious, bountiful world. The darkness and disorder that we have brought to that world give ecological literacy an urgency it lacked a century ago. We can now look over the abyss and see the end of it all. Ecological literacy begins in childhood. "To keep alive his inborn sense of wonder," a child, in Rachel Carson's words, "needs the companionship of at least one adult who can share it, rediscovering with him the joy, excitement and mystery of the world we live in."[2] The sense of wonder is rooted in the emotions or what E. O. Wilson has called "biophilia," which is simply the affinity for the living world.[3] The nourishment of that affinity is the beginning point for the sense of kinship with life, without which literacy of any sort will not help much. This is to say that even a thorough knowledge of the facts of life and of the threats to it will not save us in the absence of the feeling of kinship with life of the sort that cannot entirely be put into words.

There are, I think, several reasons why ecological literacy has been so difficult for Western culture. First, it implies the ability to think broadly, to know something of what is hitched to what. This ability is being lost in an age of specialization. Scientists of the quality of Rachel Carson or Aldo Leopold are rarities who must buck the pressures toward narrowness and also endure a great deal of professional rejection and hostility. By inquiring into the relationship between chlorinated hydrocarbon pesticides and bird populations, Rachel Carson was asking an ecolate question. Many others failed to ask, not because they did not like birds, but because they had not, for whatever reasons, thought beyond the conventional categories. To do so would have required that they relate their food system to the decline in the number of birds in their neighborhood. This means that they would have had some direct knowledge of farms and farming practices, as well as a comprehension of ornithology. To think in ecolate fashion presumes a breadth of experience with healthy natural systems, both of which are increasingly rare. It also presumes that the persons be willing and able to "think at right angles" to their particular specializations, as Leopold put it.

Ecological literacy is difficult, second, because we have come to believe that education is solely an indoor activity. A good part of it, of necessity, must be, but there is a price. William Morton Wheeler once compared the naturalist with the professional biologist in these words: "[The naturalist] is primarily an observer and fond of outdoor life, a collector, a classifier, a describer, deeply impressed by the overwhelming intricacy of natural phenomena and revelling in their very complexity." The biologist, on the other hand, "is oriented toward and dominated by ideas, and rather terrified or oppressed by the intricate hurly-burly of concrete, sensuous reality.... he is a denizen of the laboratory. His besetting sin is oversimplification and the tendency to undue isolation of the organisms he studies from their natural environment."⁴ Since Wheeler wrote, ecology has become increasingly specialized and, one suspects, remote from its subject matter. Ecology, like most learning worthy of the effort, is an applied subject. Its goal is not just a comprehension of how the world works, but, in the light of that knowledge, a life lived accordingly. The same is true of theology, sociology, political science, and most other subjects that grace the conventional curriculum.

The decline in the capacity for aesthetic appreciation is a third factor working against ecological literacy. We have become comfortable with all kinds of ugliness and seem incapable of effective protest against its purveyors: urban developers, businessmen, government officials, television executives, timber and mining companies, utilities, and advertisers. Rene Dubos once stated that our greatest disservice to our children was to give them the belief that ugliness was somehow normal. But disordered landscapes are not just an aesthetic problem. Ugliness signifies a more fundamental disharmony between people and between people and the land. Ugliness is, I think, the surest sign of disease, or what is now being called "unsustainability." Show me the hamburger stands, neon ticky-tacky strips leading toward every city in America, and the shopping malls, and I'll show you devastated rain forests, a decaying countryside, a politically dependent population, and toxic waste dumps. It is all of a fabric.

And this is the heart of the matter. To see things in their wholeness is politically threatening. To understand that our manner of living, so comfortable for some, is linked to cancer rates in migrant laborers in California, the disappearance of tropical rain forests, fifty thousand toxic dumps across the U.S.A., and the depletion of the ozone layer is to see the need for a change in our way of life. To see things whole is to see both the wounds we have inflicted on the natural world in the name of mastery and those we have inflicted on ourselves and on our children for no good reason, whatever our stated intentions. Real ecological literacy is radicalizing in that it forces us to reckon with the roots of our ailments, not just with their symptoms. For this reason, I think it leads to a revitalization and broadening of the concept of citizenship to include membership in a planetwide community of humans and living things.

And how does this striving for community come into being? I doubt that there is a single path, but there are certain common elements. First, in the lives of most if not all people who define themselves as environmentalists, there is experience in the natural world at an early age. Leopold came to know birds and wildlife in the marshes and fields around his home in Burlington, Iowa before his teens. David Brower, as a young boy on long walks over the Berkeley hills, learned to describe the flora to his nearly blind mother. Second, and not surprisingly, there is often an older teacher or mentor as a role model: a grandfather, a neighbor, an older brother, a parent, or teacher. Third, there are seminal books that explain, heighten, and say what we have felt deeply, but not said so well. In my own life, Rene Dubos and Loren Eiseley served this function of helping to bring feelings to articulate consciousness.

Ecological literacy is becoming more difficult, I believe, not because there are fewer books about nature, but because there is less opportunity for the direct experience of it. Fewer people grow up on farms or in rural areas where access is easy and where it is easy to learn a degree of competence and self-confidence toward the natural world. Where the ratio between the human-created environment to the purely natural world exceeds some point, the sense of place can only be a sense of habitat. One finds the habitat familiar and/or likeable but without any real sense of belonging in the natural world. A sense of place requires more direct contact with the natural aspects of a place, with soils, landscape, and wildlife. This sense is lost as we move down the continuum toward the totalized urban environment where nature exists in tiny, isolated fragments by permission only. Said differently, this is an argument for more urban parks, summer camps, green belts, wilderness areas, public seashores. If we must live in an increasingly urban world, let's make it one of well-designed compact green cities that include trees, river parks, meandering greenbelts, and urban farms where people can see, touch, and experience nature in a variety of ways. In fact, no other cities will be sustainable in a greenhouse world.

ECOLOGICAL LITERACY AND
FORMAL EDUCATION

The goal of ecological literacy as I have described it has striking implications for that part of education that must occur in classrooms, libraries, and laboratories. To the extent that most educators have noticed the environment, they have regarded it as a set of problems which are: (1) solvable (unlike dilemmas, which are not) by (2) the analytic tools and methods of reductionist science which (3) create value-neutral, technological remedies that will not create even worse side effects. Solutions, therefore, originate at the top of society, from governments and corporations, and are passed down to a passive citizenry in the form of laws, policies, and technologies. The results, it is assumed, will be socially, ethically, politically, and humanly desirable, and the will to live and to sustain a humane culture can be preserved in a technocratic society. In other words, business can go on as usual. Since there is no particular need for an ecologically literate and ecologically competent public, environmental education is most often regarded as an extra in the curriculum, not as a core requirement or as an aspect pervading the entire educational process.

Clearly, some parts of the crisis can be accurately described as problems. Some of these can be solved by technology, particularly those that require increased resource efficiency. It is a mistake, however, to think that all we need is better technology, not an ecologically literate and caring public willing to help reduce the scale of problems by reducing its demands on the environment and to accept (even demand) public policies that require sacrifices. It all comes down to whether the public understands the relation between its well-being and the health of the natural systems.

For this to occur, we must rethink both the substance and the process of education at all levels. What does it mean to educate people to live sustainably, going, in Aldo Leopold's words, from "conqueror of the land community to plain member and citizen of it"?[5] However it is applied in practice, the answer will rest on six foundations.

The first is the recognition that *all education is environmental education*. By what is included or excluded, emphasized or ignored, students learn that they are a part of or apart from the natural world. Through all education we inculcate the ideas of careful stewardship or carelessness. Conventional education, by and large, has been a celebration of all that is human to the exclusion of our dependence on nature. As a result, students frequently resemble what Wendell Berry has called "itinerant professional vandals," persons devoid of any sense of place or stewardship, or inkling of why these are important.[6]

Second, *environmental issues are complex and cannot be understood through a single discipline or department*. Despite a decade or more of discussion and experimentation, interdisciplinary education remains an unfulfilled promise. The failure occurred, I submit, because it was tried within discipline-centric institutions. A more promising approach is to reshape institutions to function as transdisciplinary laboratories that include components such as agriculture, solar technologies, forestry, land management, wildlife, waste cycling, architectural design, and economics.[7] Part of the task, then, of Earth-centered education is the study of interactions across the boundaries of conventional knowledge and experience.

Third, *for inhabitants, education occurs in part as a dialogue with a place and has the characteristics of good conversation*. Formal education happens mostly as a monologue of human interest, desires, and accomplishments that drowns out all other sounds. It is the logical outcome of the belief that we are alone in a dead world of inanimate matter, energy flows, and biogeochemical cycles. But true conversation can occur only if we acknowledge the existence and interests of the other. In conversation, we define ourselves, but in relation to another. The quality of conversation does not rest on the brilliance of one or the other person. It is more like a dance in which the artistry is mutual.

In good conversation, words represent reality faithfully. And words have power. They can enliven or deaden, elevate or degrade, but they are never neutral, because they affect our perception and ultimately our behavior. The use of words such as "resources," "manage," "channelize," "engineer," and "produce" makes our relation to nature a monologue rather than a conversation. The language of nature includes the sounds of animals, whales, birds, insects, wind, and water—a language more ancient and basic than human speech. Its books are the etchings of life on the face of the land. To hear this language requires patient, disciplined study of the natural world. But it is a language for which we have an affinity.

Good conversation is unhurried. It has its own rhythm and pace. Dialogue with nature cannot be rushed. It will be governed by cycles of day and night, the seasons, the pace of procreation, and by the larger rhythm of evolutionary and geologic time. Human sense of time is increasingly frenetic, driven by clocks, computers, and revolutions in transportation and communication.

Good conversation has form, structure, and purpose. Conversation with nature has the purpose of establishing, in Wendell Berry's words: "What is here? What will nature permit here? What will nature help us do here?"[8] The form and structure of any conversation with the natural world is that of the discipline of ecology as a restorative process and healing art.

Fourth, it follows that *the way education occurs is as important as its content*. Students taught environmental awareness in a setting that does not alter their relationship to basic life-support systems learn that it is sufficient to intellectualize, emote, or posture about such things without having to live differently. Environmental education ought to change the way people live, not just how they talk. This understanding of education is drawn from the writings of John Dewey, Alfred North Whitehead, J. Glenn Gray, Paulo Friere, Ivan Illich, and Eliot Wigginton. Learning in this view best occurs in response to real needs and the life situation of the learner. The radical distinctions typically drawn between teacher and student, between the school and the community, and those between areas of knowledge, are dissolved. Real learning is participatory and experiential, not just didactic. The flow can be two ways between teachers, who best function as facilitators, and students who are expected to be active agents in defining what is learned and how.

Fifth, *experience in the natural world is both an essential part of understanding the environment, and conducive to good thinking.* Experience, properly conceived, trains the intellect to observe the land carefully and to distinguish between health and its opposite. Direct experience is an antidote to indoor, abstract learning. It is also a well-spring of good thinking. Understanding nature demands a disciplined and observant intellect. But nature, in Emerson's words, is also "the vehicle of thought" as a source of language, metaphor, and symbol. Natural diversity may well be the source of much of human creativity and intelligence. If so, the simplification and homogenization of ecosystems can only result in a lowering of human intelligence.

Sixth, *education relevant to the challenge of building a sustainable society will enhance the learner's competence with natural systems.* For reasons once explained by Whitehead and Dewey, practical competence is an indispensable source of good thinking. Good thinking proceeds from the friction between reflective thought and real problems. Aside from its effects on thinking, practical competence will be essential if sustainability requires, as I think it does, that people must take an active part in rebuilding their homes, businesses, neighborhoods, communities, and towns. Shortening supply lines for food, energy, water, and materials—while recycling waste locally—implies a high degree of competence not necessary in a society dependent on central vendors and experts.

THE AIM: ECOLOGICAL LITERACY

If these can be taken as the foundations of Earth-centered education, what can be said of its larger purpose? In a phrase, it is that quality of mind that seeks out connections. It is the opposite of the specialization and narrowness characteristic of most education. The ecologically literate person has the knowledge necessary to comprehend interrelatedness, and an attitude of care or stewardship. Such a person would also have the practical competence required to act on the basis of knowledge and feeling. Competence can only be derived from the experience of doing and the mastery of what Alasdair MacIntyre describes as a "practice."[9] Knowing, caring, and practical competence constitute the basis of ecological literacy.

Ecological literacy, further, implies a broad understanding of how people and societies relate to each other and to natural systems, and how they might do so sustainably. It presumes both an awareness of the interrelatedness of life and knowledge of how the world works as a physical system. To ask, let alone answer, "What then?" questions presumes an understanding of concepts such as carrying capacity, overshoot, Liebig's Law of the minimum, thermodynamics, trophic levels, energetics, and succession. Ecological literacy presumes that we understand our place in the story of evolution. It is to know that our health, well-being, and ultimately our survival depend on working with, not against, natural forces. The basis for ecological literacy, then, is the comprehension of the interrelatedness of life grounded in the study of natural history, ecology, and thermodynamics. It is to understand that: "There ain't no such thing as a free lunch"; "You can never throw anything away"; and "The first law of intelligent tinkering is to keep all of the pieces." It is also to understand, with Leopold, that we live in a world of wounds senselessly inflicted on nature and on ourselves.

A second stage in ecological literacy is to know something of the speed of the crisis that is upon us. It is to know magnitudes, rates, and trends of population growth, species extinction, soil loss, deforestation, desertification, climate change, ozone depletion, resource exhaustion, air and water pollution, toxic and radioactive contamination, resource and energy use—in short, the vital signs of the planet and its ecosystems. Becoming ecologically literate is to understand the human enterprise for what it is: a sudden eruption in the enormity of evolutionary time.

Ecological literacy requires a comprehension of the dynamics of the modern world. The best starting place is to read the original rationale for the domination of nature found in the writings of Bacon, Descartes, and Galileo. Here one finds the justification for the union of science with power and the case for separating ourselves from nature in order to control it more fully. To comprehend the idea of controlling nature, one must fathom the sources of the urge to power and the paradox of rational means harnessed to insane ends portrayed in Marlowe's *Doctor Faustus,* Mary Shelley's *Frankenstein,* Melville's *Moby-Dick,* and Dostoevsky's "Legend of the Grand Inquisitor."

Ecological literacy, then, requires a thorough understanding of the ways in which people and whole societies have become destructive. The ecologically literate person will appreciate something of how social structures, religion, science, politics, technology, patriarchy, culture, agriculture, and human cussedness combine as causes of our predicament.

The diagnosis of the causes of our plight is only half of the issue. But before we can address solutions there are several issues that demand clarification. "Nature," for example, is variously portrayed as "red in tooth and claw," or, like the film "Bambi," full of sweet little critters. Economists see nature as natural resources to be used; the backpacker as a wellspring of transcendent values. We are no longer clear about our own nature, whether we are made in the image of God, or are merely a machine or computer, or animal. These are not trivial, academic issues. Unless we can make reasonable distinctions between what is natural and what is not, and why that difference is important, we are liable to be at the mercy of the engineers who want to remake all of nature, including our own.

Environmental literacy also requires a broad familiarity with the development of ecological consciousness. The best history of the concept of ecology is Donald Worster's *Nature's Economy*.[10] It is unclear whether the science of ecology will be "the last of the old sciences, or the first of the new." As the former, ecology is the science of efficient resource management. As the first of the new sciences, ecology is the basis for a broader search for pattern and meaning. As such it cannot avoid issues of values, and the ethical questions raised most succinctly in Leopold's "The Land Ethic."

The study of environmental problems is an exercise in despair unless it is regarded as only a preface to the study, design, and implementation of solutions. The concept of sustainability implies a radical change in the institutions and patterns that we have come to accept as normal. It begins with ecology as the basis for the redesign of technology, cities, farms, and educational institutions, and with a change in metaphors from mechanical to organic, industrial to biological. As part of the change we will need alternative measures of well-being such as those proposed by Amory Lovins (least-cost end-use analysis),[11] H. T. Odum (energy accounting),[12] and John Cobb (index of sustainable welfare).[13] Sustainability also implies a different approach to technology, one that gives greater priority to those that are smaller in scale, less environmentally destructive, and rely on the free services of natural systems. Not infrequently, technologies with these characteristics are also highly cost-effective, especially when subsidies for competing technologies are leveled out.

If sustainability represents a minority tradition, it is nonetheless a long one dating back at least to Jefferson. Students should not be considered ecologically literate until they have read Thoreau, Kropotkin, Muir, Albert Howard, Alfred North Whitehead, Gandhi, Schweitzer, Aldo Leopold, Lewis Mumford, Rachel Carson, E. F. Schumacher, and Wendell Berry. There are alternatives to the present patterns that have remained dormant or isolated, not because they did not work, were poorly thought out, or were impractical, but because they were not tried. In contrast to the directions of modern society, this tradition emphasizes democratic participation, the extension of ethical obligations to the land community, careful ecological design, simplicity, widespread competence with natural systems, the sense of place, holism, decentralization of whatever can best be decentralized, and human-scaled technologies and communities. It is a tradition dedicated to the search for patterns, unity, connections between people of all ages, races, nationalities, and generations, and between people and the natural world. This is a tradition grounded in the belief that life is sacred and not to be carelessly expended on the ephemeral. It is a tradition that challenges militarism, injustice, ecological destruction, and authoritarianism, while supporting all of those actions that lead to real peace, fairness, sustainability, and people's right to participate in those decisions that affect their lives. Ultimately, it is a tradition built on a view of ourselves as finite and fallible creatures living in a world limited by natural laws. The contrasting Promethean view, given force by the success of technology, holds that we should remove all limits, whether imposed by nature, human nature, or morality. Its slogan is found emblazoned on the advertisements of the age: "You can have it all" (Michelob Beer), or "Your world should know no limits" (Merrill Lynch). The ecologically literate citizen will recognize these immediately for what they are: the stuff of epitaphs. Ecological literacy leads in other, and more durable, directions toward prudence, stewardship, and the celebration of the Creation.

The Liberal Arts, the Campus, and the Biosphere: An Alternative to Bloom's Vision of Education

Debates about the content and purposes of education are mostly conducted among committees of the learned conditioned to such fare.
Allan Bloom changed all of that in 1987 by writing a best-seller on the
subject. Professor Bloom, as far as I can tell, believes that questions
about the content of education (i.e., curriculum) were settled some
time ago; perhaps once and for all with Plato, but certainly no later
than Nietzsche. Subsequent elaborations, revisions, and refinements
have worked great mischief with the high culture he purports to
defend. Bloom's discontent focuses on American youth. He finds them
empty, intellectually slack, and morally ignorant. The "soil" of their
souls is "unfriendly" to the higher learning.[1] And he thinks no more
highly of their music and sexual relationships.

In Professor Bloom's ideal academy, students of a higher sort
would spend a great deal of time reading the Great Books, a list no
longer universally admired. Bloom's avowed aim is to "reconstitute the
idea of an educated human being and establish a liberal education
again." But after 344 pages of verbal pyrotechnics—some illuminating
the landscape, others merely the psyche of Professor Bloom—he
leaves us only with some variation on the Great Books approach to
education. The classics, he argues, "provide the royal road to the students' hearts...their gratitude [for being so exposed is]...boundless."[2]
Exclusion of the classics, he thinks, has culminated in an "intellectual
crisis of the greatest magnitude which constitutes the crisis of our civi-

lization." Lesser minds might have related the crisis to more pedestrian causes such as violence, nuclear weapons, technology, overpopulation, or injustice. No matter. All of this was revealed to Professor Bloom while on the faculty at Cornell during the student uprising in 1969. One may reasonably infer that Professor Bloom and his Great Books were not at that moment treated kindly. One may also infer that Professor Bloom has neither forgiven nor forgotten.

Bloom has been widely attacked as a snob and as having totally misunderstood what America is all about.[3] In his defense, there is no reasonable case to be made against the inclusion of ancient wisdom in any good, liberal education. Nor can there be any good argument against the "idea of an educated human being." But questions about which ancient wisdom we might profitably consult, and about the intellectual and moral qualities of the educated person, have not been settled once and for all with Professor Bloom's book. At the end we know a great deal of what Professor Bloom is against, some of which is justified, but little of what he is for.

His vagueness about ends suggests that Professor Bloom, without saying so, regards education as an end in itself. In a time of global turmoil, what transcendent purposes will Bloom's academy serve? In a time of great wrongs, what injustices does he wish to right? In an age of senseless violence, what civil disorders and dangers does he intend to resolve? In a time of anomie and purposelessness, what higher qualities of mind and character does he propose to cultivate? A careful reading of *The Closing of the American Mind* offers little insight about such matters. Rather, it is indicative of the closure of the purely academic mind to ecological issues.

For all of his conspicuous erudition, Professor Bloom seems to regard the liberal arts as an abstraction. For example, rather than merely "reconstitute the idea" of educated human beings, why not actually educate a large number of them? Likewise, his reverence for the classics is not accompanied by any suggestion of how they might illuminate the major issues of our day. The effect is ironically to render them both sacred and unusable, except for purposes of conspicuous pedantry. It also distorts our understanding of the origins of some of humanity's best thinking. Many of what are now described as classics were produced by the friction of extraordinary minds wrestling with the problems of their day, which is to say that they were relevant in their time. Plato wrote *The Republic* in part as a response to the breakdown of civic order in fourth-century Athens. Locke wrote his *Two Treatises* to justify the English civil war. Only in hindsight does their work appear to have the immaculate qualities that they certainly lacked at birth. The progress of human thought has been hard-fought, uneven, and erratic. We have reason to believe that it will continue to be so. If our descendants five centuries hence regard any books of our era as classics, they will be those that grappled with and illuminated the major issues of our time, in a manner that illuminates theirs. Beyond complaints about education, Professor Bloom does not offer an opinion about what these issues may be. He sounds rather like a fussy museum curator, irate over gum wrappers on the floor.

Amidst growing poverty, environmental deterioration, and violence in a nuclear-armed world, Professor Bloom is silent about how his version of the liberal arts would promote global justice, heal the breech with the natural world, promote peace, and restore meaning in a technocratic world. On the contrary, he arrogantly dismisses those concerned about such issues. Yet, ironically, if our era adds any "classics" to the archeology of human thought, they will more likely than not be written about these subjects.

It is now widely acknowledged that the classics of the Western tradition are deficient in certain respects. First, having been mostly composed by white males, they exclude the vast majority of human experience. Moreover, there are problems that this tradition has not successfully resolved, either because they are of recent origin, or because they were regarded as unimportant. In the latter category is the issue of the human role in the natural world. Search as one may through Plato, Aristotle, and the rest of the authors of the Great Books, there is not much said about it. With a few exceptions such as Hesiod, Cicero, Spinoza, and St. Francis (who wrote no "Great Book"), what wisdom we have from Western sources begins with the likes of Thoreau and George Perkins Marsh in the middle years of the last century. Whatever timeless qualities human nature may or may not have, Western culture has not offered much enlightenment on the appropriate relationship between humanity and its habitat. Nor does Professor Bloom.

Professor Bloom, I believe, has also missed something basic about education. Whitehead put it this way: "First-hand knowledge is the ultimate basis of intellectual life.... The second-handedness of the learned world is the secret of its mediocrity. It is tame because it has never been scared by the facts."[4] An immersion in the classics, however valuable for some parts of intellectual development, risks no confrontation with the facts of life. The aim of education is not the ability to score well on tests, do well in Trivial Pursuit, or even to quote the right classic on the appropriate pedagogical occasion. The aim of education is life lived to its fullest. A study of the classics is one tool among many to this end.

The purpose of a liberal education has to do with the development of the whole person. J. Glenn Gray describes this person as "one who has fully grasped the simple fact that his self is fully implicated in those beings around him, human and nonhuman, and who has learned to care deeply about them."[5] Accordingly, its function is the development of the capacity for clear thought and compassion in the recognition of the interrelatedness of life.

And what do these mean in an age of violence, injustice, ecological deterioration, and nuclear weapons? What does wholeness mean in an age of specialization? It is perhaps easier to begin with what they do not mean. We do not lack for bad models: the careerist, the "itinerant professional vandal"[6] devoid of any sense of place, the yuppie, the narrow specialist, the intellectual snob. In different ways, these all too common role models of the 1980s lack the capacity to relate their autobiography to the unfolding history of their time in a meaningful, positive way. They simply cannot speak to the urgent needs of the age, which is to say that they have been educated to be irrelevant. In Gray's words, they have not grasped "the simple fact" of their implicatedness, nor have they learned to "care deeply" about anything beyond themselves. To the extent that this has become the typical product of our educational institutions, it is an indictment of enormous gravity. Professor Bloom's emphasis on the classics and preservation of high culture does not remedy this dereliction in any obvious way.

It might be possible to dismiss Professor Bloom as a harmless crank were it not for the wide impact of his book, and because he has become a spokesman for the powerful. The problem is not with Professor Bloom's ideas, which are toothless enough. The danger lies in the combination of vagueness, surliness, and the large number of things that he does not say. The result is that *Closing* can be cited by any number of ill-informed proponents of bad causes wanting to exit the twentieth century backwards. Bloom has not provided any coherent vision of the liberal arts relevant to our time. What he does offer is a sometimes insightful cultural critique in combination with a mummified curriculum with the distinct aroma of formaldehyde.

RECONSTRUCTION:
THE TASK OF THE LIBERAL ARTS

The mission of the liberal arts in our time is not merely to inculcate a learned appreciation for the classics, as Bloom would have it, or to transmit "marketable skills," as any number of others propose, but to develop balanced, whole persons. Wholeness, first, requires the integration of the personhood of the student: the analytic mind with feelings, the intellect with manual competence. Failure to connect mind and feelings, in Gray's words, "divorces us from our own dispositions at the level where intellect and emotions fuse."[7] A genuinely liberal education will also connect the head and the hands. Technical education and liberal arts have been consigned to different institutions that educate different parts of the anatomy. What passes for the higher learning deals with the neck up and only half of that, technical schools the remainder. This division creates the danger that students in each, in Gray's words, "miss a whole area of relation to the world."[8] For liberal arts students, it also undermines an ancient source of good thought: the friction between an alert mind and practical experience. Abstract thought, "mere book learning," in Whitehead's words, divorced from practical reality and the facts of life, promotes pedantry and mediocrity. It also produces half-formed or deformed persons: thinkers who cannot do, and doers who cannot think. Students typically leave sixteen years of formal education without ever having mastered a particular skill or without any specific manual competence, as if the act of making anything other than term papers is without pedagogic or developmental value.

Second, an education in the liberal arts must overcome what Whitehead termed "the fatal disconnection of subjects."[9] The contemporary curriculum continues to divide reality into a cacophony of subjects that are seldom integrated into any coherent pattern. There is, as Whitehead reminds us, only one subject for education: "life in all its manifestations." Yet we routinely unleash specialists on the world, armed with expert knowledge but untempered by any inkling of the essential relatedness of things. Worse, specialization undermines the ability to communicate "plainly, in the common tongue."[10] The academy, with its disciplines, divisions, and multiplying professional jargons, has come to resemble not so much a *uni*versity as a cacophony of different jargons. I do not believe that Whitehead overstated the case. Disconnectedness in the form of excessive specialization is fatal to comprehension because it removes knowledge from its larger context. Collection of data supersedes understanding of connecting patterns, which is, I believe, the essence of wisdom. It is no accident that connectedness is central to the meaning of the Greek root words for both ecology and religion, *oikos* and *religio*.

A third task of the liberal arts is to provide a sober view of the world, but without inducing despair. For many college freshmen, acquaintance with the realities of the late twentieth century come as a shock. This is not the happy era they have heard described by a $120 billion-per-year advertising industry and by any number of feckless politicians. This is a time of danger, anomie, suffering, crack on the streets, changing climate, war, hunger, homelessness, spreading toxics, garbage barges plying the seven seas, desertification, poverty, and the permanent threat of Armageddon. Ours is the age of paradox. The modern obsession to control nature through science and technology is resulting in a less predictable and less bountiful natural world. Material progress was supposed to have created a more peaceful world. Instead, the twentieth century has been a time of unprecedented bloodshed in which two hundred million have died. Our economic growth has multiplied wants, not satisfactions. Amidst a staggering quantity of artifacts— what economists call abundance—there is growing poverty of the most desperate sort. How many student counseling services convey this sense of peril? Or obligation? The often-cited indifference and apathy of students is, I think, a reflection of the prior failure of educators and educational institutions to stand for anything beyond larger and larger endowments and an orderly campus. The result is a growing gap between the real world and the academy, and between the attitudes and aptitudes of its graduates and the needs of their time.

Finally, a genuine liberal arts education will equip a person to live well in a place. To a great extent, formal education now prepares its graduates to reside, not to dwell. The difference is important. The resident is a temporary and rootless occupant who mostly needs to know where the banks and stores are in order to plug in. The inhabitant and a particular habitat cannot be separated without doing violence to both. The sum total of violence wrought by people who do not know who they are because they do not know where they are is the global environmental crisis. To reside is to live as a transient and as a stranger to one's place, and inevitably to some part of the self. The inhabitant and place mutually shape each other. Residents, shaped by outside forces, become merely "consumers" supplied by invisible networks that damage their places and those of others. The inhabitant and the local community are parts of a system that meets real needs for food, materials, economic support, and sociability. The resident's world, on the contrary, is a complicated system that defies order, logic, and control. The inhabitant is part of a complex order that strives for harmony between human demands and ecological processes. The resident lives in a constant blizzard of possibilities engineered by other residents. The life of the inhabitant is governed by the boundaries of sufficiency, organic harmony, and by the discipline of paying attention to minute particulars. For the resident, order begins from the top and proceeds downward as law and policy. For the inhabitant, order begins with the self and proceeds outward. Knowledge for the resident is theoretical and abstract, akin to training. For inhabitants, knowledge in the art of living aims toward wholeness. Those who dwell can only be skeptical of those who talk about being global citizens before they have attended to the minute particulars of living well in their place.

LIBERAL ARTS AND THE CAMPUS

This brings me to the place where learning occurs, the campus. Do students in liberal arts colleges learn connectedness there or separation? Do they learn "implicatedness" or noninvolvement? And do they learn that they are "only cogs in an ecological mechanism," as Aldo Leopold put it, or that they are exempt from the duties of any larger citizenship in the community of life?[11] A genuine liberal arts education will foster a sense of connectedness, implicatedness, and ecological citizenship, and will provide the competence to act on such knowledge. In what kind of place can such an education occur? The typical campus is the place where knowledge of other things is conveyed. Curriculum is mostly imported from other locations, times, and domains of abstraction. The campus as land, buildings, and relationships is thought to have no pedagogic value, and for those intending to be residents it need have none. It is supposed to be attractive and convenient, without also being useful and instructive. A "nice" campus is one whose lawns and landscape are well-manicured and whose buildings are kept clean and in good repair by a poorly paid maintenance crew. From distant and unknown places the campus is automatically supplied with food, water, electricity, toilet paper, and whatever else. Its waste and garbage are transported to other equally unknown places.

And what learning occurs on a "nice" campus? First, without anyone saying as much, students learn the lesson of indifference to the ecology of their immediate place. Four years in a place called a campus culminates in no great understanding of the place, or in the art of living responsibly in that or any other place. I think it significant that students frequently refer to the outside world as the "real world," and do so without any feeling that this is not as it should be. The artificiality of the campus is not unrelated to the mediocrity of the learned world of which Whitehead complained. Students also learn indifference to the human ecology of the place and to certain kinds of people: those who clean the urinals, sweep the floors, haul out the garbage, and collect beer cans on Monday morning.

Indifference to a place is a matter of attention. The campus and its region are seldom brought into focus as a matter of practical study. To do so raises questions of the most basic sort. How does it function as an ecosystem? From where does its food, energy, water, and materials come and at what human and ecological cost? Where does its waste and garbage go? At what costs? What relation does the campus have to the surrounding region? What is the ecological history of the place? What ecological potentials does it have? What are the dominant soil types? Flora and fauna? And what of its geology and hydrology?

The study of place cultivates the habit of careful, close observation, and with it the ability to connect cause and effect. Aldo Leopold described the capacity in these terms:

> Here is an abandoned field in which the ragweed is sparse and short. Does this tell us anything about why the mortgage was foreclosed? About how long ago? Would this field be a good place to look for quail? Does short ragweed have any connection with the human story behind yonder graveyard? If all the ragweed in this watershed were short, would that tell us anything about the future of floods in the stream? About the future prospects for bass or trout? [12]

Second, students learn that it is sufficient only to learn about injustice and ecological deterioration without having to do much about them, which is to say, the lesson of hypocrisy. They hear that the vital signs of the planet are in decline without learning to question the *de facto* energy, food, materials, and waste policies of the very institution that presumes to induct them into responsible adulthood. Four years of consciousness-raising proceeds without connection to those remedies close at hand. Hypocrisy undermines the capacity for constructive action and so contributes to demoralization and despair.

Third, students learn that practical incompetence is *de rigueur,* since they seldom are required to solve problems that have consequences except for their grade point average. They are not provided opportunities to implement their stated values in practical ways or to acquire the skills that would let them do so at a later time. Nor are they asked to make anything, it being presumed that material and mental creativity are unrelated. *Homo faber* and *Homo sapiens* are two distinct species, the former being an inferior sort that subsisted between the Neanderthal era and the founding of Harvard. The losses are not trivial: the satisfaction of good work and craftsmanship, the lessons of diligence and discipline, and the discovery of personal competence. After four years of the higher learning, students have learned that it is all right to be incompetent and that practical competence is decidedly inferior to the kind that helps to engineer leveraged buyouts and create tax breaks for people who do not need them. This is a loss of incalculable proportions both to the personhood of the student and to the larger society. It is a loss to their intellectual powers and moral development that can mature only by interaction with real problems. It is a loss to the society burdened with a growing percentage of incompetent people, ignorant of why such competence is important.

The conventional campus has become a place where indoor learning occurs as a preparation for indoor careers. The young of our advanced society are increasingly shaped by the shopping mall, the freeway, the television, and the computer. They regard nature, if they see it at all, as through a rearview mirror receding in the haze. We should not be astonished, then, to discover rates of ecological literacy in decline, at the very time that that literacy is most needed.

THE UPSHOT:
THE CAMPUS AND THE BIOSPHERE

Every educational institution processes not only ideas and students but resources, taking in food, energy, water, materials, and discarding organic and solid wastes. The sources (mines, wells, forests, farms, feedlots) and sinks (landfills, toxic dumps, sewage outfalls) are the least-discussed places in the contemporary curriculum. For the most part, these flows occur out of sight and mind of both students and faculty. Yet they are the most tangible connections between the campus and the world beyond. They also provide an extraordinary educational opportunity. The study of resource flows transcends disciplinary boundaries; it connects the foreground of experience with the background of larger issues and more distant places; and it joins empirical research on existing behavior and its consequences with the study of other and more desirable possibilities.

The study of institutional resource flows is aimed to determine how much of what comes from where, and with what human and ecological consequences. How many kilowatt hours of electricity from what power plants burning how much fuel extracted from where? What are the sources of food in the campus dining hall? Was it produced "sustainably" or not? Were farmers or laborers fairly paid or not? What forests are cut down to supply the college with paper? Were they replanted? Where does toxic waste from labs go? Or solid wastes?

The study of actual resource flows must be coupled with the study of alternatives that may be more humane, ethically solvent, ecologically sustainable, cheaper, and better for the regional economy. Are there other and better sources of food, energy, materials, water? The study of potentials must also address issues of conservation. How much does the institution waste? How much energy, water, paper, and materials can be conserved? What is the potential for recycling paper, materials, glass, aluminum, and other materials? Can organic wastes be composted on-site or recycled through solar aquatic systems? At what cost? Can the institution shift its buying power from national marketing systems to support local economies? How? In what areas? How quickly? Can the landscape be designed for educational rather than decorative purposes? To what extent can good landscaping minimize energy spent for cooling and heating?

To address these and related questions, the Meadowcreek Project conducted studies of the food systems of Hendrix College in Conway, Arkansas, and Oberlin College in Ohio. Both institutions are served by nationwide food-brokering networks that are not sustainable and that tend to undermine regional economies. In the Hendrix study, for example, students discovered that the college was buying only nine percent of its food within the state. Beef came from Amarillo, Texas; rice from Mississippi. Yet the college is located in a cattle and rice-farming region. In both studies, students uncovered ample opportunities for the institutions to expand purchases of locally grown products. Not infrequently, these are fresher, less likely to be contaminated with chemicals, and, not surprisingly, they are cheaper because shipping costs are lower. In conducting the research, which involved travel to the farms and feedlots throughout the United States that supply the campus, students confronted basic issues in agriculture, social ethics, environmental quality, economics, and politics. They were also involved in the analysis of existing buying patterns while having to develop feasible alternatives in cooperation with college officials. The results were action-oriented, interdisciplinary, and aimed to generate practical results. Both colleges responded cooperatively in the implementation of plans to increase local buying. In the Hendrix case, in-state purchases doubled in the year following the study. Through video documentaries and articles in the campus newspaper, the studies became part of a wider campus dialogue. Finally, the willingness of both colleges to support local economies helps to bridge the gap between the institutions and their locality in a way no public relations campaign could have done.

CONCLUSION

The study of institutional resource flows can lead to three results. The first is a set of policies governing food, energy, water, materials, architectural design, landscaping, and waste flows that meet standards for sustainability. A campus energy policy, for example, would set standards for conservation, while directing a shift toward the maximum use of both passive and active solar systems for hot water, space conditioning, and electricity. A campus food policy would give high priority to local and regional organic sources. A materials policy would aim to minimize solid waste and recycling. An architectural policy governing all new construction and renovation would give priority to solar design and the use of nontoxic and bioregionally available building materials. A landscape policy would stress the use of trees for cooling and windbreaks, and as a means to offset campus CO_2 emissions. Decorative landscaping would be replaced by "edible landscaping." A campus waste policy, aimed to close waste loops, would lead to the development of on-site composting and the exploration of biological alternatives for handling waste water such as that being developed by John Todd.[13]

The study of campus resource flows and the development of campus policies would lead to a second and more important result: the reinvigoration of a curriculum around the issues of human survival, a plausible foundation for the liberal arts. This emphasis would become a permanent part of the curriculum through research projects, courses, seminars, and the establishment of interdisciplinary programs in resource management or environmental studies. By engaging the entire campus community in the study of resource flows, debate about the possible meanings of sustainability, the design of campus resource policies, and curriculum innovation, the process carries with it the potential to enliven the educational process. I can think of few disciplines throughout the humanities, social sciences, and sciences without an important contribution to this debate.

Third, the study and its implementation as policy and curriculum would be an act of real leadership. Nearly every college and university claims to offer "excellence" in one way or another. Mostly the word is invoked by unimaginative academic officials who want their institution to be like some other. And for those so emulated, prestige, like barnacles on the hull of a ship, limit institutional velocity and mobility. Real excellence in an age of cataclysmic potentials, consists neither in imitation nor timidity. College and university officials with courage and vision have the power to lead in the transition to a sustainable future. Within their communities, their institutions have visibility, respect, and buying power. What they do matters to a large number of people. How they spend their institutional budget counts for a great deal in the regional economy. Through alumni, they reach present leaders; through students they reach those of the future. All of which is to say that colleges and universities are leverage institutions. They can help create a humane and livable future, rather than remaining passively on the sidelines, poised to study the outcome.

Not without irony, those who presume to defend the liberal arts in the fashion of Allan Bloom have undersold them. A genuinely liberal education will produce whole persons with intellectual breadth, able to think at right angles to their major field; practical persons able to act competently; and persons of deep commitment, willing to roll up their sleeves and join the struggle to build a humane and sustainable world. They will not be merely well-read. Rather, they will be ecologically literate citizens able to distinguish health from its opposite and to live accordingly. Above all, they will make themselves relevant to the crisis of our age, which in its various manifestations is about the care, nurturing, and enhancement of life. And life is the only defensible foundation for a liberal education.

VII

A Prerequisite to the Great Books of Allan Bloom: A Syllabus for Ecological Literacy

INTRODUCTION

1. How the World Works.

   a. *THERMODYNAMICS.* Paul and Anne Ehrlich, and John P. Holdren, "Availability, Entropy, and the Laws of Thermodynamics," in Herman Daly, ed., *Economics, Ecology, Ethics* (San Francisco: W. H. Freeman, 1980), 44–48.

   b. *ECOLOGY.* William Ophuls, *Ecology and the Politics of Scarcity* (San Francisco: W. H. Freeman, 1977), ch. 1; Eugene Odum, *Basic Ecology* (Philadelphia: Saunders, 1983); Tyler Miller, *Environmental Science: An Introduction* (Belmont: Wadsworth, 1986); Paul and Anne Ehrlich, and John Holdren, *Ecoscience: Population, Resources, Environment* (San Francisco: W. H. Freeman, 1977); Paul Ehrlich, *The Machinery of Nature* (New York: Simon and Shuster, 1986).

BACKGROUND

2. Trends, Forecasts, Probabilities, Possibilities, Uncertainties.

    a. WorldWatch Institute, State of the World: (annual) (New York: W. W. Norton, 1990); Conservation Foundation, *State of the Environment: A View Toward the Nineties* (Washington, D.C.: Conservation Foundation, 1987).

    b. Norman Myers, *Gaia: An Atlas Of Planetary Management* (New York: Doubleday, 1984).

    c. *World Resources Annual: 1989,* 1–6.

    d. World Commission of Environment and Development, *Our Common Future* (New York: Oxford University Press, 1987), 1–23.

    e. *World Military and Social Expenditures: 1987–88.*

    f. Theodore H. Von Laue, *The World Revolution of Westerniza-tion* (New York: Oxford University Press, 1987), 333–69.

    g. William Ophuls, *Ecology and the Politics of Scarcity,* ch. 2, 3, 4.

    h. Bill McKibben, *The End of Nature* (New York: Random House, 1989); and Jonathan Weiner, *The Next One Hundred Years* (New York: Bantam Books, 1990).

3. The Dynamics of the Modern World: The Project of Modernization.

    a. *AS VIEWED FROM LITERATURE.* Francis Bacon, *Novum Organum* (1620); Christopher Marlowe, *Dr. Faustus* (1604); Mary Shelley, *Frankenstein* (1817); Herman Melville, *Moby-Dick* (1850); John Steinbeck, *Grapes of Wrath* (1939); Aldous Huxley, *Brave New World* (1932).

    b. *THE IDEA OF PROGRESS.* J. B. Bury, *The Idea of Progress* (New York: Dover, 1955); Robert Nisbet, *The History of the Idea of Progress* (New York: Basic Books, 1980); and its dissenters: Isaiah Berlin, *Against the Current* (New York: Viking, 1980).

    c. *THE CORNUCOPIANS.* Julian Simon, *The Ultimate Resource* (Princeton: Princeton University Press, 1981), 3–52; and the review by Garrett Hardin, *Naked Emperors* (Los Altos: William Kaufman, 1982), 196–204; Julian Simon and Herman Kahn,

"Introduction," *The Resourceful Earth* (Oxford: Basil Blackwell, 1984), 1–49.

d. *AND THE RISK TAKERS*. Herman Kahn et al., *The Next 200 Years* (New York: Morrow, 1976), 1–25, 163–180; Aaron Wildavsky, "No Risk is the Highest Risk of All," *American Scientist* (January/February 1979); and Wildavsky and Douglas, *Risk and Culture* (Berkeley: University of California Press, 1982)

e. *PROMETHEAN SCIENCE*. H. E. Goeller and Alvin Weinberg, "The Age of Substitutability," *Science* (20 February 1976); Goeller, "The Age of Substitutability," in V. Kerry Smith, ed., *Scarcity and Growth Reconsidered* (Baltimore: Johns Hopkins Press, 1979); H. E. Goeller and A. Zucker, "Infinite Resources: The Ultimate Strategy," *Science* (7 July 1984).

4. Some Critics of the Modern World.

a. Dostoevsky, "The Legend of the Grand Inquisitor," in *Brothers Karamazov* (1880).

b. Morris Berman, *The Reenchantment of the World* (Ithaca: Cornell University Press, 1981), ch. 1, 3, 4.

c. Stephen Toulman, *The Return to Cosmology* (Berkeley: University of California Press,), 237–74.

d. Lewis Mumford, "The Reinvention of the Megamachine," in *The Lewis Mumford Reader* (New York: Pantheon, 1987), 333–47.

e. C. S. Lewis, *The Abolition of Man* (New York: Macmillan, 1947), 67–91.

f. John Livingston, *The Fallacy of Wildlife Conservation* (Toronto: McClelland and Stewart, 1982), 64–98.

g. René Dubos, "A Demon Within," in Dubos, *A God Within* (New York: Scribners, 1972), 200–16.

5. Sources of Environmental Problems.

a. *SOCIAL TRAPS AND RATIONAL ACTORS*. Robert Costanza, "Social Traps and Ecological Destruction," *Bioscience* (June 1987); Livingston, *The Fallacy of Wildlife Conservation*, 24–46; Garrett Hardin, "The Tragedy of the Commons," *Science* (1968).

b. *INSTITUTIONAL RELIGION.* Lynn White, "The Historical Roots of Our Ecologic Crisis," *Science* (10 March 1967); Wendell Berry, *The Gift of Good Land* (San Francisco: North Point Press, 1981).

c. *THE RELIGION OF ECONOMICS.* Karl Polanyi, *The Great Transformation* (Boston: Beacon Press, 1967/44), 3–76, 249–58; Daly, *Economics, Ecology, and Ethics* (1980), 1–31; Herman Daly and John Cobb, *For the Common Good* (Boston: Beacon Press, 1990).

d. *THE TRANSITION TO AGRICULTURE.* Paul Shepard, *Nature and Madness* (San Francisco: Sierra Club Books, 1982).

e. *THE ISSUE OF POWER.* Andrew Bard Smookler, *The Parable of the Tribes* (Berkeley: University of California Press, 1984), 245–71.

f. *LANGUAGE.* Wendell Berry, *Standing By Words* (San Francisco: North Point Press, 1983), 24–63.

g. *HUMAN CUSSEDNESS.* Livingston, *The Fallacy of Wildlife Conservation,* 64–98. C. G. Jung, *Memories, Dreams, Reflections* (New York: Vintage, 1965), 299–359; Lewis Mumford, "The Uprising of Caliban," in Mumford, *Interpretations and Forecasts, 1922–1972* (New York: Harcourt Brace Jovanovich, 1979), 334–50; Ernest Becker, *The Denial of Death* (New York: Free Press, 1973); Jeffrey Burton Russell, "The Question of Evil," in Russell, *The Devil: Perceptions of Evil From Antiquity to Primitive Christianity* (Ithaca: Cornell University Press, 1977), 17–35.

h. *PATRIARCHY.* Carolyn Merchant, *The Death of Nature* (New York: Harper and Row, 1980); Susan Griffen, *Woman and Nature* (New York: Harper and Row, 1978).

i. *POLITICS.* Andre Gorz, *Ecology as Politics* (Boston: South End Press, 1980), 11–53; Ophuls, *Ecology,* ch. 5, 6; Bertram Gross, *Friendly Facism* (New York: Evans, 1980); Max Horkheimer, "The Revolt of Nature," in Horkheimer, *The Eclipse of Reason* (New York: Seabury, 1974/1947); Donald Worster, *Rivers of Empire: Water Aridity and the Growth of the American West* (New York: Pantheon, 1985), 17–60; Marc Reisner, "Dominy," in Reisner, *Cadillac Desert* (New York: Viking, 1986), 222–63; Barry Commoner, "The Environment," *The New Yorker* (15 June 1987).

j. *MORAL INCOHERENCE.* Alasdair MacIntyre, *After Virtue* (South Bend: Notre Dame University Press, 1981).

6. The Question of Scientific Knowledge.

a. *FOUNDATIONS OF WESTERN SCIENCE.* Lewis Mumford, *The Myth of the Machine: The Pentagon of Power* (New York: Harcourt Brace Jovanovich, 1970), 51–129; E. A. Burtt, *The Metaphysical Foundations of Modern Science* (New York: Doubleday, 1954); Alfred North Whitehead, *Science and the Modern World* (New York: Free Press, 1967).

b. *THE PROCESS OF SCIENCE.* Thomas Kuhn, *The Structure of Scientific Revolutions* (Chicago: University of Chicago Press, 1977); Abraham Maslow, *The Psychology of Science* (Chicago: Henry Regnery, 1966); Jerome Ravetz, *Scientific Knowledge and Its Social Problems* (New York: Oxford University Press, 1973), 31–67.

c. *SCIENCE IN SOCIETY.* Robert Sinsheimer, "The Presumptions of Science," in Daly, *Economics, Ecology, and Ethics,* (1980), 146–61; Floyd Matson, *The Broken Image* (New York: Anchor, 1966); Kass, *Toward a more Natural Science: Biology and Human Affairs (New York: Free Press, 1985), 1–8; Alan Schnaiberg,* The Environment: From Surplus   to Scarcity (New York: Oxford University Press, 1980), 277–361.

d. *KNOWING.* Michael Polanyi, *Personal Knowledge* (New York: Harper and Row, 1964); Theodore Roszak, "The Monster and the Titan: Science, Knowledge, Gnosis," *Daedalus* (Summer 1974); Roszak, *Where the Wasteland Ends* (New York: Anchor, 1973), ch. 7.

e. *WISDOM.* Erwin Chargaff, "Knowledge Without Wisdom," *Harper's* (May 1980).

7. The Problem of Technology.

a. *FOREBODINGS.* Henry Adams, "The Dynamo and the Virgin," in *The Education of Henry Adams* (Boston: Houghton Mifflin, 1973).

b. *TWO VIEWS OF TECHNOLOGY.* David Ehrenfeld, *The Arrogance of Humanism* (New York: Oxford University Press, 1979); Daniel Bell, "Technology, Nature, and Society," in Bell, *The Winding Passage* (New York: Basic Books, 1980).

c. *TECHNOLOGY AS DEVICES AND PRACTICES.* Albert Borgman,

Technology and the Character of Contemporary Life (Chicago: University of Chicago Press, 1984).

d. *TECHNOLOGY AS AUTONOMOUS.* Jacques Ellul, *The Technological Society* (New York: Vintage, 1964); Ellul, *The Technological System* (New York: Continuum, 1980); Langdon Winner, *Autonomous Technology* (Cambridge: MIT Press, 1977).

e. *THE POLITICS OF ARTIFACTS.* Langdon Winner, *The Whale and the Reactor* (Chicago: University of Chicago Press, 1986), 3–58; Joseph Weizenbaum, *Computer Power and Human Reason* (San Francisco: W. H. Freeman, 1976), 17–38, 228–80.

f. *TECHNOLOGY AND RISK.* Charles Perrow, *Normal Accidents* (New York: Basic Books), ch. 9.

g. *SCIENCE AND IDEOLOGY.* Richard Levins and Richard Lewontin, *The Dialectical Biologist* (Cambridge: Harvard University Press, 1985), 197–208, 267–88.

h. *POSSESSIONS.* Erazim Kohak, "Creation's Orphans: Toward a Metaphysics of Artifacts," *The Personalist Forum* (Spring 1985); Kohak, *Embers and Stars,* 3–26.

i. *POLITICS OF SCIENCE.* Walter McDougall, *The Heavens and the Earth* (New York: Basic Books, 1985), 436–61.

RECONSIDERATIONS

8. Ideas of Nature.

a. John Stuart Mill, "Nature," in Three Essays on *Religion.*

b. Peter Kropotkin, *Mutual Aid* (New York: New York University Press, 1914).

c. Ralph Waldo Emerson, "Nature," (1837).

d. John Burroughs, *Accepting the Universe* (Boston: Houghton Mifflin, 1920).

e. Wendell Berry, "Getting Along With Nature," in *Home Economics* (San Francisco: North Point Press, 1987), 6–20.

f. Joyce Carol Oates, "Against Nature," in Daniel Halpern, *On Nature* (San Francisco: North Point Press, 1987).

g. Paul Shepard, "Place in American Culture," *North American Review* (1977).

h. René Dubos, "Humanized Nature" (1972), and Dubos, *The Wooing of the Earth* (New York: Scribners, 1980).

i. Leon Kass, *Toward a More Natural Science* (New York: Free Press, 1985), 249–75.

j. James Lovelock, *Gaia: A New Look at Life on Earth* (New York: Oxford University Press, 1979); Lovelock, *The Ages of Gaia* (New York: W. W. Norton, 1988).

k. Donald Griffin, *Animal Thinking* (Cambridge: Harvard University Press, 1984).

9. And Human Nature.

a. Barry Schwartz, *The Battle for Human Nature* (New York: W. W. Norton, 1986).

b. E. O. Wilson, *On Human Nature* (Cambridge: Harvard University Press, 1978); Kenneth Bock, *Human Nature and History* (New York: Columbia University Press, 1980).

c. *Engineering humanity.* Kass, *Toward a More Natural Science* (1985), 17–42; 299–317.

d. *Humanity in nature.* René Dubos, *So Human an Animal* (New York: Scribners, 1968); and Dubos, *Beast or Angel?* (New York: Scribners, 1974).

10. What's Natural and What's it to Us?

a. Martin Krieger, "What's Wrong With Plastic Trees?" *Science* (1973).

b. Laurence Tribe, "Ways not to Think About Plastic Trees," *Yale Law Journal* 83 (1974).

c. Holmes Rolston, "Can and Ought We to Follow Nature," *Environmental Ethics* (1979); and Rolston, "Values in Nature," *Environmental Ethics* (1981).

d. Loren Eiseley, "How Natural is 'Natural,'" in *The Firmament of Time* (New York: Atheneum, 1978), 153–81. e. Kass, "Making Babies," in Kass, *Toward a More Natural Science* (1985), 43–79.

11. The Evolution of Ecological Consciousness: Science.

a. *THE GREEKS TO 1800.* Clarence Glacken, *Traces on the Rhodi-an Shore* (Berkeley: University of California Press, 1973).

b. *1864 TO 1962.* Marsh, Burroughs, Muir, Vogt, Osborn, Carson.

c. *THE SCIENCE OF ECOLOGY.* Donald Worster, *Nature's Econo-my: A History of Ecological Ideals.* (Cambridge: Cambridge University Press, 1986), 256–348; Mark Sagoff, "Fact and Value in Ecological Science," *Environmental Ethics* (1985).

d. *KNOWLEDGE ABOUT/KNOWLEDGE OF NATURE.* Joseph Wood Krutch, *The Great Chain of Life* (Boston: Houghton Mifflin, 1978/1956), ch. 9; John Livingston, *Fallacy*, ch. 4; William Barrett, *The Illusion of Technique* (New York: Anchor, 1978).

12. Ecological Consciousness II: Religion and Ethics.

a. *THE JUDAIC-CHRISTIAN LEGACY.* Lynn White Jr., "The Historical Roots of Our Ecologic Crisis," *Science* (10 March 1967); Wendell Berry, "The Gift of Good Land," *Sierra Club Bulletin* (November/December 1979); and David Ehrenfeld, "Judaism and the Practice of Stewardship," *Judaism* (Summer 1985).

b. *ETHICS.* Aldo Leopold, "The Land Ethic," in *A Sand County Almanac* (New York: Oxford University Press, 1949).

c. *THE MORAL UNIVERSE.* Erazim Kohak, *The Embers and the Stars* (Chicago: University of Chicago Press, 1984), 179–218.

d. *LAND ETHICS/ANIMAL RIGHTS.* Baird Callicott, "Animal Liberation: A Triangular Affair," *Environmental Ethics* (1980); and Callicott, "Conceptual Foundations of the Land Ethic," in Callicott, ed., *A Companion to The Sand County Almanac* (Madison: University of Wisconsin Press, 1987).

e. *DUTIES.* Holmes Rolston, "Duties to Ecosystems," in Rolston, *Philosophy Gone Wild* (Buffalo: Prometheus Books, 1987).

f. *STANDING.* Christopher Stone, *Should Trees Have Standing* (Los Anos: William Kaufman, Inc., 1974).

g. *ANIMAL RIGHTS.* Tom Regan, "The Case for Animal Rights," in Peter Singer, *In Defense of Animals* (Oxford: Basil Blackwell, 1985), 13–26.

h. *LIFEBOATS.* Garrett Hardin, "Living on a Lifeboat," *Bioscience* (1974).

i. *CALCULATIONS.* Mark Sagoff, "At the Shrine of Our Lady of Fatima, or Why Political Questions are Not All Economic," *Arizona Law Review* (1981).

RECONSTRUCTION

13. The Concept of Sustainability.

a. *ECOLOGICAL UNDERPINNINGS.* Aldo Leopold, "The Round River," in *A Sand County Almanac* (New York: Oxford University Press, 1948), 188–202; E. O. Wilson, *Biophilia* (Cambridge: Harvard University Press, 1984), 119–40; René Dubos, *A God Within* (New York: Charles Scribners, 1972), "Arcadian Life versus Faustian Civilization," 256–91.

b. *THE EPISTEMOLOGY OF WHOLENESS.* Gregory Bateson, *Mind and Nature: a Necessary Unity* (New York: E. P. Dutton, 1979); Gregory Bateson and Mary Catherine Bateson, *Angels Fear: Towards an Epistemology of the Sacred* (New York: Macmillan, 1987); also Stephen Toulmin, *Return to Cosmology* (Chicago: University of Chicago Press, 1983), 201–16; William Irwin Thompson, "Introduction," in Thompson, ed., *GAIA: A Way of Knowing* (Great Barrington: Lindisfarne Press, 1987), 11–34; Owen Barfield, *Saving the Appearances* (New York: Harcourt Brace Jovanovich, n.d.).

c. *REDISCOVERY OF THE SACRED.* Liberty Hyde Bailey, *The Holy Earth* (New York: Scribners, 1980); René Dubos, "A Theology of the Earth," in Dubos, *A God Within* (New York: Scribners, 1972); Tom Berry, *The Riverdell Papers* (n.d.); Mircea Eliade, *The Sacred and the Profane* (New York: Harcourt Brace Jovanovich, 1959).

d. *PRINCIPLES OF DESIGN.* John and Nancy Todd, *Bioshelters, Ocean Arks, City Farming: Ecology as the Basis of Design* (San Francisco: Sierra Club Books, 1984), 19–92.

e. *RESILIENCE AS A PRINCIPLE OF DESIGN.* Amory and Hunter Lovins, *Brittle Power* (Andover: Brick House, 1983), ch. 13.

f. *ECOLOGY AND DESIGN.* Eugene Odum, "The Strategy of Ecosystem Development," *Science* (18 April 1969); Tyler Miller,

Living in the Environment 4th ed. (Belmont: Wadsworth, 1982), 21–86; C. S. Holling, "The Curious Behavior of Complex Systems: Lessons From Ecology," in Linstone and Simmonds, eds., *Futures Research: New Directions* (Reading: Addison-Wesley, 1977), 114-29.

g. *DIVERSITY AND STABILITY.* Paul Erhlich, "Diversity and the Steady-State," *Technology Review* (March/April 1980); Kenneth Watt, "Man's Efficient Rush Toward Deadly Dullness," *Natural History Magazine* (February, 1972).

h. *THE IDEA OF ORGANIC.* Lewis Mumford, *Myth of the Machine,* 384–413.

i. *SUSTAINABILITY AND SECURITY.* Lester Brown, "Redefining National Security," in *State of the World: 1986* (New York: W. W. Norton, 1986), 195–211; Dan Deudney, "Whole Earth Security," *WorldWatch Paper 55* (1983); Michael Renner, *National Security: The Economic and Environmental Dimensions* (Washington: WorldWatch Institute, 1989).

14. Tools of Analysis.

a. *LEAST-COST/END-USE ANALYSIS.* Amory Lovins, *Soft-Energy Paths* (Cambridge: Ballinger, 1977); Lovins, "The Origins of the Nuclear Power Fiasco," in Byrne and Rich, eds., *Energy Policy Studies Volume Three: The Politics of Energy Research and Development* (New Brunswick: Transaction Books, 1986).

b. *ENERGETICS.* Howard Odum, *Environment, Power, and Society* (New York: Wiley, 1971); H. T. Odum et al., *Environmental Systems and Public Policy* (Gainesville: University of Florida, 1987); Martha Gilliland, "Energy Analysis and Public Policy," *Science* (26 September 1975); Robert Costanza, "Embodied Energy and Economic Valuation," *Science* (12 December 1980); Cleveland et al., "Energy and the U.S. Economy: A Biophysical Perspective," *Science* (31 August 1984); Gene Tyner et al., "The Net Energy Yield of Nuclear Power," *Energy* (1988); Herman Daly and Alvaro Umana, eds., *Energy, Economics, and the Environment* (Boulder: Westview Press, 1981).

c. *CARRYING CAPACITY/HUMAN ECOLOGY.* William Catton, *Overshoot: The Ecological Basis of Revolutionary Change* (Urbana: University of Illinois, 1980); Catton, "The World's Most Polymorphic Species," *Bioscience* (June, 1987); John Gever et al., "Carrying Capacity and Human Systems," in *Beyond Oil* (Cambridge: Ballinger, 1986), 1–32.

   d. *ECONOMICS.* Gene Logsdon, "Amish Economics," *Whole Earth Review* (Spring 1986), and "Amish Economics," in *Orion* (Spring 1988); Wendell Berry, "Two Economies," in *Home Economics* (San Francisco: North Point Press, 1987).

   e. *REGIONAL ANALYSIS.* Lewis Mumford, *The Culture of Cities* (New York: Harcourt Brace Jovanovich, 1966/1938), 300–401.

   f. *TOWARD A SCIENCE OF SCALE, PROPORTION, HARMONY.* Paul Grillo, *Form, Function, and Design* (New York: Dover, 1960); Theodore Cook, *Curves of Life* (New York: Dover, 1979); Karl von Frisch, *Animal Architecture* (New York: Harcourt Brace Jovanovich, 1974); Ivan Illich, *Energy and Equity* (New York: Harper and Row, 1974); Leopold Kohr, *The Breakdown of Nations* (New York: E. P. Dutton, 1978); E. F. Schumacher, "A Question of Size." *Small is Beautiful: Economics as if People Mattered* (New York: Harper Torch Books, 1973), 59–70; Kirkpatrick Sale, *Human Scale* (New York: Coward, McCann and Geoghegan, 1980); D'Arcy Thompson, *On Growth and Form,* abridged edition by J. T. Bonner (Cambridge University Press, 1987/1988).

   g. *OUTRAGE.* For examples, see Abraham Heschel, *The Prophets* (New York: Harper and Row, 1969/62), volume 1, ix–xv, 3–26; volume 2, 1–78; Jeremy Rifkin, *Declaration of a Heretic* (Boston: Rutledge & Kegan Paul, 1985).

   h. *RIGHT-BRAINED ANALYSIS.* Alan Watts, *Nature, Man, Woman* (New York: Vintage, 1970); Masanobu Fukuoka, *The One-Straw Revolution* (Emmaus: Rodale Press, 1978); Gary Snyder, *Earth House Hold* (New York: New Directions, 1969), 90–93.

15. Tools for Reinhabitation.

   a. *SOCIALLY RESILIENT TECHNOLOGY.* E. F. Schumacher, *Small is Beautiful* (New York: Harper and Row, 1974), part 1; Ivan Illich, *Tools for Conviviality* (New York: Harper and Row, 1973).

   b. *LAND USE/DESIGN WITH NATURE.* Ian McHarg, *Design with Nature* (New York: Natural History Press, 1969); Walter Westman, "How Much are Nature's Services Worth?" *Science* (2

September 1977); Westman, *Ecology, Impact Assessment, and Environmental Planning* (New York: Wiley, 1985).

c. *AGRICULTURE.* Albert Howard, *An Agricultural Testament* (New York: Oxford University Press, 1943); Edward Faulkner, *Plowman's Folly* (Norman: University of Oklahoma Press, 1943); F. H. King, *Farmers of Forty Centuries* (Emmaus: Rodale Press, n.d.); Bill Mollison, *Permaculture I; Permaculture II* (Tagari Books); J. Russell Smith, *Tree Crops* (New York: Harper and Row, 1978); Wes Jackson et al., *Meeting the Expectations of the Land* (San Francisco: North Point Press, 1985).

d. *FORESTRY.* Chris Maser, *Forest Primeval* (San Francisco: Sierra Club Books, 1989); Maser, *From the Forest to the Sea* (Washington: U.S. Department of Agriculture, 1988); Richard St. Barbe Baker, *My Life My Trees* (London: Lutterworth Press, 1970).

d. *ARCHITECTURE.* Christopher Alexander, *A Pattern Language* (New York: Oxford University Press, 1977).

e. *SOLAR DESIGN.* Bruce Anderson, *The Solar Home Book* (Harrisville: Cheshire Books, 1976); Edward Mazria, *The Passive Solar Home Book* (Emmaus: Rodale Press, 1979).

e. *SHELTER.* John and Nancy Todd, *Tomorrow is Our Permanent Address* (New York: Harper and Row, 1980); Jim Leckie et al., *More Other Homes and Garbage* (San Francisco: Sierra Club Books, 1981); Farallones Institute, *The Integral Urban House* (San Francisco: Sierra Club Books, 1979); John Seymour, *Blueprint for a Green Planet* (New York: Prentice-Hall, 1987); Edward Mazria, *The Passive Solar Energy Book* (Emmaus: Rodale Press, 1979); Malcolm Wells, *Gentle Architecture* (New York: McGraw-Hill, 1981).

f. *SUSTAINABLE CITIES.* Sim Van der Ryn and Peter Calthorpe, *Sustainable Communities* (San Francisco: Sierra Club Books, 1986); Michael Corbett, *A Better Place to Live* (Emmaus: Rodale Press, 1981); Anne Whiston Spirn, *The Granite Garden: Urban Nature and Human Design* (New York: Basic Books, 1984).

g. *GOOD WORK.* Eric Gill, *A Holy Tradition of Working* (Ipswich: Golgoonoza Press, 1983); E. F. Schumacher, *Good Work* (New York: Harper and Row, 1979); Alasdair MacIntyre, *After Virtue* (South Bend: Notre Dame University Press, 1981), 169–89.

h. *RESTORATION.* John Berger, *Restoring the Earth* (New York: Knopf, 1985).

16. Models of Sustainability.

   a. *POLITICAL/DECENTRALIST.* Frederick Buttel and Oscar Larson, "Whither Environmentalism," *Natural Resources Journal* (April 1980); John Friedman, *Planning in the Public Domain: From Knowledge to Action* (Princeton: Princeton University Press, 1987), 311–88; Arthur Morgan, *The Small Community* (Yellow Springs: Community Service Foundation, 1942); Theodore Roszak, *Person/Planet* (New York: Anchor, 1979); Baker Brownell, *The Human Community* (New York: Harper and Row, 1950); William Sullivan, *Reconstructing Public Philosophy* (Berkeley: University of California Press, 1982), ch. 5, 7; Herbert Agar and Allen Tate, eds., *Who Owns America* (Boston: Houghton Mifflin, 1936); Herbert Agar, *Land of the Free* (Boston: Houghton Mifflin, 1935); Benjamin Barber, *Strong Democracy* (Berkeley: University of California Press, 1984); Peter Kropotkin, *Fields Factories, and Workshops Tomorrow* (New York: Harper and Row, 1974); Ralph Borsodi, *Flight From the City* (New York: Harper and Row, 1933).

   b. *POLITICAL/CENTRALIST.* William Ophuls, *Ecology and the Politics of Scarcity* (San Francisco: W. H. Freeman, 1977), ch., 4, 5, 6, 8.

   c. *MANAGEMENT OF THE GLOBAL COMMONS. Our Common Future* (New York: Oxford University Press, 1987), ch. 10; *World Resources: 1987,* ch. 12; *Scientific American* (September 1989)

   d. *THE SOCIAL ECOLOGY OF MURRY BOOKCHIN. The Ecology of Freedom* (Palo Alto: Cheshire Books, 1982), 16–42; Bookchin, *Remaking Society* (Montreal: Black Rose Books, 1989).

   e. *STEADY-STATE ECONOMICS.* Herman Daly, *Economics, Ecology, Ethics* (San Francisco: W. H. Freeman, 1980), 1–37; 307–72; Herman Daly and John Cobb, *For the Common Good* (Boston: Beacon Press, 1990).

   f. *AGRARIANISM.* Wendell Berry, *Unsettling of America: Culture and Agriculture* (San Francisco: Sierra Club, 1977); James A. Montmarquet, *The Idea of Agrarianism* (Moscow: University of Idaho Press, 1989). The Southern Agrarians, *I'll Take My Stand* (Baton Rouge: Louisiana State University Press, 1983) 122–54.

   g. *BIOREGIONAL.* Kirkpatrick Sale, *Dwellers in the Land* (San Francisco: Sierra Club Books, 1985); *Co-Evolution* (Winter 1981);

Mumford, *The Culture of Cities* (New York: Harcourt Brace Jovanovich, 1966/1938).

h. *SIMPLICITY.* Duane Elgin, *Voluntary Simplicity.* (New York: Morrow, 1981); Helen and Scott Nearing, *Living the Good Life* (New York: Schocken, 1954); Richard Gregg, "Voluntary Simplicity," *Co-Evolution* (Summer 1977; original article published in 1936); E. F. Schumacher, "Buddhist Economics," in Schumacher, *Small Is Beautiful* (1973).

i. *DE-INDUSTRIALIZATION.* Edward Goldsmith, *The Stable Society* (Wadebridge: Wadebridge Press, 1978).

j. *DEEP ECOLOGY.* Bill Devall, "The Deep Ecology Movement," *Natural Resources Journal* (April 1980); Bill Devall, George Sessions, *Deep Ecology* (Layton, UT: Peregrine Smith, 1985); Frank Golley, "Deep Ecology from the Perspective of Environmental Science," *Environmental Ethics* (Spring 1987); Jim Cheney, "Eco-Feminism and Deep Ecology," *Environmental Ethics* (Summer 1987); George Sessions, "The Deep Ecology Movement: A Review," *Environmental Review* (Summer 1987).

k. *AND DEEPER ECOLOGY.* Edward Abbey, "Freedom and Wilderness, Wilderness and Freedom," in *The Journey Home* (New York: E. P. Dutton, 1977), 227–38; Abbey, "Thus I reply to René Dubos," in *Down the River* (New York: E. P. Dutton, 1982), 111–21; Abbey, "The Conscience of the Conqueror," in *Abbey's Road* (New York: E. P. Dutton, 1979), 133–37; and Abbey, "The Theory of Anarchy" and "Eco-Defense," in *One Life at a Time, Please* (New York: Henry Holt, 1988), 25–32.

l. *ANTHROPOLOGY.* Marshall Sahlins, *Stone Age Economics* (Chicago: Aldine, 1972; Colin Turnbull, *The Human Cycle* (New York: Simon and Schuster, 1983); Stanley Diamond, *In Search of the Primitive* (New Brunswick: Transaction Books, 1981); Claude Levi-Straus, *The Savage Mind* (Chicago: University of Chicago Press, 1969).

17. Social Change.

a. *NONVIOLENCE.* M. K. Gandhi, *Non-Violent Resistance* (New York: Schocken, 1961); Leo Tolstoy, *Tolstoy's Writings on Civil Disobedience and Nonviolence* (New York: New American Library, 1968); Thoreau, "Civil Disobedience" (1849).

b. *CONFRONTATION.* Saul Alinsky, *Rules for Radicals* (New York: Vintage, 1972); Alinsky, *Reveille for Radicals* (New York: Vintage, 1969).

c. *PLANNING AND SOCIAL CHANGE.* Freidmann, *Planning in the Public Domain* (1987).

d. *METANOIA.* Willis Harmon, *Global Mind Change* (Institute for Noetic Sciences, 1987).

e. *GREEN POLITICS.* Any number of average sources.

RESOURCES/PERSPECTIVES

a. *WONDER.* Guy Murchie, *The Seven Mysteries of Life* (Boston: Houghton Mifflin, 1981); Loren Eiseley, *The Immense Journey* (New York Vintage, 1959); Lewis Thomas, *Lives of a Cell* (New York: Viking, 1974); Joseph Wood Krutch, *The Great Chain of Life* (Boston: Houghton Mifflin, 1978); Annie Dillard, *Pilgrim at Tinker Creek* (New York: Harper's Magazine Press, 1974); Rachel Carson, *The Sense of Wonder* (New York: Harper and Row, 1984).

b. *THE ART OF LIVING WELL.* Henry David Thoreau, *Walden; Civil Disobedience;* and *Life Without Principle.*

c. *HUMOR.* Cervantes, *Don Quixote;* Joseph Meeker, *The Comedy of Survival* (Los Angeles: Guild of Tutors Press, 1980).

d. *THE HUMAN CONDITION.* Melville, *Moby-Dick;* Miguel Unamuno, *The Tragic Sense of Life* (Princeton: Princeton University Press, 1972); Hannah Arendt, *The Human Condition* (Chicago: University of Chicago Press, 1970).

e. *TIME.* Loren Eiseley, *The Unexpected Universe* (New York: Harcourt Brace Jovanovich, 1969); *The Invisible Pyramid* (New York: Scribners, 1970);

f. *ORGANIZATION.* Lewis Thomas, *The Lives of a Cell* (New York: Viking, 1974).

g. *SPIRIT.* Thomas Merton, *No Man is an Island* (New York: Harcourt Brace Jovanovich, 1955); *Love and Living* (New York: Harcourt Brace Jovanovich, 1985); Gandhi, *Collected Writings.* Lao Tzu, *Tao Te Ching;* William James, *The Varieties of Religious*

Experience (1902); "The Will to Believe" (1896); "Is Life Worth Living" (1895).

h.   *AND HOPE*. E. F. Schumacher, *A Guide for the Perplexed* (New York: Harper and Row, 1977); René Dubos, "Optimism Despite it All," in Dubos, *Celebrations of Life* (New York: Scribners, 1981), 195–251.

i.   *CREATIVITY*. Willis Harmon and H. Rheingold, *Higher Creativity* (Los Angeles: Jeremy Tarcher, 1984); Rollo May, *The Courage to Create* (New York: W. W. Norton, 1975); Edward deBono, *Lateral Thinking* (New York: Harper and Row, 1973); Silvano Arieti, *Creativity: The Magic Synthesis* (New York: Basic Books, 1976).

j.   *EDUCATION*. J. Glenn Gray, *Rethinking American Education* (Middletown: Wesleyan University Press, 1984); Alfred North Whitehead, *The Aims of Education* (New York: The Free Press, 1975); Werner Jaeger, *Paideia: The Ideals of Greek Culture* (New York: Oxford, 1945), 3 vols.; Paulo Freire, *Pedagogy of the Oppressed* (New York: Seabury, 1973); John Dewey, *The Philosophy of John Dewey,* John McDermott, ed., (Chicago: University of Chicago Press, 1981), 421–523; Eliot Wigginton, *Sometimes a Shining Moment* (New York: Anchor, 1986); Forrest Carter, *The Education of Little Tree* (Alberquerque: University of New Mexico Press, 1989.

k.   *THE UTOPIAN TRADITION*. Frank and Fritzie Manuel, *Utopian Thought in the Western World* (Cambridge: Harvard University Press, 1979); Frank Manuel, ed., *Utopias and Utopian Thought* (Boston: Beacon Press, 1967); George Kateb, *Utopia and Its Enemies* (New York: Schocken, 1972); For representative utopias, see: Plato, *The Republic* (390 B.C.); Thomas More, *Utopia* (1516); St. Simon, *The Science of Man* (1813) and *Social Organization* (1825); Edward Bellamy, *Looking Backward 2000–1887* (1888); Samuel Butler, *Erewhon* (1872); Aldous Huxley, *Brave New World* (1932).

l.   *GIFT ECONOMICS*. Lewis Hyde, *The Gift* (New York: Vintage, 1983).

VIII

Place and Pedagogy

Thoreau went to live by an ordinary pond on the outskirts of an unre-markable New England village, "to drive life into a corner, and reduce it to its lowest terms." Thoreau did not "research" Walden Pond, rather, he went to live, as he put it, "deliberately." Nor did he seek the far-off and the exotic, but the ordinary, "the essential facts of life." He produced no particularly usable data, but he did live his subject carefully, observing Walden, its environs, and himself. In the process he revealed something of the potential lying untapped in the commonplace, in our own places, in ourselves, and the relation between all three.

In contemporary jargon, Thoreau's excursion was "interdisci-plinary." *Walden* is a mosaic of philosophy, natural history, geology, folklore, archeology, economics, politics, education, and more. He did not restrict himself to any academic pigeonhole. His "discipline" was as broad as his imagination and as specific as the $28.12 he spent for his house. Thoreau lived his subject. *Walden* is more than a diary of what he thought; it is a record of what he did and what he experienced. If, as Whitehead put it, "The learned world...is tame because it has never been scared by the facts," one finds little that is tame in *Walden*. For Thoreau, the facts, including both Walden Pond and himself, goaded, tempered and scared his intellect. Nor is this the timid objective observ-er whose personhood and intellect remain strangers to each other. For Thoreau, philosophy was important enough "to live according to its dic-tates...to solve some of the problems of life, not only theoretically, but practically." Ultimately, Thoreau's subject matter was Thoreau: his goal, wholeness; his tool, Walden Pond; and his methodology, simplification.

Aside from its merits as literature or philosophy, *Walden* is an anti-dote to the idea that education is a passive, indoor activity occurring

125

between the ages of six and twenty-one. In contrast to the tendencies to segregate disciplines, and to segregate intellect from its surroundings, *Walden* is a model of the possible unity between personhood, pedagogy, and place. For Thoreau, Walden was more than his location. It was a laboratory for observation and experimentation; a library of data about geology, history, flora, and fauna; a source of inspiration and renewal; and a testing ground for the man. *Walden* is no monologue, it is a dialogue between a man and a place. In a sense, *Walden* wrote Thoreau. His genius, I think, was to allow himself to be shaped by his place, to allow it to speak with his voice.

Other than as a collection of buildings where learning is supposed to occur, place has no particular standing in contemporary education. The typical college or university is organized around bodies of knowledge coalesced into disciplines. Sorting through a college catalogue you are not likely to find courses dealing with the ecology, hydrology, geology, history, economics, politics, energy use, food policy, waste disposal, and architecture of the campus or its community. Nor are you likely to find many courses offering enlightenment to modern scholars in the art of living well in a place. The typical curriculum is reminiscent of Kierkegaard's comment after reading the vast, weighty corpus of Hegel's philosophy, that Hegel had "taken care of everything, except perhaps for the question of how one was to live one's life." Similarly, a great deal of what passes for knowledge is little more than abstraction piled on top of abstraction, disconnected from tangible experience, real problems, and the places where we live and work. In this sense it is utopian, which literally means "nowhere."

The importance of place in education has been overlooked for a variety of reasons. One is the ease with which we miss the immediate and mundane. Those things nearest at hand are often the most difficult to see. Second, for purists, place itself is a nebulous concept. Yet Thoreau understandably spent little time trying to define the precise boundaries of his place, nor was it necessary to do so. *Walden* is a study of an area small enough to be easily walked over in a day and still observed carefully. Place is defined by its human scale: a household, neighborhood, community, forty acres, one thousand acres.

Place is nebulous to educators because to a great extent we are a deplaced people for whom our immediate places are no longer sources of food, water, livelihood, energy, materials, friends, recreation, or sacred inspiration. We are, as Raymond Dasmann once noted, "biosphere people," supplied with all these and more from places around the world that are largely unknown to us, as are those to which we consign our toxic and radioactive wastes, garbage, sewage, and industrial trash. We consume a great deal of time and energy going somewhere else. The average American moves ten times in a lifetime, and spends countless hours at airports and on highways going to places that look a great deal like those just left behind. Our lives are lived amidst the architectural expressions of deplacement: the shopping mall, apartment, neon strip, freeway, glass office tower, and homogenized development—none of which encourage much sense of rootedness, responsibility, and belonging.

Third, place by definition is specific, yet our mode of thought is increasingly abstract. The danger of abstraction lies partly in what Whitehead described as the "fallacy of misplaced concreteness": the confusion of our symbols with reality. The results are comparable, as someone put it, to eating the menu instead of the meal. Words and theories take on a life of their own, independent of the reality they purport to mirror, often with tragic results. At its worst, as Lewis Mumford describes it:

> The abstract intelligence, operating with its own conceptual apparatus, in its own self-restricted field is actually a coercive instrument: an arrogant fragment of the full human personality, determined to make the world over in its own oversimplified terms, willfully rejecting interests and values incompatible with its own assumptions, and thereby depriving itself of any of the cooperative and generative functions of life—feeling, emotion, playfulness, exuberance, free fantasy—in short, the liberating sources of unpredictable and uncontrollable creativity.[1]

By capturing only a fragment of reality, unrelieved abstraction inevitably distorts perception. By denying genuine emotion, it distorts and diminishes human potentials. For the fully abstracted mind, all places become "real estate" or mere natural resources, their larger economic, ecological, social, political, and spiritual possibilities lost to the purely and narrowly utilitarian.

The idea that place could be a significant educational tool was proposed by John Dewey in an 1897 essay. Dewey proposed that we "make each of our schools an embryonic community...with types of occupations that reflect the life of the larger society." He intended to broaden the focus of education, which he regarded as too "highly specialized, one-sided, and narrow." The school, its relations with the larger community and all of its internal functions, Dewey proposed to remake into curriculum.

The regional survey, which reflected a broader conception of the role of place in education, was developed by Lewis Mumford in the 1940s. In Mumford's words, the regional survey was not something to be added to an already crowded curriculum. It is rather (potentially) the backbone of a drastically revised method of study, in which every aspect of the sciences and the arts is ecologically related from the bottom up, in which they connect directly and constantly in the student's experience of his region and his community. Regional survey must begin with the infant's first exploration of his dooryard and his neighborhood; it must continue to expand and deepen, at every successive stage of growth until the student is capable of seeing and experiencing above all, of relating and integrating and directing the separate parts of his environment, hitherto unnoticed or dispersed.[2]

The regional survey (Mumford cites *Walden* as a classic example) involved the intensive study of the local environment by specialists and every member of the community, including schoolchildren. As the focal point for education, the regional survey was intended to create habits of thinking across disciplines, promote cooperation, and dissolve distinctions between facts and values, the past and the future, and nature and human society. Beyond education, Mumford regarded the regional survey as the basis for rational coordination and planning and as a vehicle for widespread public participation.

The integration of place into education is important for four reasons. First, it requires the combination of intellect with experience. The typical classroom is an arena for lecture and discussion, both of which are important to intellectual growth. The study of place involves complementary dimensions of intellect: direct observation, investigation, experimentation, and skill in the application of knowledge. The latter is regarded merely as "vocational education." But for Mumford and Dewey, practical and manual skills were an essential aspect of experience, good thinking, and to the development of the whole person. Both regarded the acquisition of manual skills as vitally important in sharpening the intellect. Dewey again:

> We cannot overlook the importance for educational purposes of the close and intimate acquaintance got with nature at first hand, with real things and materials, with the actual processes of their manipulation, and the knowledge of their special necessities and uses. In all this there (is) continual training of observation, of ingenuity, constructive imagination, of logical thought, and of the sense of reality acquired through firsthand contact with actualities. The educative forces of the domestic spinning and weaving, of the sawmill, the gristmill, the cooper ship, and the blacksmith forge were continuously operative.[3]

Similarly, Whitehead states that:

There is a coordination of senses and thought, and also a reciprocal influence between brain activity and material creative activity. In this reaction the hands are peculiarly important. It is a moot point whether the human hand created the human brain, or the brain created the hand. Certainly, the connection is intimate and reciprocal.[4]

In the reciprocity between thinking and doing, knowledge loses much of its abstractness, becoming in the application to specific places and problems tangible and direct.

Second, the study of place is relevant to the problems of overspecialization, which has been called a terminal disease of contemporary civilization. It is surely debilitating to the individual intellect. Mumford's remedy for the narrow, underdimensioned mind is the requirement to balance analysis with synthesis. This cannot be accomplished by adding courses to an already overextended curriculum, or by fine-tuning a system designed to produce specialists. It can be done only by reconceptualizing the purposes of education in order to promote diversity of thought and a wider understanding of interrelatedness. Places are laboratories of diversity and complexity, mixing social functions and natural processes. A place has a human history and a geologic past: it is a part of an ecosystem with a variety of microsystems, it is a landscape with a particular flora and fauna. Its inhabitants are part of a social, economic, and political order: they import or export energy materials, water, and wastes, they are linked by innumerable bonds to other places. A place cannot be understood from the vantage point of a single discipline or specialization. It can be understood only on its terms as a complex mosaic of phenomena and problems. The classroom and indoor laboratory are ideal environments in which to narrow reality in order to focus on bits and pieces. The study of place, by contrast, enables us to widen the focus to examine the interrelationships between disciplines and to lengthen our perception of time.

It is important not to stop learning at the point of mere intellectual comprehension. Students should be encouraged to act on the basis of information from the survey to identify a series of projects to promote greater self-reliance, interdisciplinary learning, and physical competence, such as policies for food, energy, architecture, and waste. These provide opportunities for intellectual and experiential learning involving many different disciplines working on tangible problems. If the place also includes natural areas, forests, streams, and agricultural lands, the opportunities for environmental learning multiply accordingly.

Finally, for Mumford and Dewey, much of the pathology of contemporary civilization was related to the disintegration of the small community. Dewey wrote in 1927: "The invasion and partial destruction of the life of the (local community) by outside uncontrolled agencies is the immediate source of the instability, disintegration and restlessness which characterize the present epoch." The study of place, then, has a third significance in reeducating people in the art of living well where they are. The distinction between inhabiting and residing drawn in Chapter 6 is important here. A resident is a temporary occupant, putting down few roots and investing little, knowing little, and perhaps caring little for the immediate locale beyond its ability to gratify. As both a cause and effect of displacement, the resident lives in an indoor world of office building, shopping mall, automobile, apartment, and suburban house, and watches television an average of four hours each day. The inhabitant, in contrast, "dwells," as Illich puts it in an intimate, organic, and mutually nurturing relationship with a place.[5] Good inhabitance is an art requiring detailed knowledge of a place, the capacity for observation, and a sense of care and rootedness. Residence requires cash and a map. A resident can reside almost anywhere that provides an income. Inhabitants bear the marks of their places, whether rural or urban, in patterns of speech, through dress and behavior. Uprooted, they get homesick. Historically, inhabitants are less likely to vandalize their's or others' places. They also tend to make good neighbors and honest citizens. They are, in short, the bedrock of the stable community and neighborhood that Mumford, Dewey, and Jefferson regarded as the essential ingredient of democracy.

Paul Shepard explains the stability of inhabitants as a consequence of the interplay between the psyche and a particular land form. "Terrain structure," he argues, "is the model for the patterns of cognition."[6] The physical and biological patterns of a place are imprinted on the mind so the "cognition, personality, creativity, and maturity—all are in some way tied to particular gestalts of space." Accordingly, the child must have an opportunity to "soak in a place, and the adolescent and adult must be able to return to that place to ponder the visible substrate of his own personality." Hence, knowledge of a place—where you are and where you come from—is intertwined with knowledge of who you are. Landscape, in other words, shapes mindscape. Since it diminishes the potential for maturation and inhabitance, the ravagement of places is psychologically ravaging as well. If Shepard is right, and I believe that he is, we are paying a high price for the massive rearrangement of the North American landscape of the past fifty years.

For deplaced people, education in the arts of inhabitation is partly remedial learning: the unlearning of old habits of waste and dependency. It requires, first, the ability to perceive and utilize the potentials of a place. One of the major accomplishments of the past several decades has been the rediscovery of how much ordinary people can do for themselves in small places. The significance of this fact coincides with the growing recognition of the ecological, political, and economic costs, and the vulnerability of large-scale centralized systems, whether publically or privately controlled. Smaller-scale technologies are often cheaper and more resilient, and they do not undermine democratic institutions by requiring the centralization of capital, expertise, and political authority. Taken together, they vastly expand the potential of ecologically designed, intensively developed places to meet human needs on a sustained basis.

Education for reinhabitation must also instill an applied ethical sense toward habitat. Again Leopold's standard—" A thing is right when it tends to preserve the integrity, stability, and beauty of the biotic community. It is wrong when it tends otherwise."—is on balance a clear standard for most decisions about the use we make of our places. From the standpoint of education, the stumbling block to development of an ethic of place is not the complexity of the subject; it is the fact, as Leopold put it, "that our educational system is headed away from...an intense consciousness of land."

Critics might argue that the study of place would be inherently parochial and narrowing. If place were the entire focus of education, it certainly could be. But the study of place would be only a part of a larger curriculum which would include the study of relationships between places as well. For Mumford, place was simply the most immediate of a series of layers leading to the entire region as a system of small places. But parochialism is not the result of what is studied as much as how it is studied. Lewis Thomas, after all, was able to observe the planet in the workings of a single cell.[7]

At issue is our relationship to our own places. What is the proper balance between mobility and rootedness? Indeed, are rootedness and immobility synonymous? How long does it take for one to learn enough about a place to become an inhabitant and not merely a resident? However one chooses to answer these questions, the lack of a sense of place, our "cult of homelessness," is endemic, and its price is the destruction of the small community and the resulting social and ecological degeneracy.[8] We are not the first footloose wanderers of our species. Our nomadism, however, is on a larger and more destructive scale.

We cannot solve such deep problems quickly, but we can begin learning how to reinhabit our places, as Wendell Berry says, "lovingly, knowingly, skillfully, reverently," restoring context to our lives in the process.[9] For a world growing short of many things, the next sensible frontiers to explore are those of the places where we live and work.

Education and Sustainability: An Approach

What will people need to know to live responsibly and well in a finite world? What skills, abilities, values, and character traits will be useful and/or necessary for the transition ahead? What does sustainability imply for technology? Politics? Community design? Social structures? Economics? Values? What is the appropriate balance between the sciences, the social sciences, and the humanities? And between intellect, spirit, and practice? What do all of these imply for the substance and process of education? In short, what does the dawning awareness of planetary limits and interrelatedness of all life have to do with the way we define, direct, and transmit knowledge? No single answer can, or should, be given to such a large question. It is possible only to propose measures by which answers might eventually be judged.

Education relevant to the transition to a sustainable society, demands first, *an uncompromising commitment to life and its preservation.* Anything less is morally indefensible. By commitment to life I mean a commitment, pervading learning and research at all levels, to health, harmony, balance, wholeness, and diversity as these qualities apply to both human and natural systems. Following Schweitzer, a commitment to life rests on a deep sense of the sacredness of life expressed as love, nurture, creativity, wonder, faith, and justice. Such a commitment can be manifested in a variety of ways throughout the structure and process of formal education. It does not describe a specific agenda so much as it does an ethos or a direction in much the same way as "north" on a compass designates a direction not an itinerary. More than an attitude, it signifies a motivating and energizing force underlying education and research transcending narrow concerns of professional acclaim, career advancement, and institutional aggrandizement. A commitment to life informs priorities in the creation and advancement of knowledge.

Difficult as it may be, we must learn how to distinguish those categories of knowledge which promote life from those which retard it or jeopardize it altogether. The task is all the more urgent in a world of widening extremes between the winners and losers, a world that is busily engaged in pulling the ecological rug from under its own feet while developing more clever and more probable ways to incinerate itself.

If a commitment to life signifies a general direction for education, students and teachers must, second, be able to read the compass—to understand the world of nature and to develop competence in thinking about natural systems. Commitment or emotional predisposition without knowledge is, in Archibald MacLeish's words, rather like "an answer without a question—meaningless." Worse, it is paralyzing, for it creates expectations without providing the means for their fulfillment. Where a commitment to life is both genuine and potent, its nurturing instincts require a thorough knowledge of the natural world based on the recognition that we are only a part of a larger whole, and that our health and prosperity are contingent on that of the entire system.

Let there be no mistake. Even in an environmentally conscious age, this is not the direction in which we are headed. Today's student is largely shut off from the natural world, sealed in a cocoon of steel, glass, and concrete, enveloped in a fog of mind-debilitating electronic pulsations.[1] Upon graduation from high school, the typical eighteen-year-old will have spent some twelve thousand hours in a classroom, but will have watched television for some sixteen thousand hours and will have witnessed the simulated violent deaths of eighteen thousand persons followed by hucksters selling deodorants, beer, cars, or other claptrap. The results—apathy, moral and physical anemia—should surprise no one. Nor should we be astonished to learn that knowledge about nature has declined markedly in the past thirty years. Overall, in the words of one study, Americans now "possess an extremely limited understanding" of animals, natural systems, and the major issues of conservation.

Nor are these shortcomings necessarily being remedied in institutions of higher learning, where the study of humankind is separated from the study of nature. Ecology has been isolated within biology departments as though it had little or nothing to do with the social sciences, the humanities, or the professions. The result is a pervasive anthropocentrism that magnifies the role of humans and their ideas, art, institutions, and technology relative to soil, water, climate, wildlife, resources, geography, energy, disease, and ecosystem stability. At its worst, the separation leads to the econocentric thinking run amuck of the Herman Kahns or the Julian Simons,[2] which assumes nature to be infinite (given an infinite supply of cheap energy and no technological blunders), and human ingenuity to be the "ultimate resource." The manifest errors in such thinking might have been eliminated with a dose of ecological literacy, a nodding acquaintance with thermodynamics, a brief study of history, and a modicum of ethical sensitivity and common sense. Lest I appear to be too hard on economists, I hasten to add that other disciplines could likewise profit from a cross-fertilization with ecology, as a number of individual scholars have demonstrated.[3]

Figure 1.

Discipline	Environmental focus
History	The effects of resource mismanagement, technological changes, effects of new sources of energy: Walter Prescott Webb, William McNeil, Donald Worster, Donald Hughes, Roderick Nash, Lewis Mumford, Carolyn Merchant
Ethics	The philosophical basis of sustainability; environmental ethics, animal rights: Peter Singer, Tom Regan, Henryk Skolimowski, Chris Stone, William Leiss, Baird Callicott
Sociology	The structure of sustainability; values, behavior effects of overshoot: William Catton, Riley Dunlap
Political Science	Politics as a resource distribution system; political structures of sustainability; balance between centralization and decentralization, freedom versus. order: William Ophuls, Walter Rosenbaum, Michael Kraft, Robert Paehlke
Anthropology	Adaptive behavior of societies and cultures; alternative values; models of sustainability: Margaret Mead, Colin Turnbull, Marshall Sahlins, Stanley Diamond, Marvin Harris
Economics	Steady-state economics, alternative pricing systems, alternatives to capitalism and communism: Herman Daly, Kenneth Boulding, Nicholas Georgescu-Roegen, Ezra Mishan, E. F. Schumacher, Robert Heilbroner

Figure 1. *(continued)*

Discipline	Environmental focus
Architecture	Design with nature, use of vernacular materials: Ian McHarg, Malcolm Wells, Bruce Anderson, Gary Coates.
Biology/Agriculture	Ecosystems management, ecological agriculture, urban food systems: Eugene Odum, Paul Sears, Paul Ehrlich, John Todd, Wes Jackson, Stephen Gliessman, Bill Mollison
World Order	Peace, sustainability, justice: Richard Falk, Rajni Kothari, Burns Weston, Johan Galtung
Natural History	Henry David Thoreau, John Muir, Roger Tory Peterson, Marsten Bates, Joseph Wood Krutch
Philosophy	Alfred North Whitehead, Gregory Bateson, Teilhard de Chardin, William James, Lewis Mumford, Loren Eiseley, John Cobb, William Irwin Thompson, Thomas Merton

To the conventional disciplines listed in Figure 1, I have added the study of world order, including problems of nuclear war, environmental sustainability on a global scale, justice, and participation. It is clear to most observers that there is no purely national solution to the macro issues on the human agenda. Nor can we deal with issues of sustainability without simultaneously confronting issues of peace, equity, cultural diversity, and the structure of political institutions. Old paradigms are everywhere in disarray, but the process of changing perceptions and of building new institutions has only begun.

I have also added the study of natural history, which falls at the micro end of the spectrum. In contrast with most academic studies, which are abstract indoor activities, natural history is concrete and requires direct involvement in nature. It requires firsthand knowledge of trees, animals, plant life, birds, aquatic life, marine biology, and geology. It is an antidote to the excessively abstract, overly quantified, and computerized, as well as the romantic view of nature derived from armchair ecologists. Natural history forces us to deal with nature on nature's terms. It also promotes the capacity not only to see but to observe with care, understanding, and, above all else, with pleasure.

Such careful observation combined with insight is no longer common. To illustrate: the editors of *Co-Evolution Quarterly* once proposed a test of bioregional knowledge which includes the following questions:[4]

1. What soil series are you standing on?
2. When was the last time a fire burned your area?
3. Name five native edible plants in your region and their seasons of availability.
4. From what direction do winter storms generally come in your region?
5. Where does your garbage go?
6. How long is the growing season where you live?
7. Name five grasses in your area. Are any of them native?
8. Name five resident and five migratory birds in your area.
9. What primary geological event or processes influenced the land from where you live?
10. What species have become extinct in your area?
11. What are the major plant associations in your region?

The fact that few of us would do well on questions of this sort highlights a widening gap between the growing power of our society over nature and the general ignorance about it among individuals. Equally remarkable is the acceptance of this condition as normal or even desirable in an age of academic and occupational specialization. In contrast, sustainability will require a much higher degree of ecological literacy throughout the entire population. In democratic societies, wise public choices about environmental issues depend largely on the extent and breadth of public knowledge of ecology and concepts such as thermodynamics and energetics and their interrelationship with economic prosperity, unemployment, war and peace, and public health. If large numbers of people do not understand the environmental facts of energy, resources, land, water, and wildlife, there is little hope for building sustainability at any level.

Grass-roots participation will be essential in the process of reorganizing systems supplying energy, water, food, resources, and economic support in order to minimize environmental damage, shorten supply lines to reduce energy costs, convert to renewable sources of energy, and to develop means for recycling wastes. Many of these things can best be done at the local or even household level. Hence the transition requires people who know a great deal about such things as solar design, horticulture, waste, composting, greenhouses, intensive gardening, food preservation, household economics, and on-site energy systems. These, in turn, will require mastery of biology, chemistry, physics, engineering, architecture, community dynamics, and economics.

Education for sustainability will, thirdly, connect disciplines as well as disparate parts of the personality: intellect, hands, and heart. Connective education must go beyond "interdisciplinary" or team-taught courses by changing the structure and purposes of education. Its goals are twofold. First, it aims toward the establishment of a community of life that includes future generations, male and female, all races and nations, rich and poor, and the natural world. The essence of community is the recognition, indeed the celebration, of interdependence between all parts. Its indicators are the requisites of sustainability: peace, harmony, justice, and participation. Obviously, such qualities are not either-or, but rather points along a continuum. The purpose of connective education is integration, or, as Gregory Bateson put it, the discovery of "the pattern which connects."[5]

A second aim of connective education is personal wholeness and transcendence. In this sense it is similar to the Greek concept of Paideia, which, in Lewis Mumford's words "is not merely a learning; it is a making and a shaping and man himself is the work of art that Paideia seeks to form."[6] The aim of Paideia was self-transformation, personal wholeness, and competence—a search for the "divine center." Its methods were those of open dialogue, participation, and experience. It was not segregated into particular places, for certain hours, during a brief segment of life. Paideia assumed no distinction between learning and living. Learning was aimed to achieve mastery in the art of life; life and culture were the school. At its best, Paideia led to persons of physical and intellectual vitality; persons capable of performing different functions with skill and grace, harboring a wealth of interests and abilities, and informed by a large view of life.

The goals of modern education stand in marked contrast. It has fractured knowledge into manageable bits and pieces. Amidst the rubble of the much-celebrated "knowledge explosion," one can find little coherent meaning or high purpose. Nor does modern education require much of the learner beyond professional competence. Knowledge has become increasingly disconnected from the person. What one knows is assumed to have little or no bearing on what or who one is. Nor is it often thought to be a unifying agent between the intellect, the emotions, and the competence of the hands.

Connective education means restructuring the learning environment in order to overcome the centripetal effects of academic specialization and the split between intellect and experience. Rearranging pigeonholes won't do. Disciplines, courses, and division do have a certain logic which makes knowledge more accessible by organizing it. But they are also barriers to wholeness. Fragmentation and specialization are diseases of the curriculum as much as of cultures. But connective education is impossible unless the learning environment itself forces the mixing of disciplines and perspectives.

Education for sustainability must, fourth, include an awareness of the tragic in human affairs. By this I mean, first, a recognition that the odds against human survival are perhaps longer than most of us would like to admit. At best we have entered a period of enormous and increasing suffering and violence. Those imbued with a tragic sense of life will face these prospects squarely but without the paralysis that comes from despair or a giddy, breathless, and often silly optimism born of technological macho or new-age hype.

The tragic sense of life, however, is neither resigned nor long-faced. It locates the sources of our suffering in ourselves, in human decisions, institutions, and above all in the pretense that we are beyond the laws of ecology, thermodynamics, or even morality. A closer reading of Homo sapiens would suggest that at best we are a spindly legged, upstart, disruptive species whose intellect exceeds its wisdom, located on a small planet attached to an insignificant star in a backwater galaxy. If we are a "promising primate," as some think, the promise, whatever it might be, is yet to be discovered. If it turns out that we were not so promising after all, our major accomplishment in the larger scheme of things might be only that we recirculated massive amounts of stored carbon in the final moments of our evolutionary career. For all of our puffed-up, self-serving talk about the "ascent of man," we have truly no idea whether it is an ascent or a descent, or, if the former, what its destination might be. If our rational consciousness is our crowning glory, we are still unable to say why, or even to explain what it is or why it has occurred. On such unstable turf we best tread lightly, without the baggage of pretense, overblown pride, or, as the Greeks called it, hubris. Prudence would lead us to take our esteemed rationality, which may serve ascent or descent equally well, with a large dose of skepticism.

Education for sustainability might do well to reflect the rhythms of life itself, moving between sobriety and mirth, wisdom and foolishness, work and play, sacred and profane, awareness of limits and limitless hope, suffering and celebration. These rhythms also suggest something of the kind of personal growth for which we should strive. Much attention has been focused on the hardware of sustainability but relatively little on the software: on the kind of people necessary for the trials of building a sustainable global civilization. In this vein, Lewis Mumford once proposed that:

> Our first job in controlling the forces that are now working such destruction and havoc...is to cultivate men [writing later he would have said persons] who are capable of exercising this control: proud, confident, self-respecting, cooperative men. Not men for sale, men

tailored and trimmed to fit the machine, but men capable of using all their powers, taking back to themselves the functions they too easily resigned to the machine and projecting human goals in the full trajectory of life. If our mode of life or our education had produced such men in sufficient numbers we should not now be living in an increasingly denuded and life hostile environment.[7]

In the two decades since those words were written, their force has grown in severity and extent. But now we hear more talk about "burnout," personal fatigue, and self-fulfillment devoid of any notion of service. Students in growing numbers in the decade of the 1980s wanted safe careers in the embrace of the corporate establishment. Educators acquiesced, offering more business courses. The calling of service, we are told by both, is quixotic, passé, unrealistic, and quite unprofitable. Such talk rests on the vain hope that one can avoid the tragedies of the future by simply ignoring them. At a deeper level, one detects the fear of disappointed hopes, shared suffering, and commitment.

A tragic sense of life turns us in a different direction, toward suffering, healing, and service in which, as Schweitzer describes it, "the soft iron of youthful idealism hardens into the steel of a full grown idealism which can never be lost." This "sobering down" process requires that "our development...make us simpler, more truthful, purer, more peace loving, meeker, kinder, more sympathetic."[8]

X

What is Education For?

"The problem" of conservation education, according to Aldo Leopold, "is how to bring about a striving for harmony with land among a people many of whom have forgotten there is such a thing as land." Nearly a half century after those words were written, we know that the problem is more complex and difficult than perhaps Leopold believed. Even in our more ecologically aware age, he would have perceived a sharp decline in the "consciousness of land" and the "striving for harmony" that he regarded as the bedrock of a durable civilization. I think he would also perceive the problem more broadly as "environmental" (not simply "conservation") education, and as more difficult now than he did in 1948.

The problem is in reality many problems, none of which can be separated from larger questions about the purposes, structure, and processes of education at all levels.

Paradigms. First, can the harmony that Leopold proposed be realized within the modern paradigm, which emphasizes human dominance over the natural world, consumption, economic growth, and science and technology, and is organized around nation-states and corporations? Or, as Lynton Caldwell puts it: "What is the significance of man's relationship to his environment, and what implications does the answer hold for present and future human behavior?"[1] Is environmentalism simply another subject or academic department, or is it potentially an integrative principle leading to a radical reconceptualization of education? For those accepting the modern paradigm, environmentalism amounts to little more than fine-tuning a good thing. Environmental education, therefore, can be easily accommodated within existing disciplines and departments. But proponents of a "biospheric" viewpoint and "deep ecologists" advocate much more sweeping changes in

141

the human relationship with the natural world and hence significant changes in education, involving the development of environmental studies as, in Caldwell's term, a "metadiscipline." These proponents are in effect advocating a postmodern paradigm.

The conflict between the two paradigms is not easily resolved, because it concerns alternative views of the proper human role in nature, differences over the potential of science and technology to rescue us from ecological malfeasance, and varying estimates of the malfeasance itself.

Values. Should we strive to teach values appropriate to sustainability, or should we present these as only one possible orientation to the world? Is it possible to treat the work of Julian Simon and economist Nicholas Georgescu-Roegen as if they are equivalent? Is value-free education possible? Is it desirable? If neither, how can values be integrated into the learning process without jeopardizing objectivity and a fair treatment of facts, data, and logic?

As difficult as these issues may be, there are good precedents for the integration of objectivity with a strong value orientation. Medical education, for example, has a clear bias toward human health, not disease. The overriding concern of reputable international relations scholars such as Quincy Wright, Kenneth Boulding, Richard Falk, and Anatol Rapaport is the promotion of peace, not war. Likewise, economics is intended to expand our understanding of the conditions for prosperity. Except by pedants, knowledge has never been regarded as an end in itself, but rather as a means to human well-being. By the same logic, environmental studies ought to have a clear direction favoring harmony between human and natural systems while preserving objectivity in the handling of facts, data, and logic.

Scope and definition of education. The aim of education is often described as teaching people how to think. But think about what? How is this learning to occur? If we strive to educate intelligence alone, which aspects of intelligence do we select?[2] What about other traits, such as character, intuition, feeling, practical abilities, and instincts, which affect what people think about and how well they think? If harmony with nature is important, how is this taught? Can ecologically appropriate values be communicated if students are passive receptors of information in a highly competitive setting? Can one teach about the interrelatedness of biological phenomena without reference to the potential for personal wholeness? Even more basic, can we teach about environmental affairs without also reworking the physical setting of education to favor greater environmental harmony?

Definition of knowledge. These questions lead to others about the definition of knowledge and the way in which research and disciplinary agendas are set. From the perspective of human survival, what is worth knowing? How do we distinguish between the trivial and the important? Implicit in much of our thinking is an assumption that knowledge grows in a neutral, Darwinian fashion in which those ideas best fitted to reality survive, while others less suited do not. This assumption ignores the political, social, and above all, economic influences on the process of paradigm creation and maintenance. For example, the Department of Defense and corporate funding for university research will bias disciplinary agendas, including hiring and tenure decisions, in favor of knowledge useful for certain interests and purposes. Other knowledge or areas of potential knowledge wither, but not because they are less interesting or less important. Alan Schnaiberg has made the same point in documenting the overdevelopment of "production sciences" and the corresponding anemia of the "impact sciences" (meaning those that study the effects of human actions).[3] We might similarly ask why we know so much about chemical-based agribusiness and so little about the means and techniques of sustainable agriculture. Or about manipulative medicine to the exclusion of preventive medicine and nutrition. Or, until recently, about energy production instead of conservation and renewable sources? Why do we spend several hundred billion dollars each year for weapons and preparations to fight wars and a fraction of one percent of that amount on peace research? In each case, the reasons cannot be found in comparative data about efficiency, or ecological impacts, or public morality.

Knowledge, for all pretensions to the contrary, is biased by the way in which we determine social and economic priorities. To respond that science is a self-correcting enterprise through mechanisms of peer review is no answer at all. Science can be directed toward life-enhancing or life-destroying research, each performed with great rigor and dedication.

But how does a society determine priorities in creating and preserving knowledge that accords somehow with ecological realities? If true understanding of ecosystems and the human role in nature require, as I believe it does, development of alternative modes of knowing and perceiving that are integrative, what does this mean? How does one "do" integrative science? How do we perceive holistically?

Structure. What do these questions mean for the structure of the learning environment? Is environmental education and the emergence of integrative science best done in separate departments, or should it be woven throughout the entire curriculum? The case for the latter, including Caldwell's proposal for a metadiscipline, lies in the "logic" of environmentalism, that is, the interaction of life processes. But this logic does not readily clarify priorities, objectives, and curricular details, let alone the transition strategy from the present discipline-centric structure to metadisciplines or whatever else.

The case for confining environmental studies within separate departments, it seems, is best made on grounds of political feasibility, intellectual coherence, and practical manageability. Moreover, it does not exclude the possibility that metadisciplines will emerge eventually through a process of intellectual and institutional maturation. Its danger lies in the possibility, even probability, that environmental studies departments will become just another jealously guarded, closed, academic fiefdom, and will fail to catalyze ecological thinking.

For members of environmental studies programs, what does ecological thinking mean? How do we recognize it in hiring decisions? Few would argue that the process of academic credentialling is without flaws. Yet attainment of a Ph.D. and publication of scholarly research do provide a benchmark to judge individual qualifications. But increasing specialization has substantially narrowed the focus of scholarship. Most active scholars communicate to a small number of colleagues with similar interests through a growing number of highly specialized journals. This system implicitly involves the assumption that bits of information can be integrated by some social-political structure or process or invisible hand into some socially useful and coherent whole. Given the present knowledge explosion, however, we are building a Tower of Babel with each discipline and subdiscipline having its own jargon, theories, and paradigms understood only by a small number of the elect. The social costs of this system are incalculable. The survival issues on the human agenda, which involve whole systems of knowledge and many disciplines, receive little attention. Given the present structure of academia and its hiring, tenuring, and promotion procedures, it is not at all clear how we will identify, debate, research, and ultimately contribute to decisions that lead to farsighted, just, peaceful, and sustainable results.

If questions of environmental education cannot be separated from the broad issues of education, the reverse is equally true: the field of education can no longer afford to ignore two challenges arising from the environmental perspective. The first is the challenge of interrelatedness. We have structured education and the entire knowledge enterprise along Cartesian lines stressing reductionism, discrete entities, linearity, and simple causation, and must now shift to perceive patterns, context, systems, and complex networks of causation that span the sciences, social sciences, and humanities. Further, we must learn to overcome the parochialism inherent in nationality, geography, generation, sex, species, race, and class. If it can be done at all, this revolution in thought, perception, and behavior will go far beyond the Copernican or Darwinian revolutions, whose effects were scarcely felt at the level of daily life, politics, or international affairs.

The second challenge posed by environmentalism concerns the essential misconception of our role in the natural world. For the past five hundred years our sciences, social sciences, and humanities alike have been committed to extending and celebrating the human domination of nature. The idea that we can dominate nature, however, is proving to be both a dangerous and paradoxical illusion. The ecological implications of the philosophy of domination now loom ahead like the icebergs before the *Titanic*. Our civilization is moving at an unprecedented velocity and mass. Any change in this course will require that we rapidly transform values, institutions, and the way we define and transmit knowledge.

We must nonetheless act before the full implications of these two challenges are fully apparent. This process may be roughly analogous to the modern Enlightenment, which reshaped the Western world. We now need an ecological enlightenment which revolutionizes our world and worldviews.

Those presuming to educate should not stand aloof from the decisions about how and whether life will be lived in the twenty-first century. To do so would be to miss the Mount Everest issues on the historical topography of our age, and condemn ourselves to irrelevance. The change I have in mind is not easy to define, but it certainly would include a broad attachment to qualities of health, harmony, balance, diversity, peace, participation, and justice. Such a commitment does nothing to weaken the objectivity with which scholars handle facts and data. To the contrary, the crisis of sustainability has occurred precisely because of flaws, incompleteness, and biases in our data, facts, and logic. The transition to sustainability will require more complete facts, broader sorts of data, a more thorough integrative logic, greater intellectual creativity, and an even deeper commitment to truth.

Environmental education is unavoidably political. At the heart of the issue is the total demand humans make on the biosphere and the way we have organized the flows of energy, water, material, food, and wastes, which in turn affects what political scientists define as the essential issues of politics: "Who gets what, when, and how?" The symptoms of environmental deterioration are in the domain of the natural sciences, but the causes lie in the realm of the social sciences and humanities. To assume that technology will absolve us from our own folly is only to compound the error. Whatever its many advantages, technology has varying political, social, economic, and ecological implications that we are now only beginning to recognize. Without political, social, and value changes, no technology will make us sustainable. More to the point, do we equip students morally and intellectually to be a part of the existing pattern of corporate-dominated resource flows, or to take part in reshaping these patterns toward greater sustainability? These represent two very different visions of postindustrial society, and two very different orientations to the political realm.

Third, for these reasons, education appropriate for sustainability will give greater emphasis to place-specific knowledge and skills useful in meeting individual local needs, and for rebuilding local communities. The rise of the modern nation-state, corporation, and megalopolis has drained talent, initiative, power, capital, and responsibility from the fine grain of society. The results have been devastating, both ecologically and socially. In the process of becoming a technologically advanced, modern society, as Paul Sears once put it: "We lengthened and elaborated the chain of technology that intervenes between us and the natural world...becom(ing) steadily more vulnerable to even the slightest failure in that chain."

A more socially and ecologically resilient society will create a greater balance between knowledge that can be applied only through large organizations and that which is widely diffused throughout society and meets local needs, culture, and ecology.[4] Professional knowledge can become another restricted commodity for purchase and another way to create incompetence and hence dependence. The relationship between local self-reliance, appropriately scaled technology, societal sustainability, and citizen competence rooted in vernacular traditions is striking. So too are the benefits, including less dependence on foreign suppliers to greater community cohesion and economic resilience.

CONCLUSION

Thomas Kuhn, in his classic *The Structure of Scientific Revolutions*, suggests that scientific knowledge grows in two distinct ways. The first, which he labels "normal science," expands like an ink blot around an accepted paradigm of shared values, methods, rules of evidence, and problems. Knowledge thus grows incrementally as successive generations of scientists are trained in the context of the dominant paradigm and explore its various implications. "Normal science" works well until "anomalies" occur. These may go unrecognized or be purposely ignored, because "no part of the aim of normal science is to call forth new sorts of phenomena; indeed those that will not fit the box are often not seen at all." When this happens, Kuhn suggests, knowledge may grow by a second process in which some scientists deviate from orthodoxy to create an alternative paradigm for solving otherwise insuperable problems. As in the case of Copernicus, Newton, and Einstein, new paradigms lead to a new understanding of the world and constitute what Kuhn describes as "scientific revolutions."

A similar process may be a work in education. The state of the planet represents a series of anomalies for contemporary education. Any adequate response to the emerging agenda of the twenty-first century will require great institutional flexibility, willingness to experiment, funding, and patience. But budget and enrollment problems for many colleges and universities can be expected to further reduce institutional flexibility and the willingness of administrators to tolerate structural chaos and experimentation—let alone to pay for it. Second, for faculty who must continue to keep up with their field, teach, research, publish, and do committee chores, finding time and resources to develop the breadth necessary to comprehend environmental studies is difficult at best. Institutions of higher education are not well structured to encourage renaissance thinking; yet the logic of environmentalism requires no less.

Third, a decent environmental studies program could acquaint students with the major issues—the sciences of ecology and thermodynamics, the social-political–economic-philosophical causes of environmental degradation, and the outlines of sustainable alternatives—and still fail because its graduates were unable to make the leap from "I know" to "I care" to "I'll do something." The first stage results from programmatic thoroughness, the second from a bonding process involving the integration of analytic intelligence, personhood, and experience, and the third from empowered get-up-and-go. Evidence overwhelmingly demonstrates that all three are essential to learning. But not all experience is educationally worthwhile. Carefully designed experiential education which reinforces intellectual and personal growth will require a deeper understanding of what kinds of experience catalyze what kinds of learning. Unfortunately, the typical campus and curriculum offer little opportunity of any sort for experiential learning, whether interaction with nature or the acquisition of competence with life-support systems.

I think the outlines of an alternative paradigm of research and education are emerging from a disparate group of university and college-based environmental studies programs and nontraditional organizations. Like the English ships before the Spanish Armada in 1588, their strength lies in their flexibility, autonomy, vision, and creativity. Despite substantial differences in size, orientation, and purpose, they share common concerns including: (1) ecological sustainability; (2) appropriate scale; (3) cultural and ecological diversity; (4) reevaluation of the goals and directions of industrial society; and (5) justice, peace, and participation. They also share a common intellectual heritage that includes ecologists such as Odum and Sears; systems theorists such as Bertalanffy and Boulding; naturalists such as Krutch and Eiseley; environmental activists such as David Brower; social theorists such as Kropotkin, Kohr, Mumford, and Bateson; and social activists such as Gandhi. Common to all of these organizations is the idea of ecology as an integrative principle and the basis for a marked shift in the perception of the human role in nature, and in the way societies deal with needs for food, energy, water, material, transportation, health care, and waste cycling.

Whatever paths the field of environmental studies follow, we must work, as Leopold observed, against "the fact that our educational and economic system is headed away from...an intense consciousness of land." Accordingly, those of us in environmental education need to renew our commitment to a sustainable human future. The foundation of sustainability, however defined, will be the clear awareness that our well-being is inseparable from that of nature. And, "If education does not teach us these things," Leopold once asked, "then what is education for?"

Is Environmental Education an Oxymoron?

For those calling themselves environmental educators, it is sobering to note that the only people who have lived sustainably in the Amazon rain forests, the desert Southwest, or anywhere else on earth could not read (which is not to say that they were uneducated). And those in the United States living closest to the ideal of sustainability, the Amish for example, do not make a fetish of education, seeing it as another source of deadly pride. On the other hand, those whose decisions are wreaking havoc on the planet are not infrequently well educated, armed with B.A.'s, B.S.'s, LL.B.'s, M.B.A.'s, and Ph.D.'s. Elie Wiesel has made the same point in a different context, noting that the designers and perpetrators of Auschwitz, Buchenwald, and Dachau, the heirs and kin of Kant and Goethe, also possessed quite substantial academic credentials.[1] It would seem, then, that the relationship between education and decent behavior of any sort is not exactly straightforward. Three possibilities are worth considering.

First, perhaps education is part of the problem. Cultures capable of generating an alphabet and written language have tended to become environmentally destructive. Written language is implicated with the rise of cities, agricultural surpluses and soil erosion, fanatical belief systems, irate and well-armed pilgrims, armies, usury, institutionalized greed, notions of collective aggrandizement, and eventually progrowth hucksters—all of which take a toll on soils, forests, wildlife, and landscape, hence Chateaubriand's observation that forests precede civilization and deserts follow it. In the larger scheme of things, education may only have made us more clever, but not ecologically wiser.

As circumstantial evidence I offer the observation that the time and expense of higher education is most often excused on the grounds that it increases lifetime earnings, a crude but useful measure of the total amount of carbon the scholar is able to redistribute from the earth's crust to the atmosphere. It is somewhat rarer for education to be extolled on the grounds that it reduces the graduates' impact on the biosphere, or because it hones their skills in the art of living simply. Such claims are indeed sufficiently rare that we may reasonably surmise that, on average, those whose lifetime earnings are enhanced by degrees do more damage to the planet than those less encumbered.

Second, it may be that, beyond some fairly minimal level, education is just not an important determinant of behavior, ecological or otherwise. There is a shelf of dust-laden studies about the difference education makes. And what difference *does* four years of higher learning make? The conclusions, given present tuition rates, are remarkably ambivalent. For the majority, peer influences seem to be a more important source of ideas and behavior than professors or courses. Most students seem to regard education as a ticket to a high-paying job, not as a path to a richer interior life, let alone one of saving the planet. We also have reason to believe that television, the automobile, and cheap energy have had more to do with ecological behavior than formal schooling.

A third possibility is that, under certain conditions, education might exert a positive influence on ecological behavior, but that these conditions by and large do not now prevail. Higher education, particularly that in prestigious universities, is often animated by other forces including those of pecuniary advantage and prestige. "Academic professionalism, specialism, and careerism," in Bruce Wilshire's words, "have taken precedence over teaching, and the education and development of both professors and students has been undermined."[2] The "moral collapse" that he describes results from the separation of the professionalized intellect from the personhood of the scholar. Moreover, the university "exists in strange detachment from crucial human realities, and perpetuates the implicit dogma that there is no truth about the human condition as a whole."[3]

The moral crisis of the university is perpetuated by faculty, and I suppose administrators, who can "rationalize away and conceal [their] stunted personalit[ies] and emotional infantilism."[4] Wilshire proposes to heal the "ethical sickness" of the university by reducing its scale so that it can "address the persons within it as beings who are immeasurably more than their professional roles" by "leav(ing) room for listening, ruminating, and silence...for wonderment and for caring"[5]—an interesting subject for a memo to the dean of graduate research. But whether a morally resuscitated university would turn out graduates better suited to the limits of the planet is not clear. I am inclined to think that moral revitalization is necessary but not sufficient.

Defenders of the generic university tend to justify it not on the quality of teaching or the moral refinement and ecological rectitude of its faculty and graduates, but rather on its contributions to what, with suitable gravity, is called the "fund of human knowledge," that is, research. And what can be said of this form of human activity? Historian Page Smith, for one, writes that:

> The vast majority of research turned out in the modern university is essentially worthless. It does not result in any measurable benefit to anything or anybody. It does not push back those omnipresent 'frontiers of knowledge' so confidently evoked; it does not *in the main* result in greater health or happiness among the general populace or any particular segment of it. It is busywork on a vast, almost incomprehensible scale. It is dispiriting; it depresses the whole scholarly enterprise; and most important of all, it deprives the student of what he or she deserves—the thoughtful and considerate attention of a teacher deeply and unequivocally committed to teaching.[6]

There is more to be said. Most research is aimed to further the project of human domination of the planet. Considerably less of it is directed at understanding the effects of domination. Less still is aimed to develop ecologically sound alternatives that enable us to live within natural limits. Ultimately our survival will depend as much on *re*discovery as on *re*search.[7] In this category I would include knowledge of justice, appropriate scale, the synchronization of morally solvent ends and means, sufficiency, and how to live well in a place.

The university's preoccupation with research rests on the belief that ignorance is a solvable problem. Ignorance is not solvable because we simply cannot know all of the effects of our actions. As these become more extensive and varied through "research and development," knowledge grows. But like the circumference of an expanding circle, ignorance multiplies as well. (This is not true, I think, for what is called "wisdom," which has to do with knowledge about the limits and proper uses of knowledge.) The relationship between ignorance and knowledge is not zero-sum. For every research victory there is a corresponding increase in ignorance. The discovery of CFCs, for example, "created" the ignorance of their effects on climate and stratospheric ozone. In other words, what was until 1930 a trivial, hypothetical area of ignorance became, with the "advance of knowledge," a critical and possibly life-threatening gap in human understanding of the biosphere. Likewise, our ignorance of how to safely and permanently store nuclear waste did not exist as an important category until the discovery of how to make a nuclear reactor. This is neither an argument against knowledge nor one for ignorance. It is rather a statement about the physics of knowledge and the peril of thinking ourselves smarter than we are, and smarter than we can ever become. In Wendell Berry's words:

> If we want to know and cannot help knowing, then let us learn as fully and accurately as we decently can. But let us at the same time abandon our superstitious beliefs about knowledge: that it is ever sufficient; that it can of itself solve problems; that it is intrinsically good; that it can be used objectively or disinterestedly."[8]

The belief that we are currently undergoing an explosion of knowledge is a piece of highly misleading and self-serving hype. The fact is that some kinds of knowledge are growing while others are in decline. Among the losses are vast amounts of genetic information from the wanton destruction of biological diversity, due in no small part to knowledge put to destructive purposes. We are losing, as David Ehrenfeld has observed, whole sections of the university curriculum in areas such as taxonomy, systematics, and natural history.[9] We are also losing the intimate and productive knowledge of our landscape. In Barry Lopez's words: "Year by year, the number of people with firsthand experience in the land dwindles...herald(ing) a society in which it is no longer necessary for human beings to know where they live except as those places are described and fixed by numbers."[10] On balance, I think, we are becoming more ignorant because we are losing knowledge about how to inhabit our places on the planet sustainably, while impoverishing the genetic knowledge accumulated through millions of years of evolution. And some of the presumed knowledge we are gaining, given our present state of social, political, and cultural evolution, is dangerous; much of it is monumentally trivial.

Conservation education need not be an oxymoron. But if it is to become a significant force for a sustainable and humane world, it must be woven throughout the entire curriculum and through all of the operations of the institution, and not confined to a few scattered courses. This will require a serious effort to rethink the substance and process of education, the purposes and use of research, the definition of knowledge, and the relationship of institutions of higher education to human survival. All of which will require courageous and visionary leadership. In the mounting battle for a habitable planet it is time for teachers, college and university presidents, faculty, and trustees to stand up and be counted.

Part Three

What Knowledge?
For What Purposes?

INTRODUCTION

The crisis of sustainability and the problems of education are in
large measure a crisis of knowledge. But is the problem, as is commonly believed, that we do not know enough? Or that we know too
much? or that we do not know enough about some things and too
much about other things? Or is it that our scientific methods are in
some ways flawed? Is it that we have forgotten things we need to
remember? Or perhaps is it that we have forgotten other ways of
knowing that lie in the realm of vision, intuition, revelation, empathy,
or even common sense? Such questions are not asked often enough. It
is widely presumed that merely by increasing the quantity of knowledge through scientific research we will solve whatever ails us, including the crisis of sustainability. The essays in Part 3 were written in the
belief that the truth is not so simple and that not everything learned
through "research" is worth knowing.

Underlying much of the public acceptance of "research" is a kind of
Darwinian faith that new knowledge is better (more fit) than old knowledge that we discarded or other kinds of knowledge that we chose not
to pursue. And sometimes it is, but not always. For example, we know a
great deal about the science of efficient killing, but relatively little about
how to make peace amidst differences of culture and politics. We have
learned a great deal about how to farm "scientifically" with chemicals
and large equipment, but have lost the knowledge of how to farm in
ecologically sound ways, which is also a matter of science. In such cases
are we to infer that the former was better than the latter? Certainly not.
The pursuit of knowledge is not always free from the influence of

power and wealth, nor is it ever free from stupidity, arrogance, personal ambition, or just wrongheadedness. That is to say that the pursuit of knowledge is infected with our human limitations. And sometimes in the march of progress we have wandered up blind alleys.

The three essays in this section deal with the pathologies of knowledge beginning with the arrogance implicit in the assumption that we can manage planet earth. If our goal is sustainability our best bet is to manage people, or educate self-managing people. This means designing the human enterprise to fit nature, not attempting to redesign nature to fit infinite human wants. The difference has marked effects on research agendas and curriculum alike.

Chapter 13 is aimed at the pathologies of professionalized social science. It should be read, I suggest, along wtih Charles Lindblom and David Cohen's *Usable Knowledge: Social Science and Social Problem Solving* (Yale University Press, 1979). The social sciences, with some notable exceptions such as Lindblom, have made by and large a remarkably underwhelming contribution to our understanding of the crisis of sustainability and to its resolution. The reasons are many, including the preoccupation with a spurious "objectivity" that is itself unscientific, and the tendency for the disciplines of the social sciences to become hermetically sealed from larger realities. Disciplinary agendas tend to implode, closing in on smaller and smaller issues. And these are often distant from lived experience. This is particularly troublesome because the issues we must now resolve have much to do with matters of governance, economics, social reconstruction, and human psychology.

The final essay focuses on a specific research project funded through the United States Department of Agriculture. The researchers are generating knowledge of a sort. But on closer examination it is rather like a Rube Goldberg device that with great huffing and puffing expensively does what we should prefer to do in simpler and better ways. The march of human understanding is not always straightforward, and in this instance one can detect regression which would continue to impoverish the countryside, farmers, and our present declining culinary standards.

XII

Having Failed to Manage Ourselves, We Will Now Manage the Planet? An Opinion from the Back Forty

There is a growing presumption that humans must now take control of the planet and its life processes. A recent issue of *Scientific American* devoted an entire issue to the subject of "Managing Planet Earth." In it one finds pleas for "adaptive" policies for planetary management which require "improving the flow of information," "technologies for sustainable development," and "mechanisms...to coordinate managerial activities."[1] Economists of a similar mind-set intend to "find the right policy levers" to manage "all assets, natural resources, and human resources."[2] Language like this conjures images of economists and policy experts sitting in a computerized, planetary control room, coolly pushing buttons and pulling levers, guiding the planet to something called "sustainable growth." At a time when humans are rapidly destroying the earth, this has an eminently sensible ring to it. The alternative to management is to sit idly by until the final whimper. Or so we are asked to believe.

I do not doubt that something needs to be managed. But I would like to raise questions about what we manage and how. For would-be planet managers, it should be a matter of no small consequence that God, Gaia, or Evolution was doing the job nicely until human population, technology, and economies got out of control. This leads me to think that it is humans that need managing, not the planet. This is more than semantic hairsplitting. Planetary management has a nice ring to it. It places the blame on the planet, not on human stupidity, arro-

gance, and ecological malfeasance, which do not have a nice ring. It
avoids the messy subjects of politics, justice, and the discipline of
moral choice. Planetary management, moreover, appeals to our desire
to be in control of things. It appeals to our fascination with digital
readouts, computer printouts, dials, gauges, and high tech of all sorts.
Management is mechanical not organic, and we like mechanical things:
they reinforce our belief that we are in control.

Plans to manage the earth are founded on the belief that ignorance
is a solvable problem. With enough research, satellite data, and computer models we can take command of spaceship earth. There is a great
deal more that we will learn about the earth, to be sure. But there are
good reasons to believe that its complexity is permanently beyond our
comprehension. A square meter of topsoil to a depth of several inches is
teeming with life-forms that still have not been studied, much less their
ecology or their relationship to the planet. The same can be said of most
of the "machinery of nature." The salient fact is not our knowledge, but
our ignorance. If we consider not only the complexity of nature, from
soil bacteria to planetary biogeochemical cycles, but also the human
impacts, with their various kinds of synergies, feedback loops, leads,
and lags, the idea of managing the planet takes on a different prospect
altogether. Managing the planet, unlike piloting a 747, requires a level of
knowledge that we are not likely to acquire.

Furthermore, even if we could acquire this knowledge, other limits
would appear. I am referring to the problem of human evil, recalcitrance, and our capacity to rationalize almost anything. There is a limit
to which we can comprehend the good, and there are other limits to
our willingness to do it. These limits do not seem to trouble the would-
be planet managers, who see the world as a set of problems solvable
by adjustments in prices or more efficient technologies. There can be
no good argument against efficiency in the use of resources or against
prices that include all environmental costs. It is a mistake, however, to
believe that we face only problems solvable by painless market adjustments and better gadgets, not dilemmas that will require wisdom,
goodness, and a rationality of a higher sort. The word "hubris," meaning overweening arrogance, is not heard much any more, but it applies
to the belief that we can sufficiently understand the complexities of the
earth to manage it for good purposes. It is also hubris to believe that
the technologies of earth management and the process of management
are neutral.

Time represents a third barrier. Assuming that we could amass the
necessary knowledge and character traits for managing earth, could we
do so in perpetuity? If not, what would happen as management sys-

tems subsequently collapse or erode? Would life systems, genetic processes, species dependent upon continued genetic improvement or upon human care die out? What might happen to the technologies of management as their guardians disappear? The shadows of that problem now lie across every nuclear plant that will have to be sealed off from human contact for centuries. Once human management replaces those older processes of evolution and the integrity and balances of natural systems, it is a mistake to assume that these could be restored if necessary. Once having crossed the threshold, there may be no going back. But the likelihood of maintaining management systems for any length of time does not appear to be very high. The same planet some would presume to manage is littered with ruins that give ample testimony to our fallibility and inconstancy. Our present scale and technology have only raised the stakes without increasing the odds of success.

There is another approach to management expressed by Wendell Berry, who states that "we are not smart enough or conscious enough or alert enough to work responsibly on a gigantic scale."[3] His answer has nothing to do with management unless we mean self-management. He says that "we must acquire the character and the skills to live much poorer than we do. We must waste less. We must do more for ourselves." There are points of agreement between Berry and the planet managers, the need to reduce waste, for example. But where Berry talks openly about living more poorly, the planet managers talk of sustainable growth as if life can continue as it has for the past four decades. Berry's emphasis on skills of self-reliance and character, which have no market value, strike an odd note in a time when we think that people act only from economic motives, not from a sense of duty, rightness, or even righteousness. Elsewhere Berry has described the environmental crisis as one of character which cannot be improved by technology or market adjustments, although they can be made worse by them.[4]

The difference between the planet managers and Berry has to do first with different judgments about the cause of the crisis. The authors in the issue of *Scientific American* noted above are silent about the origins of our plight, as if the crisis has no historical causes, no antecedents, and no roots in science, technology, economics, or politics worth mention. I think it no coincidence that the advertisements of IBM, McDonnell Douglas, General Motors, and Boeing are scattered throughout. It is difficult to avoid the conclusion that planet managers have made their peace with the powers that be and have joined the movement to extend human domination of nature to the fullest extent. It may be, however, that our impulse to manage that which cannot be managed, while leaving unmanaged that which could be, is the source of the problem.

There is good evidence that the planetary crisis is a direct result of the process whereby the countryside, small towns, and neighborhoods, here and elsewhere were drained of wealth, natural resources, people, and power with these being recrystallized in corporations and governments. The processes of urbanization, modernization, and industrialization have dominated the history of the twentieth century, as have those of militarization and planetary destruction. It is no coincidence that the twentieth century is one of unparalleled violence between people, and between people and nature. Nor is it coincidental that environmental destruction has proceeded with the growing dependence of people everywhere on products, skills, markets, capital, energy, and knowledge imported from somewhere else.

Berry's point that living poorly requires both character and skills strikes at the root of the matter. For planet managers, the only skills required are those of scientific expertise, technological ingenuity, and econometrics. Sustainable development will be delivered from on high, in the same way that Dostoevsky's Grand Inquisitor in *Brothers Karamazov* feeds the masses. Perhaps for the same reasons as well. Since people need no skills or discipline, they need cultivate no particular traits of character. The kind of skills Berry has in mind, and before him Thomas Jefferson, are those of an ecologically competent and active citizenry who know how to do for themselves and have the character traits of frugality, truthfulness, and goodheartedness necessary to be a good neighbor and good citizen. This implies management, but of the kind that grows out of the disciplines of community and stewardship.

It is worth asking how many of our global problems would have occurred if this kind of world were still substantially intact. The answer would tell us, I think, how many of our global problems can be solved only by rebuilding the foundations of our culture and patterns of livelihood from the bottom up. There are problems which can only be solved at a global level. In this category I would include efforts to protect oceans, the ozone layer, climate stability, and biological diversity. At a national level, government action will be necessary to establish "prices that tell the truth" about the environmental costs of things we consume (i.e., full cost pricing). Government action will also be essential to protect the poor who will be at greater risk, and to confront that sacred cow of distribution in a society in which growing income disparities have nothing to do with economic efficiency, personal worth, social benefit, or morality.

These imply potentially traumatic changes in the mindset of people used to avoiding real political issues and living at the expense of their children by not paying the costs of soil erosion, resource depletion, decimated wildlife, and wrecked ecologies. Honest bookkeeping or a dose of care would reduce the amount of stuff we buy and discard. This is, I think, why we must live "much poorer than we do." However necessary, these changes cannot occur without an ecologically literate public willing to support them, and, I think, demand them. We may expect any number of feckless politicians and others to argue that we can technologize or grow our way out of ecological malfeasance. The result of trying to do so, however, will only delay the day of reckoning and make that time more bitter than it otherwise had to be. After all of the energy-efficient motors, lightbulbs, automobiles are in widespread use, there will be a long distance to go before we arrive at anything like harmony with the natural world or what is being called "sustainability." That distance will be made up only through inculcating changes in public attitudes and means of livelihood which will require widespread ecological literacy and attitudes akin to what Aldo Leopold once described as a "striving for harmony with land."

Living poorly, as Berry puts it, is not the same as living in poverty. The distinction is that between bloatedness and prosperity made by Thoreau, Gandhi, and Shumacher. To live poorly but not in poverty will require different skills and different knowledge. People and communities with less cash to spend will need to know how to:

1. Distinguish basic needs from wants
2. Reduce dependencies
3. Take full advantage of the free services of nature
4. Use locally available resources
5. Rebuild local and regional economies, and most importantly
6. Rebuild strong, participatory communities.

They will need a degree of practical ingenuity that is not socially acceptable in affluent and effluent societies. They will be good scroungers, scavengers, and users of the cast-off, secondhand, recycled detritus from a wasteful society. They will need to become competent with the natural world in order to reestablish bioregional economies. This requires direct knowledge of the ecology of their places including such things as its trees, medicinal herbs, soils, wildlife, solar potentials, microclimates, availability of naturally occurring materials, and wildlife. Among the skills that must be rediscovered are those that allow people to participate in their sustenance, shelter, and healing. They will need to know how to restore damaged ecosystems. Given the numbers of battered women, abused children, and victims of industrial society, they will also need to know how to restore genuine communities.

Can we manage planet earth? Don't bet on it. But we have a

chance to manage ourselves by restoring a disciplined and loving relationship to our places, communities, and to the planet. Good sense is required to know what's manageable and what's not and to leave the latter to manage itself. The problem is not the planet. We are the problem. Throughout history, humans have steadily triumphed over all of those things that managed us: myth, superstition, religion, taboo, and above all, technological incompetence. Our task now is to replace these constraints with some combination of law, culture, and a rekindled reverence for all life. Management is then more akin to child-proofing a day-care center than it is piloting "spaceship earth."

XIII

What Good is a Rigorous Research Agenda if You Don't Have a Decent Planet to Put it On? (Apologies to Thoreau)

As the sun sets tonight over the offices of the Social Science Research Council, *Homo sapiens,* the council's primary object of study, will have: (1) deforested another one hundred and fifteen square miles, mostly in the tropics; (2) added some fifteen million tons of carbon to the atmosphere; (3) driven between forty and one hundred other species into extinction; and (4) eroded seventy-one million tons of topsoil. Because of this hyperactive biped with the big brain, the planet will be a little warmer, the rain a little more acidic, the ozone layer a little thinner, and the fabric of life a little more threadbare. Yesterday, today, tommorrow: a typical day on planet earth in the late years of the twentieth century.

Inside the offices of the council, an "executive associate," a member of the species as well as a sociologist, has recently noted that "Men and women live on the face of the Earth, breathe its air, and exploit its resources."[1] One can only applaud such a discovery, however tardy. Further, he notes that "there has been a radical change in how humans interact with their environment." And, best of all, he thinks that "the time has surely come to incorporate social perspectives more adequately into research on humans as forces in nature." If the boldness in these words is not exactly breathtaking, it is a step in the right direction and raises the possibility that the slumbering giant of the SSRC will bestir itself in a good cause.

The strategy to enlist social science in the struggle to save the planet begins with "a proposal to develop an interdisciplinary national program" to be submitted to something called "the council's committee on problems and policy." A forthright, if ponderous, beginning.

Second, he proposes that the council develop a "social science research agenda" and "develop the field." The latter is, I suppose, like a farmer fertilizing a field. Lest the reader be carried away by the controlled fervor of these words, the author cautions that:

> If the study of the interactions of humans and nature is to attract the needed level of interest among social scientists, the research problems must interest social scientists on their scientific merits. The research agenda must offer some hope of enriching social science by advancing an understanding of general socioeconomic processes.

He further notes that:

> Social scientists are no less concerned than are other citizens about the erosion of soils, the pollution of the air of cities, the hazards of earthquakes in built-up areas, the genetic dangers of biochemical control of weeds, and pests, and the long-term menace of rising global mean temperatures, these concerns in themselves have not proved enough to cause us to enlist in research endeavors in large numbers.

The gap between alleged interest and action he attributes to the lack of "a formulation of research issues that are intrinsic to the viewpoint of the social sciences." In other words, the fact that human survival now hangs in the balance is not itself of much interest to social scientists unless it can be translated into familiar terms, and converted into a well-funded research agenda. The concern for environmental quality would appear to be directly related to the potential for pecuniary rewards, a prudent consideration in financially uncertain times. His forebears, Plato, Hobbes, Rousseau and the like, were not nearly so circumspect. They, however, were not nearly so professional.

Finally, the document's author states that at least three years will be required "simply to build up a research agenda," and another five to "establish career tracks," "to recruit outstanding young researchers," and, as always, to "raise enough funding." And the results from this rescue mission? Well, by "about 1995...some reliable and useful findings...that will feed further advances in the social sciences...(and) a cohort of young social scientists from many disciplines who will be pursuing concrete, well-funded research programs."

Whether all of this well-funded activity, conferences in expensive hotels and exotic places, paper shuffling, and field building will have anything at all to do with reversing destructive planetary trends, the author does not say. One suspects that the reasons he does not say is that he has not thought much about it. He seems to regard planetary distress, and the accompanying human suffering, in the same way ambulance-chasing lawyers do automobile accidents—as an opportunity to cash in.

The proposal is remarkable first because of its timing (1988). We have known about environmental deterioration for quite some time. Since Rachel Carson's classic *Silent Spring* in 1962, there has been a tide of good books, research reports, and articles on the sources of environmental problems and alternatives to what now looms before us. (I am prepared to send my thirty-seven-page bibliography to the SSRC whenever asked.) The few social scientists who noticed and cared enough to drop other priorities to deal with larger issues, such as those mentioned below, were mostly ignored, isolated, and ostracized. If the Social Science Research Council were a fire department, they would still be pulling on their boots while the ashes cooled. This characteristic may provide a prior and enlightening subject of inquiry for the council.

Second, the author and his colleagues seem not to have noticed the excellent work done by Herman Daly in economics, Lynton Caldwell, Ken Dahlberg, and William Ophuls in political science, and Riley Dunlap and William Catton in sociology. Their work, however, has not been particularly well-funded and is not developed as a "research agenda." It was done simply by people who cared strongly and were willing to stand up and be counted while most of their professional colleagues remained seated.

This raises a third observation, which may partly explain the cool reception social scientists have given to the Dalys, Caldwells, and Dunlaps. The author proposes to "incorporate social perspectives more adequately into research on humans as forces in nature." It may be, however, that he has the cart and the horse wrongly juxtaposed. I propose that the SSRC consider taking ecological issues on their terms, not on the disciplinary convenience and nine-to-five schedule of social scientists. In other words, I propose that social scientists become ecologically literate with all that may mean for old and comfortable paradigms, theories, and research agendas. When they do, they will discover that environmental issues do not fit neatly into indoor paradigms, and that they are issues of values as much as of fact. The minimally alert may also discover that positivism as a methodology and philosophical stance is not of much help in our fumbling attempts to understand complex systems like human-biosphere interactions. Nor does it provide a basis for caring deeply about the prospects for life itself. Caring does not always lend itself to the cool aloofness and studied "objectivity" that is fashionable in the social sciences. Caring will inevitably involve sweat, personal risk, intellectual daring, and inconvenience, which run counter to "well-funded" research agendas.

Before the SSRC's posse mounts up and rides out of town to "develop the field," I propose that they sit down at the saloon, have a couple of belts, and ask themselves why the social sciences have been so late in recognizing the obvious. And whether part or all of the answer may lie in the way in which the SSRC and the individual disciplines of the social sciences have organized the search for knowledge. Perhaps the problem lies in their underlying values and assumptions, what Riley Dunlap describes as the paradigm of "human exceptionalism," which sets humans above the laws of nature. Instead of organizing a research posse at this late hour, perhaps a stroll in the woods might do as well.

XIV

Food Alchemy and Sustainable Agriculture

A specter is haunting the movement to build a durable agricultural system. That specter is the possibility of a high-technology, highly centralized, capital-intensive food system that could be justified on many of the same grounds that have traditionally been used by advocates of "sustainable" agriculture. The results of the attempt to co-opt the language of sustainable agriculture for contrary purposes have been confusion in the public mind. The first part of this chapter describes one such effort at co-optation; the second describes six approaches to a truer vision of sustainable agriculture.

FOOD ALCHEMY

In a recent article, U.S. Department of Agriculture researchers Martin Rogoff and Stephen Rawlins propose a high-technology food system based on perennials which "substantially increases carrying capacity and sustainability."[1] Perennials, they argue, are more suited to natural ecosystems, less dependent on chemicals and fuels, and minimize soil erosion. On the surface, the argument resembles those of J. Russell Smith and Wes Jackson, while reaching radically different conclusions.[2]

The system Rogoff and Rawlins propose would produce "perennial lignocellulosic plants," converting these into syrups and thence into what they call "edible products," by which I presume that they mean food, but we should not dismiss the possibility that they mean feed. Farms would no longer grow wheat, tomatoes, or corn, but rather cellulose from perennials having the attributes of "tulip poplar, kenaf, and a nitrogen fixing symbiont." Cellulose would then be converted into syrups and transported by tank car or slurry line to food factories near population centers where they would be reconstituted into steaks, french fries, and zucchini with "aesthetically necessary secondary matabolites, e.g., flavor compounds and pigments" added. Yum.

Could all of this come to pass? Rogoff and Rawlins insist that the technology necessary to convert cellulose to sugar syrups will be available within five years. The genetic research necessary for the appropriate enzymes to break down lignin seems to be well advanced. The biotechnology necessary to develop appropriate perennial plants is also progressing. Rogoff and Rawlins think that "breads, pastas, vegetable oils, sauces and beverages, or even hamburgers" will soon be within the realm of possibility, but that it may take longer to make things like synthetic apricots. Among the remaining tasks is how to convince people that this is food. For recalcitrants who remember the real thing, research proceeds on "the gustatory perception of smell," that is, taste. Slick advertising, I suppose, will do the rest.

Rogoff and Rawlins cite three major advantages of their proposal. The first is a substantial reduction in soil erosion, since perennials do not require annual tillage. The second is the lower energy cost that comes from using a large fraction of whole plants, as well as fuel saved by not having to till. The third is reduced costs for chemical fertilizers and pesticides. These, if true, are not insubstantial gains.

Despite the considerable advantages of a head start and a dependable cash flow, the United States Department of Agriculture, which employs Rogoff and Rawlins, has no monopoly in matters of culinary imagination. James Lovelock, for example, has proposed[3] that we replace farmers with chemists funded "like Star Wars—world-wide, big!" If bioengineering is still something of a mystery, well-funded chemistry is not. A number of place names registered with the EPA are an enduring testimony to its potence if not to the foresight and prudence of its practitioners. Perhaps because of this mixed record they, like certain nuclear physicists, might welcome the opportunity to recoup their personal and professional reputations. And what better way to do this than by magnanimously feeding that portion of the populace not dead or dying of various malignancies? But this is Lovelock's idea, not that of the chemists. He, however, is not reticent about its blessings on their behalf. Among these he cites the possibility of ending world hunger: "There is no need for all those poor and starving people." Most, however, do not starve because we cannot grow enough food, or even from a lack of chemists for that matter, but because of the politics and economics of food distribution.

Ending world hunger, however, is secondary to the goal of "releas(ing) the world to allow Gaia to run it." And how does one release the world? Well, by "get(ting) rid of the damned farmers," and returning farms to the wild, a wilderness that will be off-limits to the public, but not to "qualified naturalists." All of this makes sense to Mr. Lovelock because, as he puts it, "farmers are the curse of the world," and chemists, by inference, its salvation.

But what will people eat once farms have been eliminated, and what will it taste like? Well, chemists working from feedstocks of limestone or crude oil "will produce food that is really first-rate." Lovelock perceptively notes that currently available artificial foods are of uniformly dismal quality, but adds that this is so because "the chemists only produce junk food because the kids like it." And what alchemy of conscience or force of enlightened pallets will convert the present gastronomic mediocrity of chemicuisine into excellence? Lovelock does not say.

Both proposals raise a number of issues that their authors have overlooked. First, good solutions, to reiterate Wendell Berry's words, "solve for pattern," that is, they solve more than one problem while creating no new ones. But Rogoff, Rawlins, and Lovelock, albeit in different ways, aim only to maximize one thing: the production of "feedstocks." Their proposals have all of the characteristics of the one-eyed vision that has wrought so much havoc in the industrial age. Because, as the saying has it, we "can never do just one thing," it would be prudent to ask about the other consequences of these schemes. One might wonder, for example, what kind of pride and dignity growers of lignocellulose or conjurors of chemicuisine will have in their handiwork, or whether pride and dignity will be important to them at all. What products of labor, skill, and love will growers of lignocellulose exhibit at the county fair? Or will they even want to meet during fall harvest as neighbors, colleagues, and as competent farmers? The farmer in Rogoff and Rawlins's system is finally rendered into an industrialist who supplies, not food, but raw materials that enter the food system in a slurry line or tank car.

Lovelock's solution is even more stark, dispensing with farmers altogether. Not only are they a menace to Gaia, but to higher civilization as well. "Farming," he announces, "is unquestionably a profession that diminishes you. If one goes in reasonable, one comes out brutish."

On balance, however, the practical differences between Rogoff and Rawlins and Lovelock are small, reducible to matters of the speed and thoroughness with which farmers are removed from the land. Both simply accelerate existing trends. The Congressional Office of Technology Assessment argues that the entire country will be fed by fifty thousand "super farms" and five thousand "super dairies" by the year 2000.[4] The production of lignocellulose or chemicuisine, whatever their other benefits, can only accelerate this process. While Lovelock would abolish farms altogether, Rogoff and Rawlins's proposal would favor vast plantations and hence the continuing centralization of rural land ownership. Both proposals give priority to feeding urban masses as if the health of rural communities and that of cities were unrelated. They regard rural areas, if they regard them at all, as places where cheap food or chemical feedstocks can be produced, which is to say as colonies of urban civilization.

Third, synthetic foods certainly are not new. Many of us routinely eat margarine, and some of us eat things in boxes bearing labels like "Cap'n Crunch," or symmetrical potato chips served in tennis ball cans. We have been altering and adulterating basic foods for quite some time. But these proposals represent a significant extension of this trend. I am reminded, however, of the words of the Grand Inquisitor in Dostoevsky's *Brothers Karamazov,* who says to a silent Christ:

> Oh never, never can they (the masses) feed themselves without us. No science will give them bread so long as they remain free. In the end they will lay their freedom at our feet and say to us "make us your slaves, but feed us."[5]

Perhaps people willing to eat lignocellulose or crude oil transmogrified into hamburger deserve no better. But I for one think something important will have been lost in the process. Perhaps it will only be the trifling differences of taste and texture, which are, after all, matters of personal preference. But I think more is at stake, including the increased dependence of "consumers" on food engineers who will also need to engineer people through what they will call "consumer education." These are matters of politics and how we organize our commonwealth, including that of the land. Neither Rogoff and Rawlins nor Lovelock say anything about the politics of lignocellulose, slurry lines, and chemical food factories, because there is nothing very good to be said of their politics. They are the politics of technocracy and mass dependence, not democracy. We are justified in asking what happens when the knowledge of how to grow and preserve real food has been eradicated and the slurry lines run dry? The good intentions the authors profess may not be sustained by their successors in other times. Real sustainability and social resilience will not be built on mass dependence.

The authors of both proposals have made food a technological problem. A clearer reading of the evidence suggests that it is not a problem of technology, nor is it one of chemistry and biotechnology. It is first and foremost a political problem that has to do with tax and credit policies, research priorities in land-grant universities, and the distribution of power. A society in which the top one percent control thirty-five percent of the wealth of the country is one about to be fed lignocellulose or chemicuisine in one form or another. The security of the food system, which is to say its dependability and longevity, is basically the result of politics, and the relationships between people and the land which, properly cared for, sustains them.

Rogoff, Rawlins, and Lovelock believe that biotechnology and chemistry can be the basis of a stable food system. Let this be restated to read: "Vast corporations using high technology can turn practically anything into synthetic foods that meet minimal FDA requirements for nutrition for as long as it is profitable to do so and/or for as long as lots of other things work without interruption." In these terms I am inclined to believe them. Science has the capacity to turn lots of things into reasonable facsimiles of other things. And food conglomerates have learned how to sell reasonable facsimiles as "the real thing." We should not, however, confuse the results with a genuinely sustainable agriculture or culture.

TOWARD A SUSTAINABLE AGRICULTURE

A genuinely sustainable agriculture will rest on two foundations,[6] the first of which has to do with getting the metaphor right. Conventional agribusiness is not sustainable in the long run because it represents a misapplication of simplistic industrial metaphors, techniques, and expectations to complex biological and rural social systems. Farming conducted strictly as a business destroys soil, biological diversity, farmers, and farm communities as if these were simply replaceable industrial components. Given declining fertility and crop yields or increasing pest damage, the industrial farmer increases "inputs" of chemical fertilizers, pesticides, and water, all of which require more energy and more expense, and all of which have serious environmental and social side effects—what economists call "externalities."

Sustainable agriculture, on the contrary, is rooted in the metaphor of ecology, stressing coevolution with, not domination of, nature. Its scientific underpinnings are found in the emerging field of agroecology, which is an attempt to build a comprehensive theoretical framework for the study of "mineral cycles, energy transformations, biological processes, and socioeconomic relationships" at the farm level that widens the focus and lengthens the time-horizons of agricultural research.[7] In this view, human well-being is inseparable from that of the land community.

A second foundation of sustainable agriculture has to do with the set of tools, techniques, technologies, and farm practices—that is, the way farming is done. Proponents of sustainable agriculture tend to be highly skeptical of technological fixes such as herbicides, pesticides, bigger equipment, genetic engineering and no-till methods that require large amounts of herbicides. These are based on a gamble that industrial techniques can be applied indefinitely to biological systems. If the gamble pays off, we will still have an agricultural crisis, though one of a different sort. If it fails for any reason, most believe that we will have widespread famine. And it is failing. Despite a ten-fold increase in the use of pesticides since 1945, for example, insect damage to crops has risen from seven percent to thirteen percent.[8] Similar "anomalies" are becoming evident in the use of fertilizers and livestock antibiotics.

The practice of sustainable agriculture relies more on natural processes than on hardware. The differences between conventional and sustainable agriculture are summarized by Nicanor Perlas in these words:

> One will utilize the achievements of molecular biology to redesign and engineer the earth's living heritage and thus create a second green revolution. The other will seek guidance from the more holistic sciences, such as organismic biology and applied ethology and forge linkages with the various movements for individual and social transformation to create healthy and sustainable food systems.[9]

For example, sustainable farm systems will control insect predation through a variety of biological methods such as companion planting, early harvesting, and a farm design that preserves habitat for birds. Similarly, soil fertility can be sustained and regenerated by the use of legumes and tnitrogen-fixing trees. Where agribusiness relies on the extensive use of land and capital and increasingly on genetic manipulation and chemicals, sustainable agriculture uses less land more intensively with fewer inputs to achieve comparable profits.[10]

There are, however, substantial differences about the definition of the problems in (or of) agriculture, its causes, and consequently in the solutions proposed. While some of these are minor, others suggest major differences in what is often regarded as a highly unified movement. At least six different, if partially overlapping, approaches to sustainable agriculture can be discerned.

Agriculture and culture. Wendell Berry traces the problem to a disintegrating culture which no longer rewards or encourages agricultur-

al husbandry. The problem and therefore the solution are primarily matters of culture and morality. Sustainable agriculture requires farmers
who farm with care, pride, and skill, and depends on those factors that
undergird stable rural communities and stable farm families. He does
not believe that good agriculture will result from government programs
or research, but rather as a slow evolution—the cumulation of many
small changes. "The most necessary thing in agriculture," he writes, "is
not to achieve breakthroughs, but to determine what tools and methods
are appropriate to specific people, places, and needs, and to apply them
correctly."[11] Ultimately sustainable agriculture will depend on all of
those individual and cultural factors that produce good farmers who do
their work "knowingly, lovingly, skillfully, reverently." This cannot be
the outcome of any technical or social fix, but of a deeper, slower, and
more problematic process of social changes that include education,
child-raising techniques, sound economic policies that reward stewardship, and, most important, the continued existence of good farms and
farmers to pass on the knowledge and attitudes of land husbandry.

The closest example of the kind of agriculture Berry envisions is to
be found in Amish communities.[12] The Amish typically farm less than
two hundred acres, use horses instead of tractors, raise a variety of animals and crops, and have generally done very well in the poor farm
economy of the 1980s. According to the USDA this is not possible. Yet,
as Kenneth Boulding once noted, "whatever is is possible." Amish agriculture is, and is therefore a possibility for others to emulate. They
have not made agriculture a technological problem to be solved by
bioengineering schemes, slurry lines, and food factories that turn wood
chips into surrogate food. Amish agriculture is a community enterprise
within a culture that preserves humility, simplicity, moderation, prudence, frugality, hard work, neighborliness, and family stability. Farming for the Amish is a cultural problem to be solved within the context
of a tightly knit community that gives little room for egotism, vanity,
sloth, and the other deadly sins. These are also people, as Gene Logsdon notes, who find plenty of time to celebrate. From my own memories of the Amish in Pennsylvania, I recall that they do not do it as fran-
tically and as expensively as others, but perhaps with more of what
Liberty Hyde Bailey once called "heartease."[13] And, not the least, they
eat well, mostly foods grown on their own and their neighbors' farms
and gardens, and prepared in kitchens that lack microwave ovens,
trash compactors, and garbage disposals. Somehow they make do.

There are other examples of the kind of agriculture described by
Berry that preserve the long-term health of the land and rural communities.[14] In various ways, their "products" are not just "feedstocks" but

also well-tended farms, solid communities, healthy people, good citizens, and an attractive countryside. The fact that this now sounds utopian to some is a measure of how much we have forgotten about our past or choose to dismiss about future possibilities. Not all rural communities had these characteristics, but many did, a few still do, and most with care and thought could.

The food system. Researchers on "regenerative agriculture" at the Rodale Press in Pennsylvania have defined the problem of sustainability as a disorder of the entire food system that includes farmers, processors, wholesalers, retailers, and consumers.[15] The present organization of the food system relies on long-distance transport, economic concentration, high capitalization, and high technology, all of which in turn requires large amounts of energy. As a result, the system is neither efficient nor economic. Moreover, it is highly vulnerable to a variety of domestic or foreign disturbances. When all factors including environmental costs are considered, the system provides neither food cheaply as advertised, nor quality nutrition. The Rodale organization has recommended a long list of changes beginning with advice to farmers to reduce debt, stop erosion, and minimize inputs of chemical fertilizers, pesticides, and herbicides. The heart of their proposals involves the development of local and regional markets that: (1) give consumers a choice of locally grown, chemical-free, high-quality food; (2) reduce vulnerability and costs associated with long-distance transportation and processing; and (3) provides farmers profitable local markets that eliminate food brokers and retailers. The project has sponsored studies of food imports/dollar exports of several dozen states and is now beginning work to identify local markets and match these with local producers. To date, the Rodale organization through its Regeneration Project, has given the broadest analysis of the food system and the most complete blueprint for the transition to a regenerative economy.

Farm policy. Marty Strange, at the Center for Rural Affairs in Walthill, Nebraska, has taken a third approach, arguing that sustainable agriculture "must be organized economically and financially so that those who use the land will benefit from using it well and so that society will hold them accountable for their failure to do so."[16] The problem, then, is not primarily one of culture or farm techniques as much as it is the result of public policies that encouraged overproduction, absentee ownership, and the substitution of capital for labor. He proposes policy changes to encourage appropriately scaled, owner-operated, internally financed family farms with access to genuinely open markets. Farm policy, he argues, should:

1. Allow a farmer to pay for farmland by farming it well
2. Reward farmers for good farming
3. Allow a farmer to pay for land by farming it and by no other means
4. Eliminate other motives other than farming for owning farmland.[17]

Specifically, he proposes an end to subsidies for capital investment in agriculture, more sensible production controls, restrictions on concentrated ownership, greater federal regulation on farm suppliers, and changes in agricultural research that reflect social and environmental effects.[18] These objectives would require centrally planned production limits matched to consumer needs at reasonable prices, along with a quota system for producers, and particularly, substantial changes in federal tax laws. Once biases that discriminate against "smaller farms that practice a more sensible, sustainable agriculture" are removed, he suggests family farming might flourish.

Farm design. The work of John Jeavons, Bill Mollison, and the New Alchemists implicitly defines the problem of agriculture in terms of farm design, involving primarily energy use, farm structure, size, and technique. In one way or another, all stress the development of smaller farms of ten to fifty acres, perennialism, and complex polycultures that provide a diversity of products. The New Alchemists, in particular, have introduced a high degree of design sophistication by which farms would become "intensified, miniaturized, and diversified, fostering a dimension of self-repair and sustainability."[19] Similarly, Mollison proposes the development of permanent agricultural systems of self-perpetuating intensive polycultures. The results would be combinations of trees, shrubs, fiber, flours, cooking oils, timber, firewood, medicine, and dyes. This "permaculture" is intended as a low-energy, high yielding, labor-and-information intensive substitute for the present system, which is vulnerable, energy-intensive, and biologically simple. This involves "a totally new synthesis of plant and animal systems" drawing on systems ecology, energetics, and the philosophical approach of Fukuoka (see below).[20]

Soil loss and perennialism. A fifth approach to sustainable agriculture defines the problem as one of tillage and attempts to create systems that minimize its practice. J. Russell Smith in *Tree Crops* proposed the use of trees on steep slopes for food, forage, and cash crops, but did not otherwise object to plowing.[21] Wes Jackson at the Land Institute in Salina, Kansas has taken a more extreme approach which involves decades of research to create a "bio-technical fix" for "the problem of agriculture."[22] His goal is that of developing the plant materials for a domesticated prairie that would need to be retilled only once every three to five years ("at least in the early stages"). For Jackson, the problem of tillage is the problem of agriculture. Sustainable farming, in his view, can use proper tillage techniques, but, given human imperfections, proper land husbandry is rare. In this perspective, the problem is beyond education, moral exhortation, cultural changes, and government policy. The solution he proposes is to remove or minimize the need to plow by developing "polycultures of high yield herbaceous, seed bearing perennials" that resemble the original prairie. Jackson's approach applied to other bioregions would result in various applications of agroforestry, the integration of trees into what was formerly pasture, range, or cropland.

Agriculture and spirituality. The most radical approach to sustainable agriculture is that of Masanobu Fukuoka, described in *One Straw Revolution.*[23] The problem of agriculture, according to Fukuoka, is "extravagance of desire," which is to say, a spiritual problem. The goal of farming is "not the growing of crops, but the cultivation and perfection of human beings." Natural or, as he calls it, "do nothing farming" requires no large-scale research program, no legislation, no sweeping educational reforms. His proposal is at once more simple and more elusive than others: the abandonment of human will in favor of the guidance of nature. His four principles of natural farming are all stated as negatives: no cultivation, no chemical fertilizer or prepared compost; no weeding by tillage; no dependence on chemicals. Fukuoka's approach is grounded in a deep distrust of modern science, which proceeds by fragmenting reality and which cannot comprehend wholeness of nature nor grasp its perpetual flow and its local variations. His intent, reminiscent of Thoreau, is to discover and eliminate all of those things that farmers do not have to do. As a spiritual activity, farming should not be the exclusive work of a small minority, but should involve everyone. In his approach, this is possible because farms need not be larger than five to ten acres, nor require more than hand tools.

To a great extent, these six approaches are complementary, but with important differences. For both Berry and Fukuoka, sustainable agriculture requires good farmers who in turn are the product of a stable rural culture. Wes Jackson, on the contrary, assumes that the existence of good farmers will always be problematic, hence the need to minimize the potential for ecological mischief through a biotechnical fix. For Marty Strange, good farmers are in large part the product of a fair and farsighted public policy. Both the permaculturists and New Alchemists propose to redesign the farm to minimize energy use and ecological vulnerability. Advocates of regenerative farming stress changes in the entire food system and in farm techniques, but not necessarily in farm design or plant materials.

Each approach is vulnerable to somewhat different problems. Those proposing to reestablish farming as a high calling face roughly the same odds that confront other purveyors of virtue. This is not an argument against virtue, only a statement about its likelihood. Good husbandry, as Jackson argues, is rare in any place over any length of time. The destructiveness of contemporary agriculture is unique only in its scale, not in kind, from the abuses of earlier eras. Moreover, to the extent that good farming requires good farmers to pass down knowledge, attitudes, and traditions of land stewardship, the sharp decline in the number of family farms suggests that the traditional farm may already be beyond resuscitation on any large scale.

Those proposing to redesign the farm, such as the New Alchemists and Permaculturists, now face the task of building not only biologically sophisticated models on paper, but of working farms that produce food, make money, and demonstrate a high order of ecological harmony. Even if these are biologically and economically successful, serious questions will remain about their potential to feed large numbers of people. Those wishing to change the techniques of farming (almost all advocates of sustainable agriculture) must master the complex economic, social, and psychological forces by which technologies are accepted and diffused.

Likewise, those, like Marty Strange and Robert Rodale, who propose to reform the economic and financial context of agriculture or the entire food system, must show how this can be done politically. In other words, how can the policy requisites of sustainable agriculture be made politically important to a majority of Americans?

For Wes Jackson and researchers at the Land Institute, other questions arise. Do we have the fifty years said to be necessary to develop and diffuse alternative plant ensembles and the related technologies to plant, harvest, and process? Assuming that we do, how will the resulting "domestic prairies" affect the balance between family scale farming, which some regard as vital to sustainable agriculture, and large-scale corporate farming? If domestic prairies were to confer an advantage of scale to agribusiness, even temporarily, would not a biotechnical fix require a prior sociopolitical fix to limit the concentration of ownership, size of machinery, and absentee control before the last vestiges of family farms and small towns are eliminated? At issue are unresolved questions about the cause of unsustainability and whether sustainability implies mimicking natural systems or restoring them. Rutgers University

Professor Frank Popper, for example, has proposed that the prairies be restored to their original use as a buffalo preserve on grounds that partially resemble Jackson's argument.

All of the approaches to sustainable agriculture face at least three problems. Except for that of Wendell Berry and Wes Jackson, most of the discussion about sustainability revolves around questions concerning farmers' values, farm techniques, and farm ecology and design, with little said about farm communities. If, however, sustainable farming requires a supportive rural culture, as Berry persuasively argues, the larger issues of community cohesion must be faced. If durable farm communities are not rooted in religion and/or in stable traditions, how will they withstand the corroding effects of urban secularism: dish antennas, four-wheel trucks, and six-packs? Might sustainable agriculture require farmers with the same sense of place demonstrated by the Amish, along with their self-imposed limits on technology, consumption, and life-style? If so, will enough people choose such a life or accept the conditions which would allow others to do so?

Second, could a system of sustainable agriculture exist as an island in an unsustainable society that squanders not only land, but energy, resources, and biological diversity? If not, what larger sociopolitical issues must be addressed? The concept of sustainability implies the recognition of limits inherent in ecological systems. Must the same recognition become an integral part of social values, laws, and institutions that affect everyone? What different relationship must be established between agriculture and the larger society? For example, should farmers working with biological systems that are vulnerable to drought, pestilence, and ecological limits be subject to the same rigors of compound interest as those involved in the service sector or in manufacturing?

Third, the transition to sustainable agriculture will coincide with a period of high ecological instability. By the year 2000, world population will reach six billion with more on the way, liquid fossil fuels will have become more expensive, and biological productivity will be reduced by the effects of acid rain and changes in rainfall and temperature expected to begin in the 1990s due to global warming. Each of these trends will make successful farming of any sort more difficult. For example, whether energy needs for traction are supplied by alcohol fuels grown on the farm or from horses, food production will be reduced because of the acreage withdrawn for feed or feedstock. Finally, the same processes of land degradation (urbanization, soil erosion, and chemicalization) that have given urgency to the movement toward sustainable agriculture will make its success less likely. The next generation of farmers, however they choose to farm, will inherit a less-biologically resilient and productive land, and a less-predictable climate.

Finally, in coming decades farmers in all probability will be subject to unprecedented political capriciousness, born of confusion in the face of energy and water shortages, accumulating environmental stresses, and a rising tide of national debt and trade deficits, and compounded by their own political decline. They are likely to be increasingly at the mercy of a growing urban population who have come to think of cheap and abundant food as a birthright. If advocates of sustainable agriculture are to be more than merely right, if they are also to be successful in transforming agriculture, they must acquire a large constituency that understands the connections between eating well, health, and what happens on and to farms across the country. In developing that constituency, including farmers, it matters a great deal how and how accurately the problems of agriculture are defined, and what goals are proposed.

XV

Epilogue

The modern world arose as a volcanic eruption so suddenly and massively that it buried or transformed all that had preceeded it, including landscapes and mindscapes. It is difficult to know how much we have lost, but I believe that for all of the increases in convenience and speed, we have lost a great deal of the richness and experience of a life that once existed. The losses are not all visible. The most serious have to do with the way we think and what we think about. For all of our gross national product, most live increasingly barren lives in an increasingly impoverished land. Rising consumption can provide only surrogate, and ultimately destructive, satisfactions. Cultural commentator Mick Jagger once said it all: "I can't get no satisfaction." The problem Mick has analyzed seems to lie in the "I", the interiorized ego characteristic of the modern world which will never "get no satisfaction." Rational consumers will not, I think, find satisfaction because the economy we have constructed works, not by creating satisfaction, but by multiplying wants. As Lewis Mumford once noted, its moral alchemy converted the seven deadly sins (pride, envy, sloth, greed, gluttony, avarice, and lust) into economic virtues necessary for the growing economy. Its focus is the self isolated from obligation, tradition, community, and ecology. Until we confront what modernity has done to us as people and resolve to do otherwise, we can only put Band-Aids on terminal problems.

The vast majority of thought about a sustainable society, however, has to do with hardware. I think it is time to ask about the software of sustainability as well, and thus about the qualities people will need to build and maintain a durable civilization. I do not believe that a humane version of sustainability will come about solely as the result of "economically rational" behavior. It will only come about as the result of a higher and more thorough rationality. Sustainability, I think, will require a considerable increase in virtue throughout the society, by which I mean people motivated by a sense that their well-being is linked to that of others and to other life-forms. I must add, however, that a civilization resembling those described by Orwell or Huxley could perhaps be made sustainable in a purely technological sense. This shadow will haunt us in coming decades. The difference between a humane and sustainable world and a technological nightmare will ultimately be decided by people capable of acting with wisdom, fore-sight, and love, which is to say, with virtue.

Virtue, in the words of philosopher Alasdair MacIntyre, "is at vari-ance with central features of the modern economic order and more especially its individualism, its acquisitiveness and its elevation of the values of the market to a central social place."[1] In a passage worth quoting in full, MacIntyre writes:

> One of the key moments in the creation of modernity occurs when production moves outside the household. So long as productive work occurs within the structure of households, it is easy and right to under-stand that work as part of the sustaining of the community of the household and of those wider forms of community which the house-hold in turn sustains. As, and to the extent that, work moves outside the household and is put to the service of impersonal capital, the realm of work tends to become separated from everything but the service of biological survival and the reproduction of the labor force, on the one hand, and that of institutionalized acquisitiveness, on the other.[2]

Persons caught in an economy such as ours which destroys the bonds that join us together in the wider society of life cannot think well about virtue. In place of the concept of the virtuous man that MacIntyre describes or that Cicero would have recognized, we have "niceness" and the narrow, constricting, life-destroying rationality of the isolated ego. In MacIntyre's view, it is not possible to be both modern and moral since "the fully autonomous self knows no morality other than the expression of its own desires and principles."[3]

At this point there is something to be learned from older notions of virtue found in antiquity. I am referring to the sense that one's self is inseparable and inexplicable from that of a larger community which is part of an understandable cosmos. In Robert Proctor's words: "The attempt to regain moral consciousness thus becomes an attempt to regain historical consciousness as well."[4] The modern world has destroyed the sense of belonging to a larger order which must be restored as the foundation of a postmodern world. Virtue once implied actions that were harmonious in a larger commonwealth. I think it is no accident that the root for religion and for ecology similarly imply relatedness.

Now, how is virtue to be taught in the age of shopping malls and MTV? At the most basic level there is no substitute for role models, parents, teachers, and leaders who live virtuous lives. Nor is there any substitute for experiences that foster virtue and the discipline that goes with it. For all of their streetwise sophistication, the vast majority of young people have grown up in a kind of sensory deprivation chamber of the modern suburb or city. The kind of educational experiences that promote virtue are of a different sort found in some measure in schools such as Deep Springs Academy (CA), College of the Atlantic, Beria College, and Warren Wilson College. Students need opportunities to work together, to create, to take responsibility, and to lead in a community setting without which they are unlikely to comprehend the full meaning of virtue, ecology, or community. Finally, the subject of virtue needs to become a part of what we talk about with clarity and understanding. To do so will require the reintroduction of moral philosophy throughout the contemporary curriculum.[5] We cannot expect to act with virtue if we cannot think clearly about it and as a result, cannot talk articulately about it. Nor can we act virtuously if we assume that any definition of virtue is as good as any other (at this point I am inclined to agree with Allan Bloom).

Dietrich Bonhoeffer, who knew something of the subject, said that "cheap grace is the deadly enemy of our church." In its place he argued for "costly grace" that requires much of its followers. Likewise, the transition to the kind of postmodern society envisioned in this series of books cannot be done cheaply. It will cost us something, perhaps a great deal. But there is a far higher price waiting to be paid.

Notes

Introduction

1. David Ray Griffin, "Introduction," *The Renchantment of Science* (Albany: State University of New York Press, 1988), xi.

2. *Ibid.*

Chapter 1

1. The phrase is Langdon Winner's. See his *The Whale and the Reactor* (Chicago: University of Chicago Press, 1986), 10.

2. Thomas Berry, *The Dream of the Earth* (San Francisco: Sierra Club Books, 1988).

3. John G. Cross and Melvin J. Guyer, *Social Traps* (Ann Arbor: University of Michigan Press, 1980), 4; and Robert Costanza, "Social Traps, Ecological Destruction, and the Arms Race: Some Examples of Optimization Gone Awry" (Paper presented to the Environmental Studies Conference at Meadowcreek Project, October 16–19 1986). Also Robert Costanza, "Social Traps and Environmental Policy," *Bioscience* 37/6 (June 1987): 407–12.

4. Garrett Hardin, "The Tragedy of the Commons," *Science* 162 (13 December 1968): 1243–48.

5. Henry Teune, *Growth* (Newbury Park: Sage Publications, Inc, 1988), 111.

6. Peter Vitousek et al., in "Human Appropriation of the Products of Photosynthesis," *Bioscience* 36/6 (June 1986): 368–73, define net primary productivity as "the amount of energy left after subtracting the respiration of primary producers (mostly plants) from the total amount of energy (mostly solar) that is fixed biologically."

7. Walter Prescott Webb, *The Great Frontier* (Austin: University of Texas Press, 1975), 13.

8. *Ibid.,* 282.

9. Donella Meadows et al., *The Limits to Growth* (New York: Universe Books, 1972).

10. Cited in Herman Daly, ed., *Economics, Ecology, Ethics* (San Francisco: W. H. Freeman, 1980), 8.

11. Cited in *ibid.,* 7.

12. Julian Simon, *The Ultimate Resource* (Princeton: Princeton University Press, 1981), 17.

13. See Herman Daly, "The Steady-State Economy: Postmodern Alternative to Growthmania," in David Ray Griffin, ed., *Spirituality and Society* (Albany: State University of New York Press, 1988), 107–22; and Herman Daly and John Cobb, *For the Common Good* (Boston: Beacon Press, 1990).

14. Nicholas Georgescu-Roegen, *The Entropy Law and the Economic Process* (Cambridge: Harvard University Press, 1971), 281.

15. *Ibid.,* 304.

16. Fred Hirsch, *The Social Limits to Growth* (Cambridge: Harvard University Press, 1976).

17. *Ibid.,* 67.

18. *Ibid.,* 175; see also Daniel Bell, *The Cultural Contradictions of Capitalism* (New York: Basic Books, 1976).

19. Joseph A. Schumpeter, *Capitalism, Socialism and Democracy* (New York: Harper Torchbooks, 1962), 162.

20. Robert Heilbroner, *Business Civilization in Decline* (New York: W. W. Norton, 1976), 111.

21. *Ibid.,* 115.

22. Susan DeMarco and Jim Hightower, "You've Got to Spread it Around," *Mother Jones* (May 1988): 33.

23. Volkmar Lauber, "Ecology, Politics and Liberal Democracy," *Government and Opposition* 13/2 (Spring 1978): 200.

24. Wendell Berry, *Home Economics* (San Francisco: North Point Press, 1987), 68.

25. Lynn White, Jr., "The Historical Roots of Our Ecologic Crisis," *Science* 155 (10 March 1967): 1203–07. White's article created a sizeable literature in

response. See David and Eileen Spring, eds., *Ecology and Religion in History* (New York: Harper Torchbooks, 1974).

26. Lewis Moncrief, "The Cultural Basis for Our Environmental Crisis," *Science* (30 October 1970).

27. Lewis Mumford, *The Myth of the Machine: The Pentagon of Power* (New York: Harcourt Brace Jovanovich, 1970), 82.

28. *Ibid.,* 57.

29. Martin Heidigger, "The Question Concerning Technology," in David Krell, ed., *Martin Heidigger: Basic Writings* (New York: Harper and Row, 1977); Alfred North Whitehead, *Science and the Modern World* (New York: Free Press, 1967); Carolyn Merchant, *The Death of Nature* (New York: Harper and Row, 1980); William Leiss, *The Domination of Nature* (Boston: Beacon Press, 1974); Morris Berman, *The Reenchantment of the World* (Ithaca: Cornell University Press, 1981); Jacques Ellul, *The Technological Society* (New York: Vintage, 1964).

30. C. S. Lewis, *The Abolition of Man* (New York: Macmillan, 1947), 79–80.

31. Robert Sinsheimer, "The Presumptions of Science," *Daedalus* (Spring 1978): 23–35.

32. Donald Worster, "The Vulnerable Earth: Toward a Planetary History," *Environmental Review* 11/2 (Summer 1987): 101.

33. Erwin Chargaff, "Knowledge without Wisdom," *Harper's* (May 1980): 41–48.

34. Wendell Berry, "Solving for Pattern," in *The Gift of Good Land* (San Francisco: North Point Press, 1981).

35. George Orwell, *The Road to Wigan Pier* (New York: Harcourt Brace Jovanovich, 1958), 201, 210.

36. Colin Turnbull, *The Human Cycle* (New York: Simon and Schuster, 1983); Marshall Sahlins, *Stone Age Economics* (Chicago: Aldine, 1972).

37. Stanley Diamond, *In Search of the Primitive* (New Brunswick: Transaction Books, 1981), 173.

38. Paul Shepard, *The Tender Carnivore and the Sacred Game* (New York: Scribners, 1973).

39. Paul Shepard, *Nature and Madness* (San Francisco: Sierra Club Books, 1982), 124.

40. Riane Eisler, *The Chalice and the Blade* (New York: Harper and Row, 1987).

41. Ernest Becker, *Denial of Death* (New York: Free Press, 1973), 281.

42. John A. Livingston, *The Fallacy of Wildlife Conservation* (Toronto: McClelland and Stewart, 1982), 79.

43. Aldo Leopold, *A Sand County Almanac* (New York: Oxford University Press, 1971), 224–225.

44. *Ibid.,* 204.

45. David Ehrenfeld, *The Arrogance of Humanism* (New York: Oxford University Press, 1979), 105.

46. C. G. Jung, *Memories, Dreams, Reflections* (New York: Vintage, 1965), p. 341.

47. Mumford, *Myth,* 413.

48. Richard Wilkinson, *Poverty and Progress: An Ecological Perspective* (New York: Praeger, 1973), 4.

49. John Platt, "What We Must Do," *Science* (28 November 1969): 1115–21.

50. Peter Gay, *The Enlightenment* (New York: W. W. Norton), 567.

51. Leo Marx, "Does Improved Technology Mean Progress?" *Technology Review* 90/1 (January 1987): 71.

52. Lawrence Goodwyn, *The Populist Movement* (New York: Oxford University Press, 1978), 284.

53. See for example, James Miller, *Democracy is in the Streets* (New York: Simon and Schuster, 1987).

54. E. F. Schumacher, *A Guide for the Perplexed* (New York: Harper and Row, 1977), 140.

Chapter 2

1. Lester Brown, Christopher Flavin, and Sandra Postel, "Picturing a Sustainable Society," in Lester Brown et al., *State of the World: 1990* (New York: W. W. Norton, 1990), 173.

2. Lester Brown, *Building A Sustainable Society* (New York: W. W. Norton, 1980). International Union for the Conservation of Nature, *World Conservation Strategy* (Geneva: International Union for the Conservation of Nature, 1980).

3. World Commission on Environment and Development, *Our Common Future* (New York: Oxford University Press, 1987), 43.

4. *Ibid.,* 89.

5. By "modern paradigm" I mean a world based on the philosophies of Bacon, Galileo, Newton, Descartes, Adam Smith, and John Locke. Its core values are those of domination of nature through science and technology, economic growth, consumption, patriarchy, and nationalism.

6. David Ray Griffin, "Introduction," in David Ray Griffin, ed., *The Reenchantment of Science* (Albany: State University of New York Press, 1988), xi.

7. Herman Kahn et al., *The Next Two Hundred Years* (New York: William Morrow, 1976), 1.

8. Robert Repetto, *World Enough and Time* (New Haven: Yale University Press, 1986), 15.

9. See Gifford Pinchot's autobiography, *Breaking New Ground* (Washington, D.C.: Island Press, 1987/1947).

10. Quoted in Barry Schwartz, *The Battle for Human Nature* (New York: W. W. Norton, 1986), 325.

11. *Ibid.,* 317.

12. *Our Common Future,* 89.

13. James Gustave Speth, "A Luddite Recants," *Amicus Journal* (Spring 1989): 3–5.

14. Herman Daly, "Sustainable Development: From Concept and Theory Towards Operational Principles" (Paper presented in Milan, Italy, March 1988). See also Herman Daly and John Cobb, *For the Common Good* (Boston: Beacon Press, 1990), 71–6.

15. Daly, "Sustainable Development," 3.

16. A strategy Dieter Senghaas calls "de-linking. " See Senghaas, "The Case for Autarchy," in Charles Wilbur, ed., *The Political Economy of Development and Underdevelopment,* 3rd ed. (New York: Random House, 1984), ch. 13.

17. Daly, "Sustainable Development," 26.

18. Repetto, *World Enough,* 8.

19. For a notable exception, see Alan Durning, "Mobilizing at the Grassroots," *State of the World: 1989* (New York: W. W. Norton, 1989), ch. 9.

20. World Resources Institute, *Tropical Forests: A Call for Action,* pt. 1 (Washington, D.C., 1985), 1.

21. See, for example, Vandana Shiva, "Forestry Myths and the World Bank," *The Ecologist* 17/4–5 (1987): 142–9.

22. Discussion of education in the Brundtland Commission report (see note 3 above) is confined to pages 111–14.

23. Wendell Berry, "The Futility of Global Thinking," *Harper's* (September 1989): 19.

24. Ivan Illich, *Shadow Work* (Boston: Marion Boyars, 1981), 15.

25. Wolfgang Sachs, "A Critique of Ecology," *NPQ* (Spring 1989): 16–19.

26. Wendell Berry, *Home Economics* (San Francisco: North Point Press, 1987), 67.

27. Berry, "The Futility of Global Thinking," 22.

28. Lewis Mumford, *The Culture of Cities* (New York: Harcourt Brace Jovanovich, 1970/1938), 386.

29. *Ibid.*, 387.

30. John Friedmann, *Planning in the Public Domain* (Princeton: Princeton University Press, 1987), 314.

31. *Ibid.*, 374.

32. *Ibid.*, 354.

33. *Ibid.*, 375–82; see also Daly and Cobb on the issue of free trade, capital mobility, and community, *For the Common Good*, ch. 11.

34. Garrett Hardin, *Filters Against Folly* (New York: Penguin Books, 1985), 141–63.

35. Michael Redclift, *Sustainable Development: Exploring the Contradictions* (New York: Methuen, 1987), 151.

36. Quoted in *ibid.*, 151.

37. *Ibid.*, 155.

38. Richard B. Norgaard, "Risk and Its Management in Traditional and Modern Agroneconomic Systems" (Paper presented at the Society of Economic Anthropology, April 1987), 14.

39. Richard B. Norgaard, "Economics as Mechanics and the Demise of Biological Diversity," *Ecological Modelling* 38 (1987): 118; see also Margery L. Oldfield and Janis B. Alcorn, "Conservation of Traditional Agroecosystems," *Bioscience* 37/3 (March 1987): 199–207.

40. Norgaard, "Risk," 13.

41. See for example Gary Paul Nabhan, *Gathering the Desert* (Tucson: University of Arizona Press, 1987); *The Desert Smells Like Rain* (San Francisco:

North Point Press, 1982); *Enduring Seeds* (San Francisco: North Point Press, 1989).

42. John and Nancy Todd, *Bioshelters, Ocean Arks, City Farming: Ecology as the Basis of Design* (San Francisco: Sierra Club Books, 1984), 18–92.

43. John Todd, "Living Machines," *Annals of Earth* 8/1 (1990).

44. *Ibid.*

45. Amory B. Lovins, L. Hunter Lovins, *Brittle Power: Energy Strategy for National Security* (Andover: Brick House, 1982), 191.

46. Wes Jackson, "The Necessary Marriage Between Ecology and Agriculture," *Ecology* (1989).

47. Sir Albert Howard, *An Agricultural Testament* (Emmaus: Rodale Press, 1979/1943), 4.

48. Keith Critchlow, "Twelve Criteria for Sacred Architecture," *Lindisfarne letter* 12 (West Stockbridge: Lindisfarne Press, 1981). See also, *Bioshelters, Ocean Arks,* 79.

49. William Jordan et al., *Restoration Ecology* (New York: Cambridge University Press, 1987).

50. Using nature as a standard is not as easy as it once seemed. Natural systems are more influenced by random factors and disturbances than once thought. See for example, Daniel Botkin, *Discontinuous Harmonies* (New York: Oxford University Press, 1990), and Donald Worster, "The Ecology of Chaos," *Environmental Review* (Summer 1990).

51. Leopold Kohr, *The Breakdown of Nations* (New York: E. P. Dutton, 1978); E. F. Schumacher, *Small is Beautiful* (New York: Harper Torchbooks, 1974); Kirkpatrick Sale, *Human Scale* (New York: Coward, McCann and Geoghegan).

52. See Charles Perrow, *Normal Accidents* (New York: Basic Books, 1984).

53. Kohr, *The Breakdown of Nations,* 35.

54. *Ibid.,* 79.

55. *Ibid.,* 91.

56. Gregory Bateson, *Mind and Nature* (New York: E. P. Dutton, 1979); also Gregory Bateson, *Steps to an Ecology of Mind* (New York: Ballantine, 1975); and Gregory Bateson and Mary Catherine Bateson, *Angels Fear* (New York: Macmillan, 1987).

57. On the reductionism in much of recent ecology, see Donald Worster, "The Ecology of Order and Chaos" (Paper given at Evergreen State University, April 1989).

58. See Eugene Odum, *Basic Ecology* (Philadelphia: Saunders Co., 1983), 1–12.

59. William Irwin Thompson, "The Cultural Implications of the New Biology," in Thompson, ed., *GAIA: A Way of Knowing* (Great Barrington: Lindisfarne Press, 1987), 27.

60. David Gordon, ed., *Green Cities* (Montreal: Black Rose Books, 1990).

61. See Jacques Ellul, *The Technological Society* (New York: Vintage Books, 1964); Langdon Winner, *Autonomous Technology* (Cambridge: MIT Press, 1977).

62. See Langdon Winner, *The Whale and the Reactor* (Chicago: University of Chicago Press, 1986).

63. Frederick Ferre, *Philosophy of Technology* (Englewood Cliffs: Prentice-Hall, 1988), 134.

64. Donella Meadows, "The New Alchemist," *Harrowsmith* (November 1989).

Chapter 3

1. Vladimir Vernadsky, *The Biosphere* (Oracle, AZ: Synergetic Press, 1986).

2. Lynn H. Miller, *Global Order* (Boulder: Westview Press, 1985), 17–67; see Hedley Bull, *The Anarchical Society* (New York: Columbia University Press, 1977).

3. Paul Kennedy, *The Rise and Fall of the Great Powers* (New York: Random House, 1987), 446.

4. See Michael Renner, *National Security: The Economic and Environmental Dimensions* (Washington: WorldWatch Institute, 1989), 12–13.

5. Andrew M. Scott, *The Dynamics of Interdependence* (Chapel Hill: University of North Carolina Press, 1982), 33.

6. *Ibid.*, 203.

7. Robert Gilpin, *War and Change in World Politics* (Cambridge: Cambridge University Press, 1981), 162.

8. Ruth Leger Sivard, *World Military and Social Expenditures: 1987–88* (Washington: World Priorities, 1987), 15.

9. *Ibid.*, 5–6.

10. Renner, *National Security,* 21.

11. See Robert A. Dahl, *Democracy and Its Critics* (New Haven: Yale University Press, 1989), 245–51; Jay Robert Lifton and Richard A. Falk, *Indefensible Weapons* (New York: Basic Books, 1982), 139–41.

12. Anjali Sastry, Joseph Romm, and Kosta Tsipis, "Could the United States Survive a Few Nuclear Weapons?" *Technology Review* 92/3 (April 1989): 22–9. Interest in calculating the exact degree of global cooling following nuclear wars of varying magnitudes seems to me to be a waste of time. As a layman, I am struck by the fact that we were forty years into the nuclear age before anyone thought to ask whether debris and smoke might blot out sunlight and with what ecological effects. This leads me to wonder what else might happen during or after a nuclear war that no one has thought about, and may never think about. Nonetheless, I am sufficiently impressed by the explosive power of nuclear weapons and by the number of them now available to believe that nuclear war at any level would cause all kinds of effects, ecological and otherwise that we can never anticipate.

13. Arthur Westing and E. W. Pfeiffer, "The Cratering of IndoChina," *Scientific American* (May 1972), reprinted in Herbert York, ed., *Arms Control: Readings From Scientific American* (San Francisco: W. H. Freeman, 1973).

14. John Mueller, *Retreat From Doomsday: The Obsolescence of Major War* (New York: Basic Books, 1989), 9.

15. Mueller, *Retreat From Doomsday,* ch. 11.

16. Andrew Bard Schmookler, *The Parable of the Tribes: The Problem of Power in Social Evolution* (Berkeley: University of California Press, 1984).

17. Andrew Bard Schmookler, *Out of Weakness: Healing the Wounds That Drive us to War* (New York: Bantam Books, 1988), 145.

18. Schmookler, *Parable,* 262.

19. Schmookler, *Out of Weakness,* 311.

20. *Ibid.,* 320.

21. Robert Axelrod, *The Evolution of Cooperation* (New York: Basic Books, 1984), 190.

22. A similar approach was once proposed by psychologist Charles Osgood, *An Alternative to War or Surrender* (Urbana: University of Illinois Press, 1962).

23. James Lovelock, *The Ages of Gaia* (New York: W. W. Norton, 1988), 19; also L. Margulis and J. E. Lovelock, "Gaia and Geognosy," in Mitchell Rambler, Lynn Margulis, and Rene Fester, eds., *Global Ecology* (San Diego: Academic Press, 1989), 1–30.

24. *Ibid.,* 178.

25. These figures are from William C. Clark, "Managing Planet Earth," *Scientific American* 261/3 (September 1989): 50–51.

26. For a good review of the science involved, see Jonathan Weiner, *The Next One Hundred Years* (New York: Bantam Books, 1990), 1–134; and Stephen Schneider, *Global Warming* (San Francisco: Sierra Club Books, 1989).

27. Richard Kerr, "Global Warming Continues in 1989," *Science* (2 February 1990).

28. See Christopher Flavin, *Slowing Global Warming* WorldWatch Paper 91 (Washington, D.C.: WorldWatch Institute 1989).

29. Gregory H. Kats, "Slowing Global Warming and Sustaining Development," *Energy Policy* 18 (January/February 1990): 25–33.

30. F. Sherwood Rowland, "Chlorofluorocarbons and the Depletion of Stratospheric Ozone," *American Scientist* 77 (January/February 1989): 36–45.

31. Arjun Makhijani et al., *Saving Our Skins* (Washington, D.C.: Environmental Policy Institute, 1989).

32. Nathan Keyfitz, "The Growing Human Population," *Scientific American* 261/3 (September 1989): 119.

33. John and Carol Steinhart, "Energy Use in the U. S. Food System," *Science* 184 (19 April 1974): 307–16.

34. David Pimentel, "Waste in Agricultural and Food Sectors: Environmental and Social Costs" (Unpublished paper, 1989), 8.

35. Robert Repetto, "Population, Resources, Environment: An Uncertain Future," *Population Bulletin* 42/2 (July 1987): 22.

36. Lester Brown, "Reexamining the World Food Prospect," *State of the World: 1989* (New York: W. W. Norton, 1989), 41–58; and Lester Brown and John E. Young, "Feeding the World in the Nineties," in Brown et al., *State of the World: 1990* (New York: W. W. Norton, 1990), 59–78.

37. John Gever et al., *Beyond Oil* (Cambridge: Ballinger, 1986), ch. 5.

38. Joel Smith and Dennis Tirpak, "Potential Effects of Global Climate Change on the United States" (Washington, D.C.: U.S. Environmental Protection Agency, 1988).

39. Jonathan Weiner, *The Next One Hundred Years,* 158–59.

40. George Perkins Marsh, *Man and Nature* (Cambridge: Harvard University Press, 1965/1864), 36.

41. For a solid analysis of the economics of agriculture, see Marty Strange, *Family Farming* (Lincoln: University of Nebraska Press, 1988).

42. I am referring to the work of Stephen Gliessman, Robert Rodale, and Wes Jackson.

43. Albert Howard, *An Agricultural Testament* (Oxford: Oxford University Press, 1943); J. Russell Smith, *Tree Crops: A Permanent Agriculture* (1950; New York: Harper, 1978); Edward H. Faulkner, *Plowman's Folly* (Norman: University of Oklahoma, 1943).

44. For an exquisite statement read Wendell Berry, *The Gift of Good Land* (San Francisco: North Point Press, 1981)

45. Chris Maser, *The Redesigned Forest* (San Pedro: R & E Miles, 1988); also Chris Maser, *Forest Primeval* (San Francisco: Sierra Club Books, 1989).

46. Alan Savory, *Holistic Resource Management* (Washington: Island Press, 1988).

47. Aldo Leopold, *Game Management* (Madison: University of Wisconsin Press, 1986).

48. Aldo Leopold, *A Sand County Almanac* (New York: Ballantine, 1966), 197.

49. *New York Times,* 19 April 1986.

50. Jose Goldemberg et al., *Energy for a Sustainable World* (Washington: World Resources Institute, 1987), 17.

51. *New York Times,* 16 February 1989.

52. *New York Times,* 8 September 1989.

53. Charles Hall, Cutler Cleveland, and Robert Kaufman, *Energy and Resource Quality* (New York: Wiley and Sons, 1986), 28.

54. Joan Ogden and Robert Williams, *Solar Hydrogen* (Washington, D.C.: World Resources Institute, 1989).

55. Data from the office of Claudine Schneider, U. S. Congress from a report by U. S. Department of Energy, 1986.

56. Gene Tyner, Robert Costanza, and Richard Fowler, "The Net Energy Yield of Nuclear Power," *Energy* 13/1 (1988): 73–81.

57. William Keepin and Gregory Kats, "Greenhouse Warming: Comparative analysis of Nuclear and Efficiency Abatement Strategies," *Energy Policy* 16/6 (December 1988): 538–61.

58. Lovelock, *Ages of Gaia,* 19.

59. Solly Zuckerman, *Nuclear Illusion and Reality* (New York: Vintage Books, 1983), 103.

60. Daniel Deudney, *Whole Earth Security: A Geopolitics of Peace* (Washington: WorldWatch Institute, 1983), 39–40.

61. Jeremy Rifkin, *Time Wars* (New York: Henry Holt, 1987).

62. See note 21 above.

Chapter 4

1. Wendell Berry, "Solving for Pattern," in Wendell Berry, *The Gift of Good Land* (San Francisco: North Point Press, 1981), 137.

2. *Ibid.,* 140–45.

3. Marilyn Ferguson, *The Aquarian Conspiracy* (Los Angeles: J. P. Tarcher, 1980), 24.

4. *Ibid.,* 29.

5. *Ibid.,* 395.

6. Richard A. Falk, "In Pursuit of the Postmodern," in David Ray Griffin, ed., *Spirituality and Society* (Albany: State University of New York Press, 1988), 85–86.

7. Adam Smith, *The Wealth of Nations* (New York: Modern Library, 1965), 423.

8. Herman Daly, "Introduction to the Steady-State Economy," in Daly, ed., *Economics, Ecology, Ethics* (San Francisco: W. H. Freeman, 1980), 19.

9. See also Robert C. Paehlke, *Environmentalism and the Future of Progressive Politics* (New Haven: Yale University Press, 1989), 253.

10. William Ophuls, *Ecology and the Politics of Scarcity* (San Francisco: W. H. Freeman, 1977), 3.

11. For a review of poll data, see Riley Dunlap, "Polls, Pollution, and Politics Revisited: Public Opinion on the Environment in the Reagan Era," *Environment* 29:6 (July/August 1987): 11; see also Barry Sussman, *What Americans Really Think* (New York: Pantheon, 1988), 170–74, regarding the shift in attitudes on nuclear energy.

12. See Noel Grove, "Which Way to the Revolution?" *American Forests* 96/3–4 (March/April 1990): 23.

13. Walter Truett Anderson, "Beyond Environmentalism," in Anderson, ed., *Rethinking Liberalism* (New York: Avon Books, 1983), 246.

14. For an interesting statement of the issue, see Daniel Kemmis, *Community and the Politics of Place* (Norman: University of Oklahoma Press, 1990).

15. Robert Heilbroner, *An Inquiry into the Human Prospect* (New York: W. W. Norton, 1980), 175.

16. Ophuls, *Ecology and the Politics of Scarcity,* 163.

17. Garrett Hardin, "The Tragedy of the Commons," in Hardin and John Baden, eds., *Managing the Commons* (San Francisco: W. H. Freeman, 1977), 16–30.

18. Alvin Weinberg, "Social Institutions and Nuclear Energy," *Science* 177 (7 July 1972): 27–34.

19. E. F. Schumacher, *Small is Beautiful: Economics as if People Mattered* (New York: Harper Torchbooks, 1974); and Leopold Kohr, *The Breakdown of Men and Nations* (New York: E. P. Dutton, 1979).

20. Kirkpatrick Sale, *Dwellers in the Land: The Bioregional Vision* (San Francisco: Sierra Club Books, 1985), 170.

21. Lewis Mumford, *The Myth of the Machine: The Pentagon of Power* vol. 2 (New York: Harcourt Brace Jovanovich, 1970), 408.

22. See also Herman E. Daly and John B. Cobb, Jr., *For The Common Good* (Boston: Beacon Press, 1990), 209–354.

23. Lewis Hyde, *The Gift: Imagination and the Erotic Life of Property* (New York: Vintage, 1983); Marshall Sahlins, *Stone Age Economics* (Chicago: Aldine, 1972); Colin Turnbull, *The Human Cycle* (New York: Simon and Schuster, 1983).

24. Gene Logsdon, "Amish Economics," *Whole Earth Review* 50 (Spring 1986): 74–82.

25. E. F. Schumacher, *Small is Beautiful,* 50–58.

26. For a good selection of this work, see Paul Ekins, ed., *The Living Economy* (New York: Routledge & Kegan Paul, 1986).

27. Pliny Fiske, *An Appropriate Technology Working Atlas* (Austin: Center for Maximum Potential Building Systems, n. d.).

28. Benjamin Barber, *Strong Democracy* (Berkeley: University of California Press, 1984).

29. John Dewey, *The Public and Its Problems* (Chicago: Swallow Press, 1954), 213.

30. Robert Bellah et al., *Habits of the Heart* (Berkeley: University of California Press, 1985), 290.

31. Barber, 261–311.

32. Thomas Jefferson, letter to William Charles Jarvis, 28 September 1820.

33. James MacGregor Burns, *Leadership* (New York: Harper and Row, 1978), 43–44.

34. John Keegan, *The Mask of Command* (New York: Viking, 1987), 351.

35. Robert Greenleaf, *Servant Leadership* (Mahwah, NJ: Paulist Press, 1977).

36. *Ibid.,* 13.

37. Joseph Campbell, *The Hero With a Thousand Faces* (Princeton: Princeton University Press, 1968), 388.

38. *Ibid.,* 390.

39. *Ibid.,* 391.

40. Erazim Kohak, *The Embers and The Stars* (Chicago: University of Chicago Press, 1984), 170.

41. See William Sullivan, *Reconstructing Public Philosophy* (Berkeley: University of California Press, 1982), 154–80; Bellah et al., *Habits of the Heart.*

Chapter 5

1. Barry Lopez, *Crossing Open Ground* (New York: Vintage, 1989), 65.

2. Rachel Carson, *The Sense of Wonder* (New York: Harper and Row, 1984), 45.

3. E. O. Wilson, *Biophilia* (Cambridge: Harvard University Press, 1984).

4. In Charles P. Curtis, Jr. and Ferris Greenslet, eds., *The Practical Cogitator,* 3rd ed. (Boston: Houghton Mifflin Co., 1962), 226–29.

5. Aldo Leopold, *A Sand County Almanac* (New York: Ballantine, 1966), 240.

6. Wendell Berry, *Home Economics* (San Francisco: North Point Press, 1987), 50.

7. On the structure of environmental education, see Lynton K. Caldwell, "Environmental Studies: Discipline or Metadiscipline," *The Environmental Professional* (1983): 247–59.

8. Wendell Berry, *Home Economics* (San Francisco: North Point Press, 1987), 146.

9. Alasdair MacIntyre, *After Virtue* (South Bend: Notre Dame University Press, 1981), 168–89.

10. Donald Worster, *Nature's Economy* (San Francisco: Sierra Club Books, 1977; reissued by Cambridge University Press, 1985).

11. Amory Lovins, *Soft Energy Paths* (Cambridge: Ballinger, 1977).

12. For the best discussion of energy accounting, see Charles Hall et al., *Energy and Resource Quality* (New York: Wiley and Sons, 1986) 3–151.

13. In Herman Daly and John Cobb, *For the Common Good* (Boston: Beacon Press, 1990), 401–55.

Chapter 6

1. Allan Bloom, *The Closing of the American Mind* (New York: Simon and Schuster, 1987), 380.

2. *Ibid.*, 344.

3. For example, Benjamin Barber, "The Philosopher Despot," *Harper's* (January 1988): 61–65.

4. Alfred North Whitehead, *The Aims of Education* (New York: The Free Press, 1967/1929), 51.

5. J. Glenn Gray, *Re-Thinking American Education* (Middletown: Wesleyan University Press, 1984), 34.

6. The phrase is Wendell Berry's, *Home Economics* (San Francisco: North Point Press, 1987), 50.

7. Gray, *Rethinking,* 84–85.

8. *Ibid.*, 81.

9. Whitehead, *Aims,* 6.

10. Berry, *Home Economics,* 79.

11. Aldo Leopold, *A Sand County Almanac* (New York: Ballantine, 1966), 210.

12. *Ibid.*, 208.

13. Donella Meadows, "The New Alchemist," *Harrowsmith* (November 1989): 38–47.

Chapter 8

1. Lewis Mumford, "Utopia, The City, and the Machine," in Frank Manuel, ed., *Utopias and Utopian Thought* (Boston: Beacon Press, 1966), 10.

2. Lewis Mumford, *Values for Survival* (New York: Harcourt, Brace and Co., 1946), 151–152.

3. John Dewey, "The School and Social Progress," in J. McDermott, ed., *The Philosophy of John Dewey* (Chicago: University of Chicago Press, 1981), 457.

4. Alfred North Whitehead, *The Aims of Education* (New York: Free Press, 1967/1929), 50.

5. Ivan Illich, "Dwelling," *Co-Evolution Quarterly* 41 (Spring 1984).

6. Paul Shepard, "Place in American Culture," *North American Review* (Fall 1977): 22–32.

7. Lewis Thomas, *The Lives of a Cell* (New York: Viking Press, 1974).

8. Baker Brownell, *The Human Community* (New York: Harper Brothers, 1950).

9. Wendell Berry, *The Gift of Good Land* (San Francisco: North Point Press, 1981), 281.

Chapter 9

1. For all of my reservations about Allan Bloom's *Closing of the American Mind* (New York: Simon and Schuster, 1987), I am inclined to believe his lightning bolts against rock music are on target. See *Closing*, 68–81.

2. Julian Simon, *The Ultimate Resource* (Princeton: Princeton University Press, 1981); Herman Kahn et al., *The Next Two Hundred Years* (New York: Morrow, 1976).

3. For notable examples of collaboration between a theologian and an economist, and between that same theologian and a biologist, see Herman Daly and John Cobb, *For the Common Good* (Boston: Beacon Press, 1990); and Charles Birch and John Cobb, *The Liberation of Life* (New York: Cambridge University Press, 1981).

4. *Co-Evolution Quarterly* 32 (Winter 1981–2) 1.

5. Gregory Bateson, *Mind and Nature* (New York: E. P. Dutton, 1979).

6. Lewis Mumford, *The Transformation of Man* (New York: Harper Torchbooks, 1972), 187.

7. Lewis Mumford, *Interpretations and Forecasts: 1922–1972* (New York: Harcourt Brace Jovanovich, 1979), 469.

8. Albert Schweitzer, *The Light Within Us* (New York: The Philosophical Library, 1959), 25–26.

Chapter 10

1. Lynton Caldwell, "Environmental Studies: Discipline or Metadiscipline?" in *The Environmental Professional* (1983), 247–59.

2. Howard Gardner, *Frames of Mind: The Theory of Multiple Intelligences* (New York: Basic Books, 1983).

3. Alan Schnaiberg, *The Environment: From Surplus to Scarcity* (New York: Oxford University Press, 1980), 277–304.

4. Ivan Illich, *Shadow Work* (Boston: Marion Boyars, 1981).

Chapter 11

1. Elie Wiesel, "On Global Education" (Address before the Global Forum, Moscow, 18 January 1990).

2. Bruce Wilshire, *The Moral Collapse of the University* (Albany: State University of New York Press, 1990), xiii.

3. *Ibid.,* 40.

4. *Ibid.,* 85.

5. *Ibid.,* 280–82.

6. Page Smith, *Killing the Spirit: Higher Education in America* (New York: Viking, 1990), 7.

7. On this point read Erwin Chargaff, "Knowledge Without Wisdom," *Harper's* (May 1980): 47.

8. Wendell Berry, *Standing by Words* (San Francisco: North Point Press, 1983), 66.

9. David Ehrenfeld, "Forgetting," *Orion Nature Quarterly,* 8/4 (Autumn 1989): 5–7.

10. Barry Lopez, "The American Geographies," *Orion Nature Quarterly* 8/4 (Autumn 1989): 57.

Chapter 12

1. William C. Clark, "Managing Planet Earth," *Scientific American* 261/3 (September 1989): 53–54.

2. Robert Repetto, *World Enough and Time* (New Haven: Yale University Press, 1986), 8.

3. Wendell Berry, "The Futility of Global Thinking," *Harper's* (September 1989): 16–22.

4. Wendell Berry, *The Unsettling of America: Culture and Agriculture* (San Francisco: Sierra Club Books, 1977), ch 2.

Chapter 13

1. *Items* (the publication of the Social Science Research Council) 42/1–2 (June 1988).

Chapter 14

1. Martin H. Rogoff and Stephen L. Rawlins, "Food Security: A Technological Alternative," *Bioscience* (December 1987): 800–07.

2. J. Russell Smith, *Tree Crops: A Permanent Agriculture* (New York: Harper Colophon, 1978); Wes Jackson, *Altars of Unhewn Stone* (San Francisco: North Point Press, 1987).

3. *Annals of Earth* 5/3: 10.

4. Office of Technology Assessment, *Technology, Public Policy, and the Changing Structure of American Agriculture* (Washington: U. S. Government Printing Office, 1986).

5. Fyodor Dostoyevsky, *The Brothers Karamazov* (New York: Modern Library, 1950), 300.

6. For a discussion of the term, see William Lockeretz, "Defining a Sustainable Future: Basic Issues in Agriculture," *Northwest Report* 8 (December 1989).

7. Miguel Altieri, *Agroecology: The Scientific Basis of Alternative Agriculture* (Berkeley: Division of Biological Control, University of California, 1983), x; Michael Dover and Lee M. Talbot, *To Feed the Earth: Agro-Ecology for Sustainable Development* (Washington: World Resources Institute, 1987), 17–29.

8. David Pimentel, "Waste in Agricultural and Food Sectors: Environmental and Social Costs" (Unpublished paper, 1989), 8; see also Evan Eisenberg, "Back to Eden," *Atlantic* 264/5 (November 1989): 59.

9. Nicanor Perlas, "The Sustainable Agriculture Movement," *Orion Nature Quarterly* 7/2 (Spring 1988): 35.

10. A fact now recognized by the National Research Council, *Alternative Agriculture* (Washington: National Academy Press, 1989); see also Frederick H. Buttel et al., "Reduced-Input Agricultural Systems: Rationale and Prospects," *Alternative Agriculture* 1/2 (Spring 1986): 58–64.

11. Wendell Berry, *The Gift of Good Land* (San Francisco: North Point

Press, 1981); *The Unsettling of America: Culture and Agriculture* (San Francisco: Sierra Club Books, 1977).

12. Gene Logsdon, "Amish Economy," *Orion* (Spring 1988): 24–33.

13. Liberty Hyde Bailey, *The Holy Earth* (Ithaca: State College of Agriculture, 1980).

14. See F. H. King, *Farmers of Forty Centuries* (Emmaus: Rodale Press, 1990).

15. The Cornucopia Project, *Empty Breadbasket* (Emmaus: Rodale Press, 1981).

16. Marty Strange, "The Economic Structure of Sustainable Agriculture," in Wes Jackson et al., *Meeting the Expectations of the Land* (San Francisco: North Point Press, 1985), 118.

17. Marty Strange, *Family Farming* (Lincoln: University of Nebraska Press, 1988), 249.

18. *Ibid.,* ch. 10.

19. Nancy Jack Todd and John Todd, *Bioshelters, Ocean Arks, City Farming: Ecology and the Basis of Design* (San Francisco: Sierra Club Books, 1984), 146.

20. Bill Mollison, *Permaculture Two* (Tagari Books, 1979), 3.

21. J. Russell Smith, *Tree Crops: A Permanent Agriculture* (New York: Harper Colophon, 1978).

22. Wes Jackson, *New Roots for Agriculture* (San Francisco: Friends of the Earth, 1980); Jackson et al., *Meeting the Expectations of the Land;* for a good description of Jackson, see Eisenberg, "Back to Eden," 57–89.

23. Masanubo Fukuoka, *The One Straw Revolution* (New York: Bantam Books, 1985); and Fukuoka, *The Natural Way of Farming: The Theory and Practice of Green Philosophy* (Tokyo: Japan Publications, 1985).

Chapter 15

1. Alasdair MacIntyre, *After Virtue* (Notre Dame: Notre Dame University Press, 1981), 237.

2. *Ibid.,* 211.

3. Robert E. Proctor, *Education's Great Amnesia* (Bloomington: Indiana University Press, 1988), 174.

4. *Ibid.,* 175.

5. *Ibid.,* ch. 9.

Index

Shakespeare and the Nature of Time, *The New World: An Epic Poem*, and *Genesis: An Epic Poem*. He is founders professor of arts and humanities at the University of Texas at Dallas, Richardson, Texas 75083.

This series is published under the auspices of the Center for a Postmodern World and the Center for Process Studies.

The Center for a Postmodern World is an independent nonprofit organization in Santa Barbara, California, founded by David Ray Griffin. It exists to promote the awareness and exploration of the postmodern worldview and to encourage reflection about a postmodern world, from postmodern art, spirituality, and education to a postmodern world order, with all this implies for economics, ecology, and security. One of its major projects is to produce a collaborative study that marshals the numerous facts supportive of a postmodern worldview and provides a portrayal of a postmodern world order toward which we can realistically move. It is located at 3463 State Street, Suite 252, Santa Barbara, Calif. 93105.

The Center for Process Studies is a research organization affiliated with the School of Theology at Claremont and Claremont University Center and Graduate School. It was founded by John B. Cobb, Jr., Director, and David Ray Griffin, Executive Director. It exists to encourage research and reflection upon the process philosophy of Alfred North Whitehead, Charles Hartshorne, and related thinkers, and upon the application and testing of this viewpoint in all areas of thought and practice. This center sponsors conferences, welcomes visiting scholars to use its library, and publishes a scholarly journal, *Process Studies*, and a quarterly *Newsletter*. It is located at 1325 North College, Claremont, Calif. 91711.

Both Centers gratefully accept (tax-deductible) contributions to support their work.